By the Same Author

Gardens of a Golden Afternoon
Vita's Other World
The Art and Architecture of English Gardens
Eminent Gardeners
Beatrix
Lutyens and the Edwardians
The Pursuit of Paradise
The Modern Garden

Spirits of Place

*Five Famous Lives in
Their English Landscape*

JANE BROWN

VIKING

VIKING

Published by the Penguin Group
Penguin Books Ltd, 27 Wrights Lane, London w8 5TZ, England
Penguin Putnam Inc., 375 Hudson Street, New York, New York 10014, USA
Penguin Books Australia Ltd, Ringwood, Victoria, Australia
Penguin Books Canada Ltd, 10 Alcorn Avenue, Toronto, Ontario, Canada M4V 3B2
Penguin Books India (P) Ltd, 11 Community Centre,
Panchsheel Park, New Delhi – 110 017, India
Penguin Books (NZ) Ltd, Cnr Rosedale and Airborne Roads,
Albany, Auckland, New Zealand
Penguin Books (South Africa) (Pty) Ltd, 5 Watkins Street,
Denver Ext 4, Johannesburg 2094, South Africa

Penguin Books Ltd, Registered Offices: Harmondsworth, Middlesex, England

First published 2001
1

Set in 12/15.5pt Monotype Bembo
Typeset by Rowland Phototypesetting Ltd,
Bury St Edmunds, Suffolk
Printed in Great Britain by Clays Ltd, St Ives plc

A CIP catalogue record for this book is available from the British Library

ISBN 0-670-88000-0

Contents

List of Illustrations

1. Virginia Stephen at twenty, studio portrait by George Charles Beresford, 1902. (National Portrait Gallery)

2. 'Sweet Morgan': E. M. Forster in 1915, aged thirty-six, four of his six famous novels already written. (King's College, Cambridge)

3. Rooksnest, the real-life *Howards End*, a considered plan of the house and garden, drawn by Forster when he was fifteen. (King's College, Cambridge and The Society of Authors)

4. Netherhampton House, Wiltshire, the gate bearing the Gauntlett arms, from a drawing by Alys Fane Trotter. (From *The Later Life and Letters of Sir Henry Newbolt*)

5. St Ives, Cornwall, as it was when Virginia spent childhood holidays there; the figure second from the right is the painter Alfred Wallis. (St Ives Museum)

6. Rugby, the Golden Jubilee Clock Tower of 1887, the year of Rupert Brooke's birth.

7. Rugby, *Cricket on The Close*, from a painting of 1889 by Jarmyn Brooks, showing School Field, the house which

became Rupert Brooke's home in 1902. (Rugby School Museum)

8. Theatricals at Limpsfield Chart. *Left to right*, Margery Olivier, David Garnett with goblet to his face, Dora Cox in background, Daphne Oliver kneeling in foreground, Edward Garnett in dark jacket, Speedwell Black sitting in foreground, Mabel Hobson wearing beard, Brynhild Oliver, Noel Olivier, Harold Hobson wielding axe. (Richard Garnett)

9. L. P. Hartley as a Harrow schoolboy, with his father, Harry Hartley, and his sisters Enid (*right*) and Norah (*left*). Enid in part inspired the character of Hilda Cherrington. (Peterborough Central Library)

10. The Orchard, Grantchester, with tables and deckchairs set out beneath the apple trees, *c.*1910. (Tom Hinton, The Orchard, Grantchester)

11. Rupert Brooke, reading in The Old Vicarage garden at Grantchester, summer 1911. (King's College, Cambridge)

12. 'May Races' on the river Cam, *c.*1908. Rupert, in his Old Rugbeian blazer, right of the masthead, reads a letter as he leans against the stair; to his left Virginia Stephen awaits a light for her cigarette from (?) Dudley Ward. The photograph was taken by Florence Keynes, so Geoffrey and possibly Maynard are there too. (King's College, Cambridge)

13. Carrington: *Hill in Snow, Hurstbourne Tarrant*, the view from Ibthorpe House, watercolour, 1916. (Private collection)

14. Carrington on the high hedge ladder at Ibthorpe in Hampshire, *c.*1913. (National Portrait Gallery)

15. Carrington, *Hoeing Vegetables*, fresco panel at Ashridge House, Hertfordshire, 1912. (Ashridge Management College)

16. Henry Lamb's studio portrait of Lytton Strachey, 1914. (Trustees of the Tate Gallery)

17. *Kew Gardens*, written by Virginia Woolf, decoration by Vanessa Bell, first published by the Hogarth Press, 1917.

18. Vanessa Bell, *Summer Camp*, oils on board, 1913, captures the mood of a camp in Suffolk that summer, which included the Olivier sisters and others of the Brooke circle. (Private collection)

19. Rupert Brooke making Helena Cornford look at the camera, Cley-next-the-Sea, August 1914. Frances Cornford on the left. (King's College, Cambridge)

20. Asheham House, Sussex, photographed in 1927 when it was the quarry manager's house: Virginia and Leonard Woolf had given up their lease in 1919. (Private collection)

21. Vanessa Bell, *The Open Door*, oils on board, 1926, one of the many images she painted of Charleston Farmhouse and its garden. (Bolton Museum and Art Gallery)

22. Vita Sackville-West in her garden at Long Barn, Sevenoaks, as she was when she met Virginia Woolf and became Orlando. (Nigel Nicolson)

23. Knole, the Sackville family home in Kent, the Brown Gallery filled with portraits of Elizabethan notables – the historic setting for *Orlando*. (Nigel Nicolson)

24. The Abinger Pageant, 1934, E. M. Forster and Dr Ralph Vaughan Williams – Forster said that R.V.W. looked like a wily cattle dealer getting the better of a simple rustic (himself). (King's College, Cambridge)

25. L. P. Hartley (in the light suit) and his father at the entrance to Fletton Tower, with the directors of the Whittlesea Central Brick Company and their presentation on Harry Hartley's retirement. (Peterborough Central Library)

26. Rex Whistler, *Conversation at the Daye House*: left to right, Edith Olivier, Lord David Cecil, Lady Ottoline Morrell and the artist; Hartley longed to be part of this world but was kept at the fringes. (From *Without Knowing Mr Walkley* by Edith Olivier, 1937)

27. Left to right, Carrington, Saxon Sydney Turner, Ralph Partridge and Lytton Strachey: Sunday morning at Ham Spray, 1929. (National Portrait Gallery)

28. L. P. Hartley after receiving his CBE at Buckingham Palace. (Miss Mary Wellesley)

Illustrations in the Text

(page 8) The development of Hyde Park Gate, based on the Ordnance Survey of 1894–6, showing the Stephen home, no. 22, third from the end of the cul-de-sac. (From *The Survey of London*)

(page 85) Rugby School, the layout of The Close with School Field in the lower right-hand corner. (From H. W. Bradby, *Rugby*, 1900)

(page 135) A plan of Charleston Farmhouse gardens drawn by Quentin Bell from his memories of it in the early 1920s (From Quentin Bell: 'Life at Charleston', in *Charleston Past and Present*, 1987

(page 178) Tidmarsh Mill, Berkshire: Carrington's sketch of the house front and plan of the garden, 1917 (From Carrington, *Letters and Extracts from her Diary*, ed. David Garnett)

Acknowledgements

Spirits of Place needed the evidence of its subjects' words and so I am particularly grateful to the following: the Society of Authors and Random House for extracts from the journals and essays of Virginia Woolf; the Provost and Scholars of King's College, Cambridge and the Society of Authors as the Literary Representatives of The E. M. Forster Estate; to Faber and Faber Limited as the publishers of the poems and letters of Rupert Brooke; to the Trustees of the National Portrait Gallery and of the Tate Gallery. These and other detailed sources appear in the Notes on pages 277–300.

For permissions to reproduce the illustrations my thanks go to Brian Stevens at the St Ives Museum, Rugby School Museum, Richard Garnett, Richard Hillier at Peterborough Central Library, Tom Hinton of The Orchard, Grantchester, Bolton Museum and Art Gallery, Nigel Nicolson, Miss Mary Wellesley, and the Provost and Scholars of King's College, Cambridge (Modern Archive Centre), as well as to the several owners of private collections.

There is no denying that *Spirits of Place* was a difficult book for me and so often the help and expectations of others pulled me through: my personal thanks go to Wendy Titman (for producing Edith Cobb's book), to Mac Griswold (for spotting the Willa

Cather quote at the right moment), and most especially to my editor, Eleo Gordon, for her patience and encouragement in right measures.

For expeditions and insights my thanks go to my cousin Eve, for her beloved New Forest, and for Netherhampton, to Patricia Reed and Linda and Brian Guest for Virginia Woolf's Sussex, to Jonathan Lovie for Rugby School, to Shirley Evans for Eagle's Nest and Zennor, to Barry and Millicent Sillince for Lulworth Cove and to Charles and Rachel Morris for Blo' Norton.

As a stranger to Cambridge and its surroundings I have been introduced by experts – my thanks to John Drake, Dona Haycraft, Peter Avery, Mary Munro, Lavinia Nourse, Mary Archer, Gillian Sutherland and Biddy and Denis Marrian.

My visit to Ashridge Management College to see the restored gardens and Carrington's mural was, as ever, gracefully conducted by the archivist Kay N. Sanecki: Kay has now retired and I would like to acknowledge both her unrivalled knowledge and her generosity, which were the mark of her long stewardship. Quite late in the book I discovered that Jane Hill, author of *The Art of Dora Carrington*, lived in a neighbouring village, and Jane's wisdom and enthusiasm have been a warm encouragement.

My wonder at the treasures of the London Library grows unceasingly, and page 55 records a sparkling example: to my perennial thanks to the staff at 14 St James's Square are added those to Peterborough Museum (for L. P. Hartley connections), Peterborough Central Library, the Cambridgeshire Collection at Cambridge Library and the University Library in Cambridge.

All the above helped me to write, and illustrate, *Spirits of Place*; my thanks to Clara Farmer, Christine Groom, Annie Lee and many others, without whom it would not be readable.

Jane Brown, Elton, February 2001

Introduction

Spirits of Place presents brief lives of five people who were motivated by a powerful sense of their own surroundings, and consequently have left their memories and legends in our landscape. They are three novelists, one poet and one painter, who have been examined more as if they were the conventional creatures of place, the gardeners, landscape designers or architects, that have been my previous subjects. Indeed they have been subjected to the tricks of the garden historian, who seizes on the sepia snapshot or photograph, salutes the subject, then uses a magnifying glass to examine beyond skirts and over shoulders to see the background, what is going on behind the pose.

My five pivotal subjects – Virginia Woolf, E. M. Forster, Rupert Brooke, Carrington and L. P. Hartley – have, to a great extent, chosen themselves. They have three qualifications in common: first, they are so famous that their works, words and very thoughts are freely available, so often in published form, and their existences have been illuminated and confirmed by an avalanche of biographies, memoirs and mythologies scattered down the years. Second, they are connected: their lives and places are interwoven and crossed by a cast of subsidiary – at least here – characters to form a web of association known as the wider Bloomsbury Group. The wider 'Bloomsbury' – as many as forty people – has unquestionably influenced much of what has been written and read, thought morally or immorally, dictated styles for living and been hung on walls, for most of the last century.

Third, all five – though they were never called 'environmentalists' because that word had not been dragged from dictionary depths in their days – possessed an acute sense of place. So acute that in each of their cases it was a motivating force in their lives; perhaps even directing their fates. They were the kind of people that the behaviourist Edith Cobb called 'individual men and women [who] ultimately create cultural and social history in terms of their particular world imagery', and they also 'possess the capacity to lead others to participate in the world as they see it'.[1]

Edith Cobb (1895–1978) spent her life studying children in their surroundings, all kinds and conditions of children in all sorts of settings. She collected and read autobiographies of childhoods – from John van Druten to Gwen Raverat, from Alison Uttley to Christie Brown, from Nabokov's *Speak Memory* to Proust, Helen Keller, Sean O'Casey and hundreds more, not all so famous. She came to believe in what she called 'the genius of childhood', meaning that in our earliest encounters with the physical world we programme ourselves for the perceptions and achievements of our entire lives.[2] The old adage was right – 'Give me a child for the first seven years, and you may do what you like with him afterwards.'

That is not to say that the following pages feature such moments as Rupert Brooke's first steps or Carrington's infant efforts with crayons – some things are best left to the behaviourists. I am more concerned with circumstance and surroundings, the colours and textures of their lives that are pierced by events; usually the events, meetings, partings, things said and done, take centre stage, but here they are consigned to the wings. To quote Edith Cobb, my five subjects are immersed in their own ecologies to see how they are affected, how they will react and move to the next scene. The patterns that emerge are all vividly different. The setting is almost always England. They appear chronologically, though sometimes clarity takes precedence: the time-span is essentially from Morgan Forster's birth in 1879 to Leslie Hartley's death in 1972, with some necessary preliminary background. Sadly, the other three had foreshortened lives.

The unwritten contrasts and understood connections between these five lives – of Virginia Woolf, Morgan Forster, Rupert Brooke, Carrington and L. P. Hartley – are the buoyancy of this book. Though I have the deepest admiration for many of the individual books about each of them, there were times when reading them I felt that both the subjects and I were overwhelmed; bombarded, engulfed, simply by the proliferation of words and pages. At one of my worst moments Willa Cather's succinct advice was sent by a merciful friend who was herself waiting to fly from Heathrow: 'In constructing a story, as in building an airship, the first problem is to get something that will lift its own weight.'³ Because so much of the ballast of conventional biography has been discarded, each of my subjects requires a personal introduction, and an *aide-mémoire*.

My life was untouched by Virginia Woolf until one day in 1982 when, upon entering Nigel Nicolson's small, rather dark writing-room at Sissinghurst, I was confronted by a huge poster of George Charles Beresford's portrait photograph of her in 1902, when she was twenty, winsome and beautiful, with a huge sweep of hair. I was there, trembling with nerves, to ask if I might write a book about Nigel's mother, Vita Sackville-West, though as I had but a hazy notion of what I wanted to do, and struggled to explain it, his 'Oh, not another book about my mother!' sent my gaze scurrying to Virginia for help. The eventual outcome, *Vita's Other World* (1985), was entirely happy, so perhaps I owe her something.

My first chapter, 'Virginia Stephen', illustrates her life from its beginning, 1882, to 1904: ostensibly all she did in those years was move from Kensington to Bloomsbury, but as the chapter is rather long, she will prove herself an excellent justification of Edith Cobb's theories. Though Virginia began writing professionally in 1905, her major books belong to the years after her marriage to Leonard Woolf in 1912: *The Voyage Out* (1915), *Night and Day* (1919), *Jacob's Room* (1922), *Mrs Dalloway* (1925), *To the Lighthouse* (1927), *Orlando* (1928), *The Waves* (1931) and *Flush* (1933). *The Years* (1937) revealed her powers and health in decline. On 28 March 1941 she cast herself, her pockets weighted with stones, into the river Ouse at Rodmell, and she drowned. *Between the Acts*, which she had just completed, was published posthumously later that year.

Edward Morgan Forster (1879–1970) was one of Virginia's favourite six people (the others were Leonard, Vanessa and Clive Bell, Duncan Grant and Lytton Strachey). Forster was born in London but found his famous paradise of childhood at 'Howard's End' in Hertfordshire; he went up to King's College Cambridge when he was eighteen. After a continental tour and four summer months employed as a tutor by the Count and Countess von Arnim at Nassenheide in Pomerania (she being Elizabeth of *German Garden* fame), he returned to England. Four of his six major novels were published within five years: *Where Angels Fear to Tread* (1905), *The Longest Journey* (1907), *A Room with a View* (1908) and *Howards End* (1910). *The Celestial Omnibus*, in a volume with five other stories, appeared in 1911. He then wrote *Maurice*, but it was not published until 1971; *A Passage to India* was completed and published in 1924. That year the fates conspired to move Forster to Abinger in Surrey, to the only house his architect father is known to have built, and it was with Abinger that he became identified, through *Abinger Harvest* (1936) and the Abinger edition of his works.

The places, of course, are the threads connecting me with my subjects; how else could I have come to any pretence of knowing these long dead souls? Forster left Abinger in 1948 and it became my home some twenty years afterwards. Searching out the legendary Pilgrims' Way meant exploring Hackhurst Downs behind his house, my 'home' turning off the A25 to Holmbury was his everyday view, his pageant of Abinger was renewed annually in the medieval fair, and in Holmbury itself I trod in the footsteps of Lucy Honeychurch and Mr Beebe whenever I cared to remember them. In peeling off the layers of memories to find Edwin Lutyens's and Gertrude Jekyll's Abinger, for my *Gardens of a Golden Afternoon* (1982), Forster and his contemporaries, Sir Max Beerbohm, Ralph Vaughan Williams, Clifford and Marjory Allen, the Gibbs family living in Lutyens's Goddards, and many other enduring names surfaced over and over again in this landscape of sandy heights wreathed in an alluring mix of feudalism and Fabianism.

I had a previous taste of that alluring mixture at Limpsfield in most easterly Surrey: this too was a Fabian forcing ground 100 years ago, producing David Garnett and the four Olivier sisters, childhood playfellows who are fateful influences in several regions of this book, especially Chapter 3. My third subject, Rupert Chawner Brooke (1887–1915), seemed netted in a similar political dichotomy, named for a Cavalier prince and a Roundhead ancestor: Brooke, with his looks of a screen idol, who was never to make it into the age of the silver screen, seems the victim of his own boyish rhetoric and the sycophantic passions which, in life and death, he inspired in others. It was actually his elder brother, Richard England Brooke, who held the family middle name, and whose death left Rupert feeling 'ill with age' when he was barely out of school: Rupert would not have wished to usurp it.

Brooke spent his life almost entirely in Rugby and Cambridge, with a few significant and sparkling exceptions; only *Poems 1911* and his contributions to the first two volumes of *Georgian Poetry* were published in his lifetime. Of my five subjects, Brooke was the most susceptible to places; I have tried to release him on 'The Roman road to Wendover by Tring and Lilley Hoo' as a free man.

> I shall desire and I shall find
> The best of my desires;
> The autumn road, the mellow wind
> That soothes the darkening shires,
> And laughter, and inn-fires.[4]

With Brooke I share my love for my present home, the former Huntingdonshire and Cambridgeshire, and for Cambridge itself. My feelings are expressed by Constance Black, the future translator of Tolstoy and Ibsen and mother of David Garnett, who became a student at Newnham College in 1879 and whose words come winging across the years:

The beauty of Cambridge was overwhelming, it made me feel too much moved. I was constantly wanting to cry. I had never imagined such a lovely place. I had never seen a beautiful building before.[5]

In a very real sense the beauty of Cambridge – a combination of past ghosts and present visions – assumes a potent guise in the following pages. That it was the fenland branch of Bloomsbury contributes to this, but there is also the contiguity of ancient enmities, of the Puritan and the romantic, the dour waterland and vain, lavish medieval glories of carved and gilded wood and stone, of an institutionalized caution that allowed spaces to Hawksmoor, Wren and James Gibbs, of legions of dull and sober men who somehow 'sired' flaming genius. There is a very well-worn spot, beside the Queen's Road, at the 'back' entrance to King's College, where this can all be taken in at one glance: it can be guaranteed that Virginia Woolf, Morgan Forster, Brooke and Carrington, and many others mentioned here, stood on this spot and experienced this view. A foot-stopping and camera-clicking view, beautifully contrived between the beech avenue of King's and the clustering trees of Clare's gardens. No techno-rubbish nor even modern building intrudes on the lordly magnifi-cence of Gibbs's Palladian rectangle and its companionable King's College Chapel – which Ruskin likened to a billiard-table with its legs in the air. The view defies the centuries; the only movement might be a passing punt-pole – for the river is low, out of sight – or the stately shuntings of a few large brown cows. In late afternoon it is a common trick of the westering sun to paint the façades and spires into a city of gold, shining across meadows and lawns. In the dear dim days before television and coloured film this was a life-transforming view; it is a good surviving example of hundreds of other emotive views that con-tribute to *Spirits of Place*.

If, with Brooke and Forster, I share a new love, then with my fourth subject it is an old love, for the Hampshire and west Berkshire border country between Newbury and Hungerford, which illumined my childhood. Dora de Houghton Carrington (1893–1932) was the possessor of a tremendous talent: she was artist, portrait painter, muralist, decorator, sign-painter, engraver, craftswoman, a writer of vivacious letters and a gardener. Carring-ton had to remedy the deficiencies of her childhood in adult life, with the result that she seemed never quite to grow up. In Bloomsbury terms she came from nowhere, and purloined – to general amazement and disbelief – their prized man of promise, Lytton Strachey (1880–1932). Strachey must be unique in having the largest biography for the smallest literary output; indeed, he is now more famous as Michael Holroyd's subject★ than for his own, rather faded works – *Landmarks in French Literature* (1912), *Eminent Victorians* (1918) and *Elizabeth and Essex: a Tragic History* (1928). Carrington's life with Lytton was her triumph, brought about by the combination of her talents and shortcomings, and the downland countryside which they both loved. Chapter 5, 'Carrington', is a celebration: for here, the ending, mentioned once only, is that Carrington killed herself with a borrowed shotgun, shortly after Lytton had died from cancer.

My final subject differs from the others in many ways, but he knew them all: Leslie Poles Hartley (1895–1972) has his epitaph in the opening line of his novel *The Go-Between*: 'The past is a foreign country: they do things differently there.'[7] The work of Hartley's life was to throw events, experiences and people into the air, letting them fall and then arranging them differently. He despised his native country, Peterborough and the surrounding area, and yet his writing evokes the paradise of childhood in all its bitter-sweetness, most skilfully of all. Hartley may deserve sympathy, for in my *arriviste* enthusiasm for the Peterborough area I have pounced on him and his story with all the despicable energies of the detective new on the case.

Hartley could not surmount Camden's early-seventeenth-century verdict on the Fenlanders: 'A kind of people according to the nature of the place where they dwell, rude, uncivil, and envious to all others whom they call upland-men, who stalking on stilts, apply their minds to grazing, fishing and fowling.'[8] He could not raise the remotest interest in Roman hoards, in Saxon saints or the great Norman abbey of St Peter's 'Gildenburgh' – all lazing beneath these vast and entertaining skies, in the countryside

---

★ Michael Holroyd's study of Lytton Strachey[6] began its distinguished journeying in 1967, and has been reprinted and revised many times.

of John Dryden and John Clare. He escaped as soon as he could, to Harrow School and Oxford, but his time there was interrupted by the war. He never needed to work, and saw himself in the mode of Henry James, so he spent much time in Italy, and wrote a novella, *Simonetta Perkins* (1925), in a Jamesian vein. When the war forced him home, he reinvented his childhood for his first great novel, *The Shrimp and the Anemone* (1944), and introduced us to Eustace Cherrington, surely one of the most enchanting children in English fiction. Eustace's adventures in Oxford appeared in *The Sixth Heaven* (1946), and in Venice in *Eustace and Hilda* (1947). His other boy anti-hero, Leo Colston, *The Go-Between*, appeared in 1953, and *A Perfect Woman* and *The Hireling* followed in 1955 and 1957 respectively. Hartley continued to write, increasingly astringent, sometimes bitter, even cruel, stories and novels; he lived out his life near Bath with little affection for anywhere but his garden, which was beside the river Avon, hardly ever returning to where he was born.

These evocations of an England of long ago have present purposes, which are the substance of my final chapter. I have taken to heart the young Virginia Woolf's disdain of 'literary geography' as parasitical, intrusive into a personal and private writer's country, 'the territory within [her] own brain', and the consequent likely disillusion. The more intriguing questions arise in the real world that she pillaged for her images, where she found her creativity. Morgan Forster addressed the future of this world in his Abinger pageant of 1934; what effect, if any, did his words have? Rupert Brooke had so little time, and had only just located the places of his heart: the remembrance of him in some of them is still vibrant, but have we made best use of his legacy? Could his memory, should it, have made any difference to the fate of his beloved Lulworth? Carrington was at her happiest as an artist in the midst of life, in the community, but would she have painted a sign for a Virginia Woolf teashop or a Rupert Brooke inn? In denying his birthplace did Leslie Hartley miss the greatest opportunity of his literary lifetime – which was so lovingly grasped some forty years later in Graham Swift's *Waterland* (1983)? Has the Peterborough 'effect' taken its revenge?

Ultimately, the purpose of creativity is to pick up the stones on our path and polish them, so that those that come after may find treasures: these five sorcerers of our emotions and sensibilities – Woolf, Forster, Brooke, Carrington and Hartley – have attracted hundreds of thousands of devotees, and pilgrims still gather; but does our landscape, with its cheapened and inadequate notion of 'heritage', do them justice? If seeking a sense of place is a search for a sense of ourselves, have we any chance of discovering the best of our heroes, at all?

1

Virginia Stephen

Virginia Stephen was born at her family's home, 22 Hyde Park Gate, Kensington, on 25 January 1882. She was a second daughter, and third child, of the second marriage of both her parents, Leslie Stephen and Julia Duckworth. Her infant cries echoed down the pillared and porticoed vistas of speculators' stucco in Queen's Gate and the Gloucester Road: her eyes opened on an heroic streetscape, built in the preceding thirty years or so in answer to the Prince Consort's vision of a new suburb for the arts and sciences, his Albertopolis. The stucco-fronted mansions also represented successes, residences for rich portrait painters and richer engineers, and all the clustering terraces and 'gates' were firmly in the top echelon of London addresses.

South of 'the Park' (there is no other of equal status) has long had the social edge over the north side: Hyde Park Gate is south, about half-way between Knightsbridge and Kensington High Street. It comprises a short stretch of the Kensington Road and two culs-de-sac, with a convenient foot-gate into Kensington Gardens on the opposite side of the road. Coming from the Albert Hall, the first, eastern cul-de-sac is long and narrow; modern times have unpicked the regulation rows of nineteenth-century stucco fronts and inserted red brick, with even some sixties restrained brutalism in rebuilding. This has been a sought-after spot, much altered until conservation became official, and now the commemorative blue plaques are dotted about – for the playwright Enid Bagnold, the hero of Mafeking and scouting pioneer Robert Baden-Powell and the sculptor Jacob Epstein, who all lived here, and for Winston Churchill, who died at his home here on 24 January 1965. At the end of the cul-de-sac, on the left opposite Churchill's red brick house, the tall semi-detached stucco villas are intact, and shine whitely in the noonday sun: the third from the end was the Stephen home.

Childhood in the cul-de-sac was the first affecting factor of Virginia Stephen's life. The rumble and rush of the Kensington Road is muffled by distance, a consolation for grown-ups, but kindling the suspicion in a child's mind that the adventures of life, other children, the blossoms in the park, are at a distance, somehow at one remove. There is little greenery at this end of the cul-de-sac, the developers left no way out, not even a footpath through to the next street, Queen's Gate Mews; it is a walled dead end, where the dust and litter swirl and settle. In a childhood of goings-out there was ever only one way to go, no choice but to pass the vicious dog or twitching curtain, ever the same line of 'good mornings' to the same elderly denizens. Long after she had grown out of prams and nannies Virginia seemed hardly ever to take the long walk alone, her days were ruled by someone else's going out, invariably her father or Vanessa to walk the dog: dogs were a hazard, with their obsessive noses for trouble, and once with their beloved Shag they were chased all down the cul-de-sac by a 'wicked spotted creature' intent on a fight, until, screaming and beating umbrellas, they found refuge in their own front door. Indoors, in her gloomier moods, Virginia found her horizon was fixed on Mrs Redgrave (widow of the painter Richard Redgrave) washing her neck in her bedroom at No. 27 across the cul-de-sac; more cheerfully, hugging her nightgown round her legs like Clara at the Nutcracker Ball, she watched parties in the big houses in Queen's Gate. In her mind's eye she joined the chatter and dancing in the lighted rooms, spilling out into the garden that she looked down on from her ivory tower, and she much preferred this kind of ball to the real thing. For a budding writer – and there was never any doubt about that – the cul-de-sac was an apprenticeship in detachment, but for a child there is an unhealthy atrophy. Trapped by the stucco cliffs the breezes of life flutter and die, the smells accumulate; most of all it is the smell, the age-old lunchtime fish-and-cabbage smell rising from a dozen basement kitchens that permeates these pavements and these walls, wafting the years away.

Virginia's father, Leslie Stephen, had spent his own early child-hood in this part of Kensington, and remembered the village 'where children could stroll through country lanes and where deer nibbled the grass in Kensington Gardens'.[1] He remembered the high wall around the gardens – he would have been five in 1837, when on a midsummer morning the young Princess Victoria, living in Kensington Palace, heard that she was Queen. Almost immediately she was removed to Buckingham Palace, for Ken-sington was a second-class royal residence, relegated to cousins and aunts by her uncles George IV and William IV, who had allowed the 'respectably dressed' public into the gardens during daylight hours. The Round Pond (really the oval Great Basin) and the Broad Walk (an avenue of magnificent elms until the 1950s) owed much to the landscaping passion of George II's Queen Caroline of Anspach – and they were soon taken to the hearts of Kensingtonians and other Londoners: Queen Caroline had great skill at getting the Prime Minister, Sir Robert Walpole, to pay for her gardening, so perhaps they were the people's gardens all the time. The eighteenth-century mood prevailed around the Palace, and in future days Virginia and her sister, Vanessa, amused themselves by tying ribbons across their chests and mincing along the Broad Walk pretending to be the Misses Bertram of *Mansfield Park*, addressing each other in Austen-speak.

The development of Hyde Park Gate was a microcosm of the transformation of rural Kensington in the nineteenth century: in 1801 the population of the 'village' was a mere 8,556; it trebled by 1841, leapt again by 1851, the year of the Great Exhibition in Hyde Park, and in the next thirty years soared up to just over 163,000.[2] By then, by Victorian standards, it was full up, filled with the rows and streets of stucco-fronted houses of the speculative developers. Hyde Park Gate took its name from the old tollgate on the Kensington Road, a ramshackle countrified wooden barrier that halted the coaches and took their dues until the early 1860s; the gatemen lived in a white clapboarded shed, with a big chimney for their brazier, and if there was any trouble they had a neighbouring cavalry barracks to call out for reinforcements. The culs-de-sac were in separate ownerships and the larger (six acres) was developed first, in 1835 for the Campden Charities, with villas around a circular drive. The long, narrow plot was three and half acres, where sometimes donkeys grazed on thin grass and thistles, and was owned by a gunmaker named Durs Egg, with little interest in building.[3] However, he sold it to a schoolmaster turned speculator, fresh from building Regency Square, Brighton and Campden Hill Square,[4] Joshua Flesher Hanson, who built himself a house (now demolished) on a large plot half-way down the cul-de-sac, and let off the rest in building leases. The strip of land was just wide enough to allow the road down the middle, giving 100-foot-deep lots on either side; the end plots, Nos. 19–24 in the south-east corner, were bought by a Hammersmith builder, Henry Payne, who put up three pairs of semi-detached stucco-fronted villas, miniature outliers of the great cliffs of Queen's Gate and its attendant ranges to the east, south and west. No. 22 was first let in 1846, but it must have been like living in a building site, as Kensington Gate (1850–52), Queen's Gate Terrace (1856–8) and the north end of Queen's Gate (1859–63)[5] arose.

This intensity of house-building, paralleled on the north and west sides of Kensington Gardens, put great pressures on the green open space, making it certain that the public's hold on the once-royal fiefdom would never be surrendered: the wall came down and for practical purposes the boundary with Hyde Park disappeared. However, Queen Victoria's vigilance over royal Kensington never lapsed, and with the arrival of her beloved and thrice-gilded Albert on his memorial podium opposite the new Albert Hall in the summer of 1872, just over ten years after his death, the seemliness of the public's behaviour became a sensitive matter. Royal displeasure was exercised over the proposed refreshment kiosks and 'disfigurements', the blow-holes for the underground electric railway – 'If the Line cannot be made without blow-holes,' came the command, 'it must not be made at all.'[6] Ministers with an empire in tow spent hours fussing over the parks and gardens matters, time vastly out of proportion to the comparatively minute acreages concerned: so much so that the Royal Parks became a cipher for the relationship between the Queen Empress and her nearest and dearest people, a gracious blessing on walking the dog, sailing a model boat, courting (for the many with no other opportunity or place), boating on the Serpentine, and even permission to bury pets in the animal cemetery near the Victoria Gate. All the Royal Parks were special, but Hyde Park was the playground of the nation, and Kensington Gardens retained a royal cachet of their own: Virginia Stephen always 'walked in the gardens' in her diaries and letters, for they were the natural habitat of her neighbours and friends, a preserve of gentility for families with nannies, the rightful inheritance of the residents of such as Hyde Park Gate.

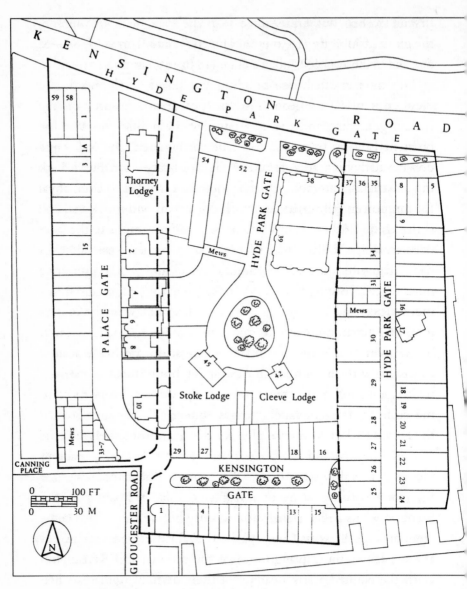

The development of Hyde Park Gate, based on the Ordnance Survey of 1894–6, showing the Stephen home, No. 22, third from the end of the cul-de-sac.

And no one was more suited to Hyde Park Gate – to bask in the glow of Albert's gaze out over his sub-city of sciences and arts, dubbed 'Albertopolis' – than Leslie and Julia Stephen, who settled at No. 22 just after their marriage in March 1878. For Leslie Stephen it was a homecoming: the five-year-old boy who had picked wild flowers in rural Kensington was forty years older, chastened by his traumatic surrender of his belief in God – and consequently his academic career – at Cambridge, arduously earning a living as a literary critic and journalist. Added to all this was the most recent blow, the death of his first wife, Minny Thackeray, at the age of thirty-five in 1875. Minny was the younger daughter of the novelist William Makepeace Thackeray, and she and Leslie had a daughter, Laura, now eight, who was looked after by a nurse: there are few photographs of Laura but they do suggest that she was born with Down's syndrome, and that she was what was then called a 'mongol' child.

The widower Stephen had found sympathy, and subsequently renewed happiness, with a widowed neighbour, Julia Duckworth, who was in her early thirties and the possessor of that familiar melancholic Pre-Raphaelite kind of beauty. Julia came from Kensington's own élite tribe, the Holland Park circle – her mother, Maria Jackson, being one of the five celebrated Pattle sisters, who included the photographer Julia Margaret Cameron and Sara Prinsep and Virginia Somers, muses and intimates of George Frederic Watts and Thackeray. With some irony, in view of Leslie Stephen's 'godlessness', while Julia was comforting him she was also modelling the Virgin for Edward Burne-Jones's *The Annunciation*: the painting took nearly three years and in the later stages Julia was convincingly pregnant with Vanessa Stephen, born on 30 May 1879.[7]

Vanessa was duly followed by Julian Thoby on 8 September 1880, Virginia in early 1882 and Adrian Leslie on 27 October

1883. This was the Stephen family completed, and united with Laura – who seemed to be part of nursery life when her step-brothers and sisters were small (but later spent long periods away from home) – and the three Duckworths, Georgie, Stella and Gerald, who were fifteen, fourteen and twelve respectively. In the year of Virginia's birth, 1882, Leslie Stephen had become editor of the *Dictionary of National Biography*, which he was to see completed in twenty-six volumes, an enormous labour which broke his health but brought him success and fame. This great task was accomplished at home, rather dominating domestic life: to make room for his growing family and find some peace for working, he added two storeys to the top of No. 22 (in brick with a curly Dutch gable, which infuriates architectural historians), making himself a light and airy study at the very top.

Undoubtedly, as breadwinner and master, Leslie had the right to the sun and air, but it meant that the five storeys, including the basement, below, were a tower of increasing babel and constrictions. Julia Stephen had brought with her unaccountable belongings in what Virginia called 'the Watts-Venetian-Little Holland House tradition' of red plush velvet, heavy dusty curtains, prickly pompous chairs and ebony-black woodwork which Vanessa recalled was only enlivened by the thinnest of gold lines.[8] Their rooms were packed with big wardrobes, chests, dark cupboards – all bursting with the belongings of the past, nothing was ever thrown away. The addition of Julia's mother, Mrs Jackson, to the household brought more baggage: tin chests full of letters and papers put down on landings stayed put, their contents all too easily upset down the stairs, and hoards of unused china and glass rocked alarmingly on shelves as the children, being children, rushed by. It was rather as if the dead were loath to give space to the living, who had to inhabit the increasingly box-like spaces in between the collections. Not surprisingly the house was dark and oppressive: Vanessa recalled that 'many of the rooms were pitch dark' even in daylight – and the Virginia creeper hung down over the back drawing-room window – on the first floor – like a thick curtain. Lower rooms and the kitchens were so dim as to be always lit by candles or lamps, not helped by the very dim, if not actually black, paint. The house accrued a gloom – Vanessa thought of the atmosphere as 'melancholy in every way'.⁹

The light and dark were endemic.* Neither Leslie nor Julia Stephen could be called cheerful people, and luxuriating in their past losses brought mutual sympathies. Leslie Stephen's biographer, Noel Annan, has called Stephen's living 'a virtuous life' despite the abandonment of his Christian beliefs 'his most notable achievement'.¹¹ It was certainly noted by his family, to whom he too often personified an injured martyr, as if God had cast a personal slight by deserting him, rather than the other way around. He was an absurdly sentimental husband and father at times, rather fey and feigning shyness and eccentricity, until his martyrdom overtook him and he exploded into harsh irrational dictums that disturbed everyone's lives. Because his first wife, Minny, had had the temerity to die on his forty-third birthday, he vowed never to celebrate it again, which made all birthdays suspect. He was 'blind to the visual arts',¹² left the room if any note of music or song should somehow arise, and he could spit out the most withering remark and kill any conversation stone dead. His children learned to cling staunchly to their views, a good training for those inclined to the law and literature, but for the young Vanessa the daily snipes and cuts that clipped corners off her painter's heart must have been agonies: they toughened

* Lord Annan's biography of Leslie Stephen¹⁰ contains a brilliant and sinister evocation of the home life at 22 Hyde Park Gate.

her ambition, inured her to her father's scorn of the Bohemian, and of emancipated women, but inevitably as she was his daughter marked her too with a talent for martyrdom that her life was to fulfil. Virginia wrote of her own passionate affection for her father alternating with an equally passionate hatred, 'all tingling and vibrating in an atmosphere of youthful bewilderment and curiosity'.[13] She was symbiotically a prey to his mood swings simply because she had inherited his writer's genes: in some ways she divined the best in him, she loved his reading aloud, the Waverley novels of Scott at a stretch, then around again, and their competitive shoutings of Kipling:*

> Winds of the World, give answer! They are whispering to and
> fro –
> And what should they know of England who only England
> know?[14]

Most precious of all, there was a corner of his heart that seemed to be especially hers: he had kept up friendships made in America with Emerson, Thoreau, President Eliot of Harvard, Whitman and James Russell Lowell, the latter having come to London as American minister in 1880, and having become Virginia's 'dear Godpapa' (officially, as Stephen had no God, her Sponsor, but he did not impose his godlessness upon his children, at least not when they were only six, as here). Virginia's earliest surviving letter is this six-year-old 'spontaneous production of Miss Stephen' which her father forwarded to Lowell, in Boston, dated 20 August 1888: 'My dear Godpapa have you been to the Adirondacks and have you seen lots of wild beasts and a lot of birds in their

---

* There was a robust attitude to Tennyson, Newbolt and Browning, among others, in the Stephen household.

nests . . .'[15] His love of mountains, beautiful landscapes and wild nature redeemed Leslie Stephen, and his distinguished American connections, based upon Harvard University's pre-eminence in the natural sciences at this time, were always to be shared with his youngest daughter.

It was no accident that this miniature of a fond father and daughter was dated August, and it is certain that the setting was not Hyde Park Gate, but rather the remembered Eden of Virginia's childhood, Talland House at St Ives in Cornwall. 'The felicitous family of Stephen' abandoned London for St Ives, and were transformed in the process, for about six weeks of every summer, from 1882, the first summer of Virginia's life, until 1894. Their gloomy, cluttered Kensington home, the nursery imprisonment, the endless trails down the cul-de-sac for the brief oasis of the grassy, flowery gardens, then the long, reluctant return, were all forgotten. The dust of London was replaced by the sparkle of the sea, and a limitless blue sky: no matter if the weather was not always fine, though in Virginia's memories it often seemed to be – St Ives was where she was happiest, where she was to be 'allowed a taste of paradise'.[16]

Her infant greediness for experience let her absorb the mounting excitement of the coming holiday long before she could understand. The ritual pilings of clean clothes, the finding and claiming of buckets, spades and rubber shoes, the packing and unpacking to check a missing jumper or irreplaceable toy, all grew with her as she grew from a pink and chubby, gurgling infant into a lanky, long-faced, long-haired girl, full of questions and happy anticipation. Getting ready to go away was to hold a lifelong fascination for her, from these early years: her last-minute shopping, her book collecting – in which she invariably exceeded her luggage allowance – and the art of packing a suitcase were all part of the delicious expectation that never failed. The first peak of excitement came as the holiday train, packed with the paraphernalia of their lives, steamed out of Paddington Station; to the adults' relief, exhaustion set in soon after Reading and the blessedly soporific rhythm of the railway took over, at least to the crossing of the Tamar by Brunel's bridge at Saltash, and entry into the newly 'discovered' countryside of Cornwall. The Stephens were amongst the first in the Great Western Railway's holiday venture: the branch line from St Erth (the depot for thousands of gallons of Cornish milk to leave daily for London) to St Ives had been opened in 1878. The railway company had apparently bought Talland House for a 'station hotel' but soon transferred their ambitions to the magnificent eighteenth-century 'folly' Tregenna Castle, which became available at the opportune moment. Leslie Stephen's arrival in St Ives on a walking tour in the spring of 1881 had been equally opportune, as he acquired the unwanted Talland House, a substantial early-nineteenth-century mansion, with rather pretty gothic balconies, and a many-'roomed' hillside garden.

On the holiday-bound train all were wide awake for the last lovely stretch of the journey, from St Erth. The line wound in a tantalizing way, past the Lelant Saltings, around the Hayle estuary, and through Carbis Bay, to repeated exaltations of 'The Sea! The Sea!' Then there was little else, the whole glorious sweep of St Ives Bay unrolling from distant Godrevy and its lighthouse (built after the wreck of the *Nile* in 1854, and the loss of forty lives) to the far 'Island' or St Ives Head, projecting beyond the clustering little seaport. Once the train arrived all was clatter and laughter and screams of delight, as they renewed their acquaintance with 'our house' by the sea.

Leslie Stephen, with stout intellectual's disregard for looks or views, chose Talland House because it was large, near the station, and yet convenient for long walks across the gorse moors and beside the sea. It was a high, light and airy house, standing among green terraces, wreathed in those faintly exotic shrubs that love the Cornish seaside, griselinias, olearias, hydrangeas, escallonias, pittosporums and stout, spiky yuccas and phormiums. Yet it was neither beautiful – rather bulky in fact – nor a romantic house by the sea: it was really rather suburban, with other capacious villas set around, and demanded an exhaustingly steep trek down to the beach. Nor was it much connected, visually or physically, to St Ives – the jumble of rooftops over cottages and sail-lofts clustering round the harbour, the picturesque piles of fish-baskets, the ever-present stink of fish. The Stephens were as far removed from that life of brutish extremes as the dress circle from the stage: if the pink and plump Virginia had really belonged in St Ives she would have been sunburned and scrawny, and married at fourteen to prevent her being 'corrupted', a mother at fifteen, and likely a widow before she was twenty. Only when Julia Stephen made a Lady Bountiful expedition to the cottages, or when on a fine day they were taken out to the Godrevy light in a fishing boat, as a great treat, did they touch the St Ives reality. Their seaside happiness was a warmly private happiness, for which they were self-sufficient, or supported by visiting cousins and aunts, or Kensington neighbours like the Holman Hunts, all transformed into amusing and playful people by the sea breeze.

The Stephens and their friends were not, of course, the only expeditioners to St Ives, and it seems to have not a little irony that Leslie Stephen the anti-Bohemian and art-hater, at least when he was in Kensington, should have lighted upon an artists' colony, and even associated with them on rare occasions. Years later Walter Sickert was to mention to Vanessa, his pupil at the time, that he had once seen her in St Ives – the presumption being that it was from afar, and that the grand and sombre elevation of the Stephens had not allowed them to meet. Sickert and the Australian painter Mortimer Menpes had worked as assistants to James McNeill Whistler in St Ives for the first time in the autumn of 1883: Whistler, recovering his career from the humiliation of Ruskin's jibe about 'flinging a pot of paint' in the public's face and the lawsuit that won him the damages of a farthing, was giving credence to the fashion for *plein air* painting, made popular at Newlyn but then shifting to St Ives. The fishing scenes of Newlyn were popular at the Royal Academy: Stanhope Forbes's *A Fish Sale on a Cornish Beach* received great acclaim in 1885, and the following year's spring exhibition was also 'a triumph for Newlyn'.[17] The appeal of St Ives was different, only partly in the picturesque fishing-port life and more in the fabulous sea coast itself, in capturing 'that strange beauty of the coast, made magic by the ever-changing light and weather and the many moods of the sea'.[18] Whistler's brilliance proved the challenge: 'I have seen a wave that Whistler was painting,' Sickert remembered, 'hang dog-eared for an incredible duration of seconds while the foam curled and creamed under his brush.'[19] Virginia's years at St Ives thus produced dozens of images, images that she was probably never to see on their canvases, but which she understood perfectly: Anders Zorn's dainty boats in the lapping shallows, Adrian Stokes's *St Ives by Moonlight*, and Sickert's own storm-washed rocks of *Clodgy Point*, which was always to be one of her favourite places. As the painterly adoration of the St Ives seascape steadily grew, from the 1880s and into the early 1890s (by which time the St Ives Arts Club was housed in permanent premises on Westcotts Quay, which Leslie Stephen once visited), so Virginia's parallel sensibilities to the same wonders also developed. Strangely, it was not to be the older Vanessa, 'the painter', who was to be infected by St Ives, for she had a practical determination of a Kensington kind, based upon sound figure drawing and portraits rather than vapourish views and zephyr breezes. It was the non-visual Virginia who 'saw' with eyes of youthful artistry the place she so loved, and converted her visions into memories which would one day be revealed in words.★

In the early autumn of 1894, when Virginia was twelve, the Stephen family left after their holiday, never to return. As far as St Ives was concerned they disappeared into the ether, almost as though they had never been there at all. Talland House was bought by a Scot who had abandoned the law for art and become associated with the rebellious Glasgow Boys, Thomas Millie Dow, his wife, Florence Pitcher, and their large family, particularly for the benefit of an asthmatic son. Millie Dow painted ethereal, spiritual seascapes (such as Virginia might later have described) 'to make you creep with the strong quietness and mystery of nature' . . . 'pictures [that] touch us as a summer evening touches us, as a melody heard over still water'.[21]

Leslie Stephen had banned any returns to St Ives and sold Talland House after his wife's death in May 1895. Julia Stephen was forty-eight, and her resolute saintliness, her determination to keep faith with her workhouse charities in Southwark and Kensington, added to the burdens of her crowded household and her increasingly querulous husband, meant that she succumbed to influenza from overwork and exhaustion. Leslie, groaning with grief, announced that the rest of his life would be consecrated as a memorial to her, memories were to be kept sacred – and in his morbidity he, all too typically, 'forgot everyone but himself'.[22] The house, 'tangled and matted with emotion', became prey to his mad whims; Virginia, in pitiable self-defence, sank into a 'nothingness' of depression of which we can know little: she began

---

★ *The Voyage Out* (1915), *To the Lighthouse* (1927) and *The Waves* (1931) show the permanence of the influence upon her. Hermione Lee's biography is very strong on the development of this theme.[20]

her diary for the following year, 1896, but gave up after about three weeks (not, in itself, an unusual failing) and it has not survived. The thought arises that too much has been made of this first 'breakdown', for which she had good enough reason, and though 1896 is a silent year, she bursts forth on 1 January of 1897, joyfully riding her new bicycle to join the crowds of young cyclists in Battersea Park with Vanessa, Adrian and Georgie (Duckworth) as a lively and energetic young lady with the hope and promise of having a very good time.

London became her playground: besides cycling there was skating on the Round Pond, daily walks turned into explorations, a circuit of the Serpentine, or to the Chelsea Embankment and Royal Hospital grounds then home via her canny sense of direction or by 'my great skill we traced our way through the slums of a Southwark description, till we came to the South Kensington Station'.[23] Hopping on and off buses gave her seven-league boots – to Bond Street for shopping, to the Regent's Park Zoo, to the National Gallery to see 'everything', and back to Kensington High Street for buns for tea, flowers or hot chestnuts for Adrian. Vanessa, the committed art student, cycled to Onslow Square three mornings a week for lessons and dragged Virginia, not unwillingly, to every gallery and exhibition. The twenty-fifth of January was her fifteenth birthday, a day of informal pleasures and affections; Stella Duckworth took her to buy an armchair, her present, and Virginia took delivery of a 'gorgeous' tome, a biography of Queen Elizabeth written by Mandell Creighton, the Bishop of London, and from her father, Lockhart's life of Walter Scott – '10 beautiful little blue and brown gilt leathered backs'[24]; the Creighton proved heavy to hold and read and difficult to house, but she treasured the little Lockharts and enjoyed every one. Her serious reading, which her father selected from his own library and questioned her upon, was hardly for the feeble-minded: a stint of Thomas Carlyle (her father took her to see his house, 24 Cheyne Row in Chelsea: 'went over the house with an intelligent old woman who knew father and everything about him'[25]), J. D. Campbell's life of Coleridge, Macaulay's *History of England* in five volumes, and, for light relief, the newly published complete edition of Samuel Pepys's *Diary*. These and more were devoured in less than three months along with her work on Greek, Latin and German texts, plus novels of her own or Stella's choice from their subscription library, such as Thackeray's *The Newcomes* and Washington Irving's *Bracebridge Hall*, and not forgetting Leslie's readings to the family in the evenings.

Besides all this Virginia manages to appear also as what we would identify as 'a typical teenager': she adored the Drury Lane pantomime *Aladdin*, and *Peter Pan*. *Peter Pan* was something she never forgot – in her last book, *Between the Acts* (1939), the tour of the Swithuns' old house in the country reaches the nursery, but everyone else is out in the garden:

. . . the room was like a ship deserted by its crew . . . Dodge crossed to the fireplace and looked at the Newfoundland Dog in the Christmas Annual that was pinned to the wall. The room smelt warm and sweet; of clothes drying; of milk; of biscuits and warm water . . . a rushing sound came in through the open door . . . he left the door open for the crew to come back . . .[26]

But Virginia lived in the Christmas Annual too, for she met the Barries walking their Newfoundland, the inspiration for Nana in *Peter Pan*, in the gardens; she knew Peter Pan himself, the little Michael Llewelyn Davies, and his brothers, and their mother, Sylvia, who inspired the whole fantasy in the Barries' woodland garden in Surrey.* Oxford Circus meant coffee at the ABC café

---

* Andrew Birkin's *J. M. Barrie and the Lost Boys* contains the whole story.[27]

and the fledgling cinema 'the animatograph' in Regent Street; she relished riding on the top of a bus down Piccadilly eating fresh Bath buns, she hated having to stand still at the dressmaker's, she was the mainspring of the family's Entomological Society, loving all creepy-crawlies and curious beasts, finding the baby crocodiles being sold by a dealer in Covent Garden rather more exciting than those in the Zoo; and she would career passionately across the park in the crowds to catch a glimpse of Queen Victoria's hat. London became her, and though her prose record is clipped and staid, surely she was having a wonderful time?

The excitement of that spring of 1897 centred around Stella Duckworth's marriage to Jack Hills, which was to be at St Mary Abbots, Kensington on Saturday, 10 April: Stella had taken her mother's place as best she could and Virginia adored her, loving to be useful company on the endless errands and trips, tryings out and tryings on in preparation for the big day. The Misses Stephen, who had turned out godless after all, only managed to get to church in time for the last reading of the banns, but on the day they were dutiful attendants and all seemed well. The Hillses came home from their honeymoon to live at 24 Hyde Park Gate, at the end of the cul-de-sac, virtually extending the territory of No. 22; the innocently virginal Stella was 'unwell', and the family doctor diagnosed peritonitis. Through May and June Virginia became Stella's self-appointed slave, running errands, sitting with her, reading to her, working at flower boxes to cheer her, even working hard to make the dusty yard that passed for the back garden pretty with borders of pansies and sweet peas, and sprinkling grass seed. The weather turned hot, conditions were against the home garden, but Kensington Gardens were shady and there the flower walk was enchanting; Virginia went to the gardens two and even three times some days, and Stella too, as she got better. The Queen's Diamond Jubilee procession took over London on

22 June, and Virginia seemed to enjoy the splendour, but the tone of her diary is nervous: Stella's condition is low again, and now the peritonitis is complicated by pregnancy. Virginia's last entry is for the day of the Eton versus Harrow cricket match at Lord's on 10 July; she became ill herself, feverish, 'miserable & achey', and for a few days she and Stella watched over each other. In the early hours of Monday morning, 19 July, Georgie Duckworth and Vanessa woke her to say that Stella was dead. Two days later she was buried beside their mother in Highgate cemetery. None of them went.

Godlessness, which Stella herself did not share, had its drawbacks, and the rituals of funeral and farewell might have helped Virginia, but her father ruled otherwise. Her diary is resumed ten days later, she fills in the gaps, and then it stutters tersely to the year's end. Stella's death, of which Virginia's doting seemed to give her a terrible foreknowledge, broke her joyful heart. Most of all it destroyed her belief in life in Kensington, the only life she had known, life at the hub of the intellectual aristocracy, where never a nonentity crossed the threshold, but only the likes of Henry James, Octavia Hill (for whom Stella had been financing a housing project), the young composer Ralph Vaughan Williams, courting their cousin and Stella's best friend, Adeline Fisher, all the professors and artists, cousins and aunts from Holland Park and Campden Hill . . . the Hollands, Stephens, Milmans, Lushingtons, Holman Hunts, Freshfields, Vaughans – who had rolled through the house like a river to view the wedding presents and eat the Charbonnel & Walker (of Bond Street) tea. What had any of them done to help Stella? Virginia's fifteen-year-old's disgust with Kensington was the first flutter of Bloomsbury, and her anger did not lessen: over twenty years later, after reading something by Edith Sichel, she wrote, 'the breath of South Kensington lives in her pages . . . where they would not speak of copulation or wcs

. . . she makes me consider that the gulf which we crossed between Kensington and Bloomsbury was the gulf between respectable mummified humbug and life, crude and impertinent perhaps, but *living*.'[28]

Stella's death destroyed the Kensington Virginia, who stood on the summit of her privileges and might have done almost anything. All the happy memories of the things she did with Stella were buried with her, and Virginia relocated her affections to other parts of her native London, to Chelsea or Westminster. Almost thirty years later she housed *Mrs Dalloway* in Westminster; the Dalloways had lived there for over twenty years so she brings time full circle, and the sheer exuberant happiness of walking across the park to Mayfair, as she had done with Stella, is reborn. Clarissa Dalloway exults in the frisson of being at the centre of things, of knowing that important telegrams are flying from the Admiralty, and garden party invitations are issuing from Buckingham Palace; she revels in the lightness of step that the sunny greenery imparts to everyone, how hats are raised to a woman of substance. Virginia, the writer, reframes herself as the coltish teenager in awe of her lovely stepsister, and the hat-raising and bowing Henry James – 'Well, how d'ye do, Miss Duckworth' – emerges from her memory as he had from the passers-by in the park. Just as she used that walk to Bond Street on a sparkling London morning to evoke the insubstantialities of Clarissa Dalloway's life, were the missed opportunities not her own? For Virginia, as that clever, coltishly enchanting fifteen-year-old, did seem to have so many opportunities: she might have put her mind to her photography, for the great-niece of Julia Margaret Cameron would never have been short of subjects or scenes from life; she might have gone to Cambridge, like her brothers, for both Newnham and Girton would have welcomed her, operating as they did on the old girls' network of the Kensington Society, the pioneering forum for women's education to which all the founders belonged. Virginia's cousin Katharine Stephen was on the staff at Newnham and her connections with Girton were equally close: with her Greek she might have emulated Jane Harrison's adventures in mythology,[29] or her Latin might have led her to medieval history, as it did Eileen Power,[30] the close friend of the psychiatrist Karin Costelloe, who was to marry Adrian Stephen.* If Virginia had had the slightest wish to be a garden-artist, then her Hyde Park Gate neighbours, the Muir-Mackenzies, were related to Gertrude Jekyll, then at the peak of her fame and an *habitué* of the circle around Princess Louise and Jacques and Leonie Blumenthal, based at the Blumenthals' 43 Hyde Park Gate in the adjoining cul-de-sac. Horticulture was close to science, and Virginia could so well have swapped a Fortuny dress for a white coat, or worn each in turn, and pursued her bug-hunting and mothing into biochemistry or zoology at the Natural History Museum on the Cromwell Road. She might even have sailed for America, into the arms of her father's Bostonian and Harvard friends, where her welcome, and the sheer expanse and wonder of the American landscape, would have released her mind into flights of philosophic naturalism, the beginnings of the science of ecology, then so much in vogue.†

None of these fancies were to become realities. Stella's death, inexplicably linked, to the young Virginia, with the dark mysteries of sex and marriage, implanted a deeper fear – who would look after her now? When she herself was ill, collapsed into the nothing-ness of breakdown, why would she be treated any differently to

---

* Karin Costelloe (1889–1953) married Adrian Stephen in 1913, and they had little time for the Bloomsbury mainstream; her sister Ray, married to Oliver Strachey, was the feminist writer, author of *The Cause*.

† Her Lowell godparentage would have made her a place in Boston Brahmin society, where Mariana van Rensselaer (1851–1934) was a respected writer on travel, architecture and landscape architecture, the vogue in careers for women.

her stepsister, Laura – who was now confined to a mental hospital for long stays, and allowed home only under the strict supervision of a nurse-gaoler? Faced with what must have seemed like nightmare alternatives, from somewhere deep in her very being she instinctively took her only certain route, into her books and her writing.

The English landscape loosed her pen. In the last summers of Leslie Stephen's life the vacuum left by the forbidden St Ives (which, unspoken, seemed to extend to all seaside venues) was filled by landlocked wanderings in August, when the remnants of the once felicitous family of Stephen and Duckworth explored the art of the rented house, borrowing bits of other people's lives. The turn of the century was a vintage period for this social phenomenon: houses in the prettiest, but invariably agriculturally depressed, bits of the Cotswolds, Surrey or Norfolk, left vacant by deaths or departures to the outposts of Empire, awaiting colonial dreams of retirement, could be cheaply acquired, complete with their books and belongings, polished cutlery and freshly folded linen. By some miracle of holiday leasing fresh milk and vegetables always seemed to materialize from a neighbouring farm, and the same willing hands, nameless to posterity, took away the dirty washing. There was a peculiar detachment to this kind of holiday, as if one was floating in a strange existence, trying it for size and suitability. The rented house was the perfect place for writing.

On a wet afternoon in early August 1899 Virginia noted their arrival in Huntingdonshire: 'how we snorted the air with our soot-sated nostrils, and revelled in the country damp, cool and quiet.'[31] This countryside, by some unconscious instinct surrounding another St Ives, was to fill page after page of her Warboys notebook: they had arrived at St Ives station from London via Cambridge (Thoby Stephen was destined for Trinity College after the holidays) and had to drive some six miles northwards to

Warboys rectory, their goal. Immediately the writer is trying her wings – 'as we drove along the sun shot a shaft of light down; and we beheld a glorious expanse of sky – this golden gauze streamer lit everything in its light; and far away over the flat fields a spire caught the beam and glittered like a gem in the darkness and wetness.'[32]

The Fen edge landscape was of such individuality that she was forced to notice; she was wary – 'Monotony, so methinks, dwells in these plains. Such melting gray of sky, land and water is the very spirit of monotony'[33] – and realistic: 'I am, at the present moment (the emotion is fleeting I know, so I must chronicle it) in love with a country life; I think that a year or two of such gardens and green fields would infallibly sweeten one and soothe one and simplify one into the kind of Gilbert White old gentleman . . .'[34] She was also driven to spoof reportage –

Extract from the Huntingdonshire Gazette
TERRIBLE TRAGEDY IN A DUCKPOND

in which herself, Adrian and their cousin Emma Vaughan load up the punt on the rectory garden pond with armchairs, for a leisurely cruise; it seems there was an 'incautious movement' on the top-heavy craft and 'the angry waters of the duckpond rose in their wrath to swallow their prey'.[35]

The setting for seven weeks that needed such enlivening is little changed. Warboys rectory is a bulky, yellow-brick representative of its Fenland type, at the end of the village, surrounded by trees, opposite the medieval church of St Mary Magdalene (and a curious seventeenth-century house of Flemish bricks that looks as if it sailed across the North Sea ready built): here they met the Curate, who was so pleased to dine, who lived up to Virginia's expectations drawn from novels by his 'gift of humorous sarcasm' and admission that his life was only made tolerable by the rabbit-shooting. This end of Warboys has a roof-of-the-world feeling, for the rectory is on the very edge of the Fens, with westward views through its sheltering trees of miles of vaguely undulating Huntingdonshire: to the east the drains and droves cut horizontally to Ely. In that summer of 1899 sometimes it was hot – Virginia exaggerated 'the hottest day I have yet lived thro' to her cousin Emma[36] – and her August ennui left her 'sinking into the Sky': it was the sky, the ever-fascinating canopy, that so delighted her and drove her pen. For, if the days were long, the country flat, perfect for day-long cycle rides, for floating on the river at Hartford or St Ives – languidly lovely meadow stretches of the Great Ouse – or simply reading in a hammock in the garden's shade, there was so much space and time in which to write. So much that she ran out of things to write about, entered into discussions with her pens, her ink and even the pages of her journal, and by early September she was counting the days, twice over. But how lucky she was, full of 'contentment and creamy potatoes', to have all this spaciousness: 'I shall think of it as a test for friends . . .' she wrote teasingly to Emma Vaughan, 'whether they can appreciate the Fen country. I want to read books about it, and to write sonnets about it all day long.'[37] They never returned to Warboys rectory, but this countryside remained familiar through visits to Lady Stephen at Godmanchester, and to another aunt, Miss Emilia Stephen, who lived at The Porch in Newnham in Cambridge. Both these aunts were to care for Virginia in her times of fragile health, and so this languid, dreaming countryside became tinged with a dangerous lassitude in Virginia's later estimation.

For the last, and predictably difficult, summer of Sir Leslie Stephen's life, for August and half of September 1903, they had a soothing interlude at Netherhampton, in the Nadder valley, west of Salisbury. For the first time Virginia is inspired to architectural detail: Netherhampton House was all that she hoped,

a little gray stone house, too humble to be itself ornate, but evidently dating from an ornate period . . . There is some kind of architectural device of urns at intervals on the gables; there is a hollowed recess in the wall, meant perhaps, were things on a larger scale, to stand a statue in. The garden gate too, is uncommon gracefully wrought in blue green iron, and surmounted by a coat of arms . . . the coat of arms, besides various small statelinesses within and without, proclaim its aristocratic connections.

The house had, in fact, been built by the Gauntlett family, prosperous clay-pipe makers, of whom one was an Elizabethan mayor of Salisbury and another had added the ornate touches in about 1670, including the gateway with the Gauntlett arms. The little grey front was deceptive, and the house was red brick at the back, with mellow old brick walls and spacious rooms around a garden court. Because the house belonged to the Wilton Estate (as it still does) Virginia imagined 'various old countesses' living in it: the history was rather more interesting, especially for a nineteen-year-old literary girl, in that after the Gauntletts died out it was bought by Thomas Grove for his niece Mrs Philippa Grove, who was in turn aunt of Harriet, Shelley's cousin and first love. Shelley was seventeen, Harriet eighteen at the time of their romantic meetings at Netherhampton; they were separated by their parents, and Harriet was married off to the cloddish William Helyer of Coker Court in Somerset. Harriet's lovely ghost was believed to return.[38]

The long-term tenant of Netherhampton was the sculptor Henry Furse, brother of the painter Charles Furse, who had done a portrait of Vanessa in 1902 and had a great success at the Royal Academy in that summer of 1903. Virginia felt that the Furse way of treating the house was perfect – 'The wide rooms are furnished not too profusely with dignified old chairs and solid tables: crimson and white is the scheme of the whole place, with a touch of ruddy old wood.'[39] There were long drifts of white 'Mrs Sinkins' pinks beside a wide grass walk in the garden, with a lawn and beds of roses, lilies and lavender; there were lime trees and hornbeams in a little 'wilderness' and merely a sunken fence separated garden from meadows.

Virginia wrote a series of topographical 'chapters' on Nether-hampton: 'Wilton – From Outside the Walls', 'The Water Meadows', 'The Downs', 'Stonehenge', and even 'The Wilton Carpet Factory' – the last a description of what she saw on a public tour. She succumbed to the beauty of Salisbury Cathedral and its mesmerizing presence in her landscape, found Romsey Abbey 'a fine place; Milton might have written it, in stone',[40] and returned to Stonehenge – where, having the whole place to themselves, they walked across and sat inside the circle: 'the solitary policeman whose strange lot in life it is to mount guard over Stonehenge had taken shelter behind one of his charges'.[41] Most interestingly she examined her response to the balmy surroundings, feeling that such an abundance of the spirit of Nature surrounded them that they could only breathe it peacefully; she was more sensitive to heat and cold, sun and rain:

If I lived here much longer I should get to understand the wonderful rise and swell and fall of the land. It is like some vast living thing, and all its insects and animals, save man, are exquisitely in time with it. If you lie on the earth somewhere you hear a sound like a vast breath, as though it were the very inspiration of earth herself, and all the living things on her.[42]

Netherhampton did not disappear entirely from Virginia's later life: Charles Furse died the following year, aged thirty-six, leaving his widow Katharine and her sons to live with Henry Furse and his sister at Netherhampton. When Katharine and the maiden sister moved out, Henry was joined by Henry and Margaret Newbolt (Sir Henry's 'Drake's Drum' was a great favourite of Leslie Stephen and Virginia, as was the poet himself, and Margaret Newbolt was the Duckworths' cousin). The Newbolts went for a summer and stayed for twenty-seven years.[43]

Virginia's twenty-first birthday, 25 January 1903, had passed with little mention and less celebration; she appreciated Thoby's present of fine old volumes of Bacon's and Montaigne's essays, and her cousins' greetings on her breakfast plate meant more than Gerald Duckworth's 'magnificent' pearls, immediately broken, and the rest 'jewels of some kind'. What a curious 'childhood' it had been, more of the eighteenth century than the brink of the twentieth, and perhaps she was more fitted to be swept off her feet by a young Shelley than anything else. But she knew no young Shelleys, nor any young men to her taste: hedged in by her brothers – Thoby, 'a charming great inarticulate creature, with torrents of things shut up in him', and Adrian, who 'grows too fast to think or feel, or do anything but eat', with Gerald Duckworth courting an American millionaire for the good of his publishing business and George courting Lady Margaret Herbert – her feelings were corralled into 'schoolgirl' crushes, on her cousin Emma Vaughan or her six-foot-tall 'my woman', Violet Dickinson. No. 22 Hyde Park Gate was her home and school and everything; she had grown tall and willowy herself, drawn up like some hothouse flower, reared on light gossip and heavy literature. The world beyond Kensington was seen only through those August windows: she had only 'the vaguest idea of your or anybodies geography' as she admitted to Emma Vaughan who was in Switzerland[44] – and apparently alighted on their holiday houses without a glance at a map.

Her discovery of places was almost entirely instinctive, venturing out from wherever she had arrived, or been taken, groping in the manner of a blind puppy. The freshness of her observations on the places came from her, slightly assumed, ignorance, which in itself was a writer's tool. Places could be damned through no fault of their own, usually because they held some association with her captivity in convalescence after one of her bad spells of depression: Surrey fell into this category – 'a sham country. This place [Chilworth, near Guildford] isn't so bad as Hindhead, but its over run with Cockneys and Culture. Everyone artistic seems to retire here, and build a red brick house with sham Elizabethan white and black.'[45] Sussex began very badly in her estimation with 'muddy misty flat utterly stupid Bognor',[46] until she discovered that Sussex too, like Wiltshire, had downland. The downs became like old friends, her green seas: while at Netherhampton they had driven to Broadchalke, along the Ebble valley through Bishopstone, beneath the great shoulders of Stoke and Fifield downs, and Knighton and Middleton hills, and without geography or geology, she wrote:

I kept likening the downs to the long curved waves of the sea. It is as though the land here, all molten once, and rolling in vast billows had solidified while the waves were still swollen and on the point of breaking. From a height it looks as though the whole land were flowing . . . the villages have all sunk into the hollows between the waves; and the result is a peculiar smoothness and bareness of outline. This is the bare bone of the earth.[47]

She took time to come to terms with the ancient downs; their green waves brought back the old losses of her mother and the sea, their very timelessness mocked her own all too often fragile hold on life, they did not care and would go on being magnificent and beautiful, even if she wasn't there. Conversely, she found the New Forest was always a greatly comforting place, its ancient woods like some old timbered houses, full of age and sympathy. The Forest's high and heathery northern plain was probably recommended by Sir Leslie Stephen's doctors, and they were there for three summers, two at Fritham House, a big and new sham Elizabethan (to Virginia) Arts and Crafts house with timbered verandahs and marvellous views. There were splendid walks in all directions, to Bramshaw, Brook, the Rufus Stone, Minstead and Castle Malwood, and excellent opportunities for bug-hunting and mothing in habitats very different from the Ouse and Nadder valleys. Virginia, however, somehow made her way to the sea, and fell in love with Christchurch Priory, seen 'from afar like a ship riding out to sea'. She turned her impressions into one of her first published pieces, ending with the view from the roof: 'Here out on the leads, with the sharp spine of the church running out beneath you, you look to the sea on two sides; and directly at your feet the rivers Stour and Avon loop and cross and entangle themselves like a silver chain.'[48] She loved it 'planted' so sturdily with only 'a breadth of flats, dun-coloured with feathery bulrushes' to save it from the waves, and inland 'an undulating shadow' that marked the beginning of the Forest.

After Sir Leslie Stephen's death on 22 February 1904 Virginia was senseless with remorse and grief, wishing she had done more for him, wishing she could have other chances. She clung to Violet Dickinson, she was irritable even with the healing wildness of Pembrokeshire, and Venice and Florence in April only struck glancing impressions: she could not believe Venice was real and wandered about open-mouthed – 'I don't think Florence will come up to this' – but the view from Fiesole was 'almost more beautiful than anything I have seen'.[49] She thought Florence 'a pretence', unsurprisingly, because they found Kensington

'Prinseps, Lytteltons, Humphry Wards, Cambridge Undergraduates, Carnarvons . . . and finally to make us feel quite at home, Aunt Minna Duckworth'.[50]

Italy as a country was unsurpassed in beastliness, and then after returning via Paris in early May she descended into nothingness again. Sir Leslie's will had made provision for Laura to be kept in a hospital (where she was to survive until 1945, longer than Virginia). Sir George Savage, who treated Virginia, was consultant to the Bethlehem Royal Hospital, and it seems that Virginia only escaped because there was money for nurses and Violet Dickinson, and her aunts, were prepared to house her: she attempted to kill herself by throwing herself out of a window at Violet's cottage in Welwyn. The October move to Bloomsbury was accomplished by the others with Virginia largely as spectator; however, it was Aunt Minna Duckworth who was to restore Virginia to joy in life, by lending them her house at Bank, near Lyndhurst, for Christmas and for the Forest to work its healing ways. Bank was a tiny hamlet of four or five houses and the Royal Oak on the edge of ancient Gritnam Wood, reachable from Lyndhurst Road station. 'It is the loveliest place,' she admitted; 'we have beech trees practically poking their heads in at the front door . . . and Forest ponies come when you call them.'[51] The Forest gradually won her, even from missing Violet Dickinson whom she clung to still, but almost for the last time: Aunt Minna's house was called Lane End, only such a different ending here – free to walk in the woods and commune with the trees, and even chat with the locals. It turned into a chaotically happy Christmas, a first Christmas for Bloomsbury in the country, when sweet independence was first tasted. Dinner was the traditional turkey but eaten so late that it merged into teatime. The hollies, oaks and beeches of Bank, its velvety lawns and sandy paths, crunching with frost, magical in snow, rescued her. The paths into medieval, mysterious woods, and the exhilaration of the high heather moors with purply-ochre waves, released her to life in her new world, and they became a byword for Bloomsbury heaven among friends yet to come.

So it was, in the way of sacred histories, that in the first week of October 1904 the four Stephens, Vanessa, Thoby, Virginia and Adrian, took possession of a home new to them at 46 Gordon Square in the parish of St Pancras, just south of Euston Station in west central London.* From their front door, on the east side of the square, it was a few steps southwards into Woburn Square, and they had crossed the invisible boundary into the parish of St George's, Bloomsbury: the Stephens, who had little time for parishes or boundaries of any kind, told their friends that they lived in Bloomsbury, and so Bloomsbury their new territory became.

Virginia supposed that Vanessa had looked at a map to see how far from Kensington they could get, and chose Bloomsbury: Vanessa was perhaps attracted by the Slade School of Art nearby (though she was soon disillusioned by Professor Henry Tonks and lost interest), or their mother's cousin, Adeline, the widow of the 10th Duke of Bedford, may have had a hand in the arrangements. Their western part of Bloomsbury was the well-managed London estate of the Dukes of Bedford, with family names and connections, Russell, Woburn, Tavistock, Endsleigh (after their Devon

---

* The Bedford Estate archives have no record of the Stephens as tenants of 46 Gordon Square; the lease was assigned in 1892 to the Alliance Economic Investment Company, who must have sub-let, until the house was sold to the University of London in 1949. Adeline, Duchess of Bedford (for whom they have no papers either), lived at Chenies in Buckinghamshire and was an early client of Edwin Lutyens and Gertrude Jekyll; it seems possible that she had an interest in the welfare of her cousin, Julia Stephen's, children, and may have suggested Gordon Square.

properties), and Gordon was the family name of the 6th Duke's second wife. 'Bloomsbury' was (and is) bounded on the north by the Euston Road, by Tottenham Court Road on the west, New Oxford Street and Bloomsbury Way to the south, and it filters eastwards through Brunswick and Mecklenburgh squares (named in honour of the Hanoverian territories – George III's Queen Charlotte of Mecklenburg-Strelitz, the Princess of Wales Caroline of Brunswick) to the Gray's Inn Road – which became Clerkenwell and the East Central postal district, where they would not have dreamed of living.

Gordon Square was almost completely filled by musty clerics running crammers or lecturing at University College in Gower Street: if Kensington was red plush and great elms in the gardens, Gordon Square was worn leather and London planes. Their house, No. 46 on the east side of Gordon Square, was the end one of a block in grey brick, banded in creamy-grey stucco below the three tall first-floor windows, with a small iron balcony, and entered by a square-headed front door. This particular style, with Corinthian columns dividing the blocks, and the same as the west side of Tavistock Square, was the most successful of the great builder Thomas Cubitt's developments across the open fields north of Bedford House and the British Museum (and may have been designed by his brother, Lewis Cubitt, the designer of King's Cross Station). The houses on the east side were the last to be finished, after Thomas Cubitt's death in 1855, and leased by his estate in 1857: the square's garden had been particularly well planted – the 7th Duke being very keen on this aspect – with ash, birch, sweet chestnut, pink-flowered horse-chestnut, limes, planes, lilacs, thorns and flowering cherries. The rectangular garden had a more intimate feeling than the larger 'squares', with paths, seats and a small summerhouse offering a private green retreat for the keyholders.

In October 1904 Virginia felt that Gordon Square was the most beautiful, romantic and exciting place in the world; it was a life of her own, alone with her sister and brothers, after six months of depression and being constantly nursed and chaperoned. For Vanessa there had been the healthier catharsis of turning out, sorting, selling, throwing out and burning the contents of 22 Hyde Park Gate, and actually relishing the sight of men with hammers demolishing cupboards and partitions that had imprisoned them. They only kept what they wanted, a first freedom, and in the space and bareness of the rooms at No. 46 their treasures – some Watts paintings, a Dutch cabinet, their blue and white china – shone out with a new life. In their large drawing-room with the tall windows on the first floor they entered the 'Sargent-Furse era' under Vanessa's direction with green and white chintzes and plainly distempered walls. It was, in those days almost 100 years ago, a room so far removed from the Victorian age as to be completely familiar today: a comfortable sofa and armchairs spaciously set around the gracious 'Georgian' fireplace, and a (real) coal fire: a room of cool plain surfaces, and many reflections, sunlight or firelight playing on a silver candlestick or three roses in a glass – 'those tall clean rather frigid rooms' that Vanessa recalled, that released them to new life.[52]

One of the first tasks of her new life for Virginia was to revisit her memories of St Ives – released from her father's ban, with hazy images of herself as a plump and happy child playing in a rock pool, of a young girl tall for her age shrieking with excitement at a game of tag among the escallonia hedges, or of herself calmly reading on a sunny terrace – those young and fleeting summers had to be verified. From a return visit, staying on her own in a boarding-house, she discovered the joy of a strenuous walk against the wind, of how gorse bushes smelt of nuts 'as George Meredith says they do', and how, taking shelter in a druid's cave, she saw 'the singular beauty of leafless but budding trees against a deep blue sea'.

'The sea is a miracle,' she concluded, 'more congenial to me than any human being.'[53] She passed the barrier of guilt to rediscover her father at his best, the Leslie Stephen that tramped and recited, shouting Meredith, Tennyson and Wordsworth to the wind . . . she now heard their lines in his voice, and rescued some of his beliefs as guidance. It was at St Ives, she remembered, that her father had taught her to walk, stretching her thin legs along the shore path to Godrevy and beyond, and through the Celtic countryside of West Penwith to Trencrom Fort and Carn Galver and out west to Zennor and Gurnard's Head. From the inspiration of these walks Virginia learned a surpassing skill, for she could write as she walked, or walk and write, both impossibilities: writing as if she was walking was to be one of her most revelatory accomplishments, beautifully displayed in an essay, 'A Walk by Night', published in the *Guardian* of 28 December 1905, and a midwinter night's dream of a piece: she uses a memory of the previous late summer when, with Vanessa, Thoby and Adrian, they had left their walk to Trevail so late that the return was engulfed in the dark. She composes the gathering uncertainties as the known world disappears into the gloom – 'a solemn procession of great cliffs fronting the night and the Atlantic waves with what seemed an almost conscious nobility of purpose, as though yet once more they must obey some immemorial command'. They are on a road that is familiar enough by day, but soon 'even the white surface beneath us swam like mist, and our feet struck somewhat tentatively as though they questioned the ground': sensual confusion mounts, companions recede . . . 'one strode on alone, conscious of the pressure of the dark all around, conscious, too, that by degrees resistance to it grew less and less; that the body carried forward over the ground was some thing separate from the mind which floated away . . .' Disorientation releases her brain to search for words, and she digs into the intensity of the experience: they struck off – 'if a word implying definite action can be used of anything as indefinite as our course' – across the fields of daytime, now 'the trackless ocean of the night'. Sight and hearing were suspended, for they were no longer reliable – then some lights appeared; incomprehensibly 'they hung, floating without anchorage, in soft depths of darkness in a valley beneath us; for directly that the eye had proved them true the brain woke and constructed a scheme of the world in which to place them' . . . familiar St Ives. The strangest part was over, for though the people they met 'were not as the people of the daytime', and the farmer bidding them good night 'recalled us as though a firm hand had grasped ours, to the shores of the world', then within two strides was gone, they were in the village. It was a different village in the dark –

. . . how puny were the rays of the lamp against the immeasurable waves of darkness . . . A ship at sea is a lonely thing, but far lonelier it seemed was this little village anchored to the desolate earth and exposed every night, alone, to the unfathomed waters of darkness.

Virginia's diary adds the ending that she did not include in the published piece:[54] it was indeed a 'different' village and 'there seemed to be a film between us and the reality' – as if they were but coming home their steps led them by instinct to Talland House, where they peer through the hedge:

There was the house, with its two lighted windows; there on the terrace were the stone urns, against the bank of tall flowers; all, so far as we could see was as though we had but left it in the morning. But yet, as we knew well, we could go no further; if we advanced the spell was broken. The lights were not our lights; the voices were the voices of strangers.[55]

They 'hung there like ghosts' then turned away, walking on to their roof of exile in Carbis Bay, where the darkness was most intense. When they arrived indoors, at this other temporary lodging 'the walls of the house were too narrow, the glare of the lamps too fierce' . . . 'we were as birds lately winged that have been caught and caged'.[56]

This was a stolen visit, for in a little more than a year the foursomeness of the Stephens was to be broken by Thoby's death from typhoid and Vanessa's engagement to Clive Bell. It was almost as if Virginia clung to her love of St Ives to replace the completeness of 'the felicitous family of Stephen' that was crumbling away, and her love was more for the symbol than the reality. For whatever reason she loved St Ives, it was in reconstructing her childhood Eden that she grappled with the inner and outer experiences of anticipating, passing through, or simply being in, places. Only the unforced love of a personal landscape can teach this, foster this need to know, this depth of curiosity: though Virginia may have ignored much of the life of St Ives, the locals not fitting her cast of likely characters, she interpreted the experience and moods of the St Ives seascape as surely as the best of the painters, and she plundered her store of beloved images of the sea and all its trappings for the rest of her life. As a writer she resented the intrusion of identification into her fictional settings; she felt very definitely that 'a writer's country is a territory within his own brain; and we run the risk of disillusionment if we try to turn such phantom cities into tangible bricks and mortar'.[57] While respecting her sensibility, it seems not far-fetched to add that without Godrevy, the far lighthouse that 'flashed its golden pathway through the mist', lighting her life there would have been no novels, no writer's territory, nor perhaps any Virginia Woolf, at all.

2

Edward Morgan Forster

Morgan Forster was unable to talk and marry his way into the Bloomsbury circle, like Clive Bell, and though he may appear to have been an outsider, his credentials from the Clapham Sect intellectuals, a mélange of Thorntons, Venns, Grants, Babingtons and Macaulays, was equal to Virginia's or Lytton Strachey's. Forster could also match Virginia's childhood paradise of St Ives: his was a rather plain, modest brick house set in a soft stretch of Hertfordshire countryside and called Rooksnest. He lived there for ten years, from just after his fourth birthday and almost until his fourteenth: he called it 'a kind of paradise', it symbolized 'my childhood and safety', and he and his mother were denied it because the owners, the neighbouring family of Poston, wanted it for their daughter. It was a fair enough reason, and Forster later became friends with the Postons, but to a sensitive, introverted and rather lonely boy, it was an appalling crime; he took his revenge, and Rooksnest, which had formerly been called Howard's after the family that farmed the land for 300 years, was to be spirited into fame as the definitive house to be loved and lost, and eventually refound, *Howards End*.

Rooksnest gave Morgan Forster a love of the English countryside, with all the foibles and peculiarities of life within it, for unlike Virginia Stephen's sea view, his paradise was firmly on earth set amid farming life. It gave him a belief in a home, in what he called 'the Thornton sense' of a home as the be-all and end-all of life: Rooksnest, and the big wych elm which filtered the western sun so that it dappled and danced on the drawing-room windows and carpet, connected him, the small boy Morgan, to the ancestral glories of the Thorntons' pride. This, he had learnt, almost as soon as he could understand, from his great-aunt Marianne, was a big house in Clapham, called Battersea Rise. It was an Adam-style mansion, with always precisely thirty-four bedrooms and a large bow-windowed library once graced by Wilberforce and Pitt. The garden was 'a perfect playground' of grand and spacious lawns and wondrous flower-beds, but most singularly a magnificent tulip tree, a *Liriodendron tulipifera*, then rare enough to be remarked upon by every observant visitor. One by one the Thornton children were inducted into the mysteries of the tree as a kind of ritual, remarking not only its size and shade, but the peculiarly beautiful blunt-fingered leaves, the green and orange tulip flowers, and how autumn turned the leaves to gold. Aunt Marianne had told him that 'to the day of my death I shall think nothing so lovely as the tree and the lawn at Battersea Rise'. She too had suffered exile, for appearances' sake, from her childhood home because of her brother's 'disgraceful' second marriage to his deceased wife's sister: her brother, Morgan's great-uncle, Henry Sykes Thornton, MP, had proposed a bill through Parliament to rectify his misdemeanour but had died in the attempt.★ [1] The tulip tree and the lawn, and Battersea Rise itself, were soon all gone – Morgan went to look for the house once but could find no sign

---

★ The North American *Liriodendron* was introduced in 1688; to be a large and impressive tree in Marianne's youth, i.e. the early 1800s, this must have been an early full-grown specimen. H. S. Thornton, MP died in 1881; his amendment did not enter the statute book until the Marriage Act 1907.

– only the name survives in the section of the A3 between Spencer Park and Clapham Common Northside. The memory was passed to Morgan as a sacred trust.

Morgan Forster really owed his very existence to Aunt Marianne, for it was she who had taken an interest in a poor but spirited twelve-year-old of her acquaintance, Alice Clara Whichelo: Alice Clara, who had no hope in her own bleak circumstances, became Miss Thornton's unofficial ward, unofficially intended for the rich spinster's favourite nephew, Eddie, a son of her sister Laura and the Revd Charles Forster. Fate was to have it that Eddie and Alice Clara, known as Lily, met of their own accord, at Abinger Hall in Surrey, where she was staying as companion to Ida Farrer (who was to marry Charles Darwin's youngest son, Horace), and to where Eddie was summoned on architectural work. Eddie Forster enjoyed life, he had enjoyed his vicarage childhood, his school, Charterhouse, and Trinity College at Cambridge, and he was now working in the architect Sir Arthur Blomfield's genial office (where Thomas Hardy had been for five years), where his Principal was President of the Westminster Abbey Glee Club and allowed plan drawing to be enlivened by glees and catches, there was much sporting talk and the usual morning greeting of the young men began with 'Any spice in the papers?'* Blomfield's style was high Gothic Revival, with a lot of church work and impeccable connections; freehand sketching and watercolours of buildings were thought important.[2]

So the cheerful Eddie and the rather more practical Lily Whichelo were duly married, on 7 November 1876, and after a

---

* The brief career of Eddie Forster (and apparent lack of interest on the part of his son) is to be regretted, for despite the gothic grounding of Sir Arthur Blomfield's office and *bonhomie*, the house that Eddie built, West Hackhurst at Abinger, demonstrated his astute observance of vernacular traditions, about to flower in the Arts and Crafts movement.

first child was stillborn their second, Edward Morgan Forster, arrived on 1 January 1879 at their home, 6 Melcombe Place, off Dorset Square, just south of Regent's Park. Eddie Forster died of tuberculosis in October the following year, 1880.

It was defiant determination to be neither snubbed nor smothered by Forsters and Thorntons that led Lily to escape to Hertfordshire with her little son: it seems possible that she had heard of Stevenage from Eddie, for Blomfield did a lot of work in Hertfordshire, including Holy Trinity church in Stevenage, a little flint and red brick building of 1861 – for which a larger nave was under discussion in the last year of Eddie's life. However she found it, it was a great adventure for a little boy: Forster later had, or at least thought he had, a clear memory of his arrival in March 1883, of the train journey, of seeing the old flint church, St Nicholas, high on the Bury at the far top of the High Street, of passing the farm and seeing Rooksnest for the first time. He did not remember entering the house, only playing with bricks on the drawing-room floor.

Rooksnest was not as pretty as memory and films have made it – to put in a word for Eddie Forster the architect, largely forgotten from now on, it was nowhere near as pretty as the house he built in 1877 for the Farrers at Abinger, where Morgan was later to live. Rooksnest was a rectangular brick house, facially of the nineteenth century (but with older timbers and a bricked-up inglenook fireplace inside), with three main rooms in line along the front, downstairs and up, and two perky dormers in the roof for attic bedrooms. It faced slightly west of due south, with St Nicholas's leaded spire and crenellations in view; one of the nicest things was the approach from the side, from the east end, which meant that the front of the house, with a modest bay window for the dining-room and front porch, gave on to flower-beds, which spilled their seedlings out into the gravel, with fruit trees and the 'front' lawn, which was big enough for tennis. Forster later recalled 'nothing peculiar' about the dining- and drawing-rooms but that they were 'nice': he loved the large L-shaped cupboard in his nursery, and the storeroom next to his mother's bedroom which had 'a mingled odour of apples, mice and jam'.[3] Rooksnest was very wholesome and fruitful.

When he was fifteen Forster made himself draw a plan of the garden★ – 'the chief fault of which is that the house is too big for the garden and the back garden should be larger than it is'.[4] (He may have been testing his own architectural talents, for his accompanying description of the house concentrates upon structure and alterations: he mourned the blocked-up inglenook and the cottage-style door on the stairs, which mystified visitors, but hinted at going to bed as some kind of secret vice!) Such realism ousted his infant ability for expanded scale – had the modest bay of the dining-room and the wych elm done duty for Battersea Rise's famed floor-to-ceiling curve of glass and the tulip tree? Was the meanly cupboard stairway an aberration of the usual pride of a house?

On the garden part of the plan he lavished tender care, marking every tree and secret treasure: outside the back door, the corner of the kitchen plot is named 'my garden': the evidence of his practical skills appeared early on in *Where Angels Fear to Tread*, where Mrs Herriton, disaster impending, concentrates upon the peas: 'We will save the peas to the last; they are the greatest fun,' comes out of the mouth of some forgotten Rooksnest gardener . . . or perhaps his mother? '. . . Mrs Herriton was very careful to let those peas trickle evenly from her hand, and at the end of the

★ Forster's Rooksnest plan is included as illustration 3. The memoir and plan are in the Modern Archive Centre, King's College, Cambridge.

row she was conscious that they had never been sown better. They were expensive too.'[5]

The whole of the back, kitchen garden and orchard is studded with fruit trees, apple, damson, cherry and more greengage, some outside the fence, indicating that the fruit orchard was once much larger, and some of the trees are of great age. At the farthest extreme of the garden is the small, wild pond. Neither old grey photographs nor Morgan's little plan do Rooksnest's garden justice: one can only imagine how enchanting it must have been with its 'end' atmosphere, for though the lane wound on to Weston, there was little but hedgerows, woods and fields in between. To the west it was only dipping fields, the prettiest small-scale landscape towards Graveley and the Wymondleys: it was contained within its hedges, with its trees, fruits and flowers, and bosky secret corners.

What a difference an end makes? Whereas the walled-in cul-de-sac of Hyde Park Gate became a prison, Howards End was a magical, secure burrow with windows on a beautiful landscape. Forster was keenly aware of the little community of which he was a rather special part: the Plums, the gamekeeper's family, with Baby Plumbun 'a truly hateful child', and the farmers, the Franklins, who fascinated him most. Their farm was chaotic, but he liked it: the yard full of mud and manure 'in the midst of which wallowed enormous pigs', passing which Morgan saw as a test of his courage. Once past the pigs, there were the great barns full of 'dim religious light' and curious machines with big wheels; Frankie, the farmer's grandson, 'used to spread himself out on them like Ixion and whirl around while I stood by wishing I dare do it too'. And he 'never tired of poking about in the barn for eggs', with the warmth and exultation at finding a buried treasure, still warm, and that a mere human could rumble the merry Hen at her wily game! The Franklins, he decided, 'were an odd mixture', mean, yet making good money on their sheep's wool, never refusing a beggar and tolerant to a fault of boys' games, tumbling in the hayricks. And yet they charged Lily Forster over the odds for two pails of drinking water a day. The water shortage – they had to catch every drop of rainwater for everything but drinking – and the overly populous mice were the drawbacks of life at Rooksnest, but neither could seriously threaten the young Forster's contentment with the place.[6]

Just as he could not spreadeagle himself like Frankie Franklin, so the young Forster learnt he could never be a farmer, they were a different kind of being. He felt both inferior and superior at the same time, knowing that the farmhouse sported 'antimacassars of vivid awfulness' and 'frightful tablecloths' in the rooms he saw (though he later discovered 'a light and warm and very nice' intimate sitting-room which small boys were forbidden). He came to know, as he later wrote, that such as the Franklins belonged to 'an elder race', to be viewed 'with some disquietude' by those, like himself, who loved the countryside for the views from their windows and from the paths they walked. The Franklins *belonged*; for them 'the graver sides of life, the deaths, the partings, the yearnings for love, have their deepest expressions in the hearts of the fields'.[7] Morgan, who would never break his heart, or his bank balance, over an aborted pedigree calf or a ripe wheatfield smashed by an August storm, could never earn the right to belong in the same way.

For the first four years of his life at Rooksnest, Aunt Marianne Thornton lived in fading Thornton splendour at 'ducally dominated' Milton Bryan, a hamlet on the edge of the Bedfords' park at Woburn. It was about twenty miles across country from Stevenage and Rooksnest by carriage, a journey which extended his views of the friendly, small-scale rolling country of Hertfordshire, where it merges into Bedfordshire. He remembered Milton Bryan as a 'resort for ageing ladies', where his Thornton pride and

Thornton prospects were aired amongst yapping lapdogs and the chink of teacups: he could only have hazily understood, but Aunt Marianne lived just long enough to impart her middle-class and atavistic slant on society into his young mind. Happiness at Rooksnest made him absorbent, well able to construct his own 'paradise of childhood', as psychologists have it, out of his present comforts, allied to a mystical sense of a proud past and image of himself as its small and special heir. Even the apparent subtlety that his was an inheritance of intellect and means, but not – as the ducal glories of Woburn outside Aunt Marianne's windows – of rent rolls, pheasant shoots and pine plantations seemed to be perfectly understood.

Between the Thorntons and the Franklins, between the view and the furrow, the young Morgan Forster constructed his poetic persona, somewhat in the Wordsworthian manner, but more aptly in the way of Walt Whitman:

> There was a child went forth every day,
> And the first object he looked upon, that object he became . . .
> The early lilacs became part of this child,
> And grass and white and red morning glories, and white and red
>   clover, and the song of the phoebe-bird.[8]

Though he was more of remote Hertfordshire, the loveliest, most lovable, landscape of England, with 'hedges full of clematis, primroses, bluebells, dog-roses, may, bryony and nuts', and all these things he became. This love for a countryside that he could not own, and would not have wanted to, but for which he feared, was to be the theme of his life's writing: it became a theme with a name, 'Forsterian'.

The break with Rooksnest came at a doubly traumatic time, when he was thirteen and a half and he had to pack up and leave, and start at his bewilderingly large public school, Tonbridge in Kent, all in quick succession. Rooksnest had only been rented and was owned by a stockbroker named Charles Poston, who lived in a house called Highfield, about a mile away; the Postons – and another family, the Jowitts – were the 'only families whom Lily had consented to know'.[9] Charles Poston, who had remarried after the death of his first wife, needed the house for his daughter Clementine and her children Elizabeth and Ralph. (Something of Charles Poston went into the character of Henry Willcox in *Howards End*.)

Forster's biographer, Nicola Beauman, notes that Forster, when he was fifty-three, had declared that if he had been able to stay at Rooksnest his life would have been quite different: Beauman feels that 'he did not say this flippantly, as meaning he would have been happy, he would have been "normal"; he also meant that by staying in rural, dusty, sensually rich surroundings he would not have acquired his fear of women's sexuality'. Leaving as he did, just when he needed a country education into the facts of life, was an emotional disaster: he headed off into an exclusively male world and women remained a mystery – he admitted that 'not till I was thirty, did I know exactly how male and female joined'.[10]

Of course, if he had stayed and learnt to belong in leafy Hertfordshire, comfortable and unconcerned, chairing meetings of the local preservation society, he would never have written a word.

Instead, as Nicola Beauman writes, 'the departure from Rooksnest made Morgan fall back on the cerebral'.[11] His relationship with his mother was based upon mutual neediness, rather than anything more noble, and Lily Forster mishandled his education because she needed his problems to fuss over. Unlike her son, she hated damp paths and misty fields; her milieu was polite suburbia, pleasant parades of shops, convenient trains and small doses of culture. At Tonbridge, where he was a day-boy, they lived within sound of the chapel bell at 38 Dry Hill Park Road, an 1860s villa, with a sloping garden, four large pine trees and a tennis court. The garden – and the view to 'a black line of hill that stretched across the country from right to left, like a great thick billow that was going to break over the wavelets and wrinkles of the green sea below' – were the only things that Morgan liked.[12]

Eddie Forster's share of the Thornton inheritance meant that his widow and son were comfortably off: Aunt Marianne had died in 1887, aged ninety, leaving Morgan the enormous sum of £8,000, which invested was to pay for his schooling and Cambridge, as well as sustain his early life. He was to go up to King's College in the autumn of 1897; Lily moved into heavenly Tunbridge Wells – 'Filthy, self righteous place, full of Dorothy Perkins roses,' sniffed Morgan,[13] who set about hating what he categorized as suburbia.

The Cambridge that was to seduce Morgan Forster into the happiest three years of his life so far appeared in many different guises. It was the city of the Darwins, in which he had an ally, the former Ida Farrer of Abinger, who had known both his parents, and been so despairing of Lily's and her son's prospects at Eddie's death. Ida was married to Charles Darwin's youngest son, Horace, who had founded the Cambridge Scientific Instrument Company; they lived in The Orchard, a large and comfortable house on the Huntingdon Road, and had two daughters, Ruth and Nora, aged fourteen and twelve.[14] Next door at Wychfield was Frank Darwin, whose daughter Frances, born 1886, was to become close friends with her cousin, Gwen, born 1885, daughter of George Darwin at Newnham Grange, and both were to become essential members of the Rupert Brooke circle. The ages of the girls was a critical point, for these first offspring of married dons were still too young for Forster's undergraduate generation. His King's College years would bring him many friendships, notably with Lytton Strachey,

Leonard Woolf, Thoby Stephen, J. M. Keynes, G. E. Moore and Desmond MacCarthy, but theirs was a Cambridge of formidable wives and mother-figures – Mrs Nora Sidgwick at Newnham, Florence Keynes, mother of John Maynard and Geoffrey, and her friend Mary Paley Marshall, Mrs Alfred Marshall, at Balliol Croft in the Madingley Road, a house that fostered philosophic discussions on economics. Though the women's colleges, Girton and Newnham, had been established over twenty years earlier, their very right to be there, as potentially part of the university, was still bitterly disputed. In an ugly scene of mob rule, in 1897, thousands of young men waving boaters and baying at the effigy of a woman undergraduate on a bicycle, hanging from the upper window of what is now the University Press building opposite the Senate House, threatened the fellows going to vote on the admission of women to degrees. The women lost, by 662 votes to 1,713, and the mob marched on Newnham, battering the barricaded gates, before returning to the market square to light a bonfire – made of market stalls and other people's property.[15] Underlying this awful day was the very real and vicious hostility to women, which was played out in cat-calls and nasty tricks on an everyday basis in the streets; Girton, at a safe distance of the 'elastic mile' out on the Huntingdon Road (2 miles/3.2 kilometres to Trinity Street), bravely celebrated their castle of defiance in a college song, to the tune of 'The Vicar of Bray' (sir):

> Yet stranger sight for don or ped
> Agogue was never seen, sir,
> Than Girton's buildings blushing red
> Behind a veil of green, sir.[16]

Forster arrived in Cambridge as this all-male society was about to crumble: women were not recognized as sisters or cousins, but viewed as the barbarian hordes, and the natural reaction of the men was to retrench, slam the doors on their lunch parties, fireside teas, secret societies and homosexual dalliances. The rituals were heightened by the effrontery that some bright young women might peep in on them and laugh. How else could they defend such delights as the Apostles, the ultimate secret ... 'I have just been elected to a secret society,' Roger Fry confided in glee to his mother. 'It is an extremely secret society, so you must not mention it much ... it has a wonderful secret ritual the full details of which I do not yet know but which is highly impressive ...'[17]

In addition to the delicious secrets, Cambridge loved its young men, and spoiled them: they came, like Forster himself and his hero Rickie in *The Longest Journey*,

cold and friendless and ignorant out of a great public school ... and praying as a highest favour that he might be left alone. Cambridge had not answered his prayer. She had taken and soothed him, and warmed him, and had laughed at him a little, saying that he must not be so tragic yet awhile, for his boyhood had been but a dusty corridor that led to the spacious halls of youth.[18]

She had transported him from the common world, the station, in the tram that dropped him at his own college gate: he was conducted to his rooms, with his name already over the door, and still distinguishable 'like a grey ghost' the name of his predecessor underneath:

... with a sigh of joy he entered ... there was a beautiful fire, and the kettle boiled at once. He made tea on the hearth-rug and ate biscuits which Mrs Aberdeen had brought for him up from Anderson's ... with his head on the fender and all his limbs relaxed, he felt almost as safe as he felt once when his mother killed a ghost in the passage by carrying him through it in her arms.[19]

On leaving this cocoon by day or evening he walked with an ever jauntier step, walking tall down stony vistas and across great courts, growing into the footsteps of famous men.

Outside, the worldly temptations clustered at the very gate of King's College: picturesque and rickety dun-coloured buildings, their overhangs darkening the cramped and poky shops, stacked with scented mysteries, nothing was forbidden here. Decks the chemists had been in King's Parade from before the nineteenth century began, offering lemon juice for punch, and negus (hot port, lemon and spices), Icelandic moss and chocolate for coughs and colds and perfumed soaps and shaving luxuries. Decks were so pleased with the young men that they put on a firework display at the gate of King's to welcome each fresh year. But the tobacconists were even deeper caverns of delight; tobacco in many fantastic guises and wrappings was the staple of youthful existence – there were dozens of tobacconists but Bacons at the corner of Rose Crescent and Market Hill was the most popular, proudly displaying Charles Stuart Calverley of Christ's (1835) 'ode' to tobacco on a brass plaque on the wall.

This Edwardian Cambridge comes to life in Forster's *The Longest Journey* (reached through the Tardis of the dark green cloth binding of the London Library's first edition of 1907, which turns out to be James Strachey's own, with his spidery neat signature inside). Forster, or Rickie, has risen from the fender to the window-seat, and the room is filled with tobacco smoke and friends discussing the reality of an ancestor of one of those elegantly shuffling brown cows: 'he could see the court . . . and the college cat teasing the college tortoise, and the kitchen-men with supper trays on their head' . . . hot food for one, cold for three . . . 'not a breath stirring' in the tranquil October air. 'The great elms were motionless' – Cambridge was a city of elms and some few remain at the back of Queens' College – 'the great elms were motionless and seemed still in the glory of midsummer, for the darkness hid the blotches on their leaves, and their outlines were still rounded against the tender sky'. Forster (Rickie) was convinced the elms were female – 'lady trees' – and had fooled the college authorities for years.[20] At times the whole of Cambridge seems like some beneficent courtesan, raddled and infinitely wise, an embodiment convincingly adopted by a few of the merrier dons, when wreathed in smoke haze and port fumes – it was little wonder that they did not wish their sisters to intervene.

Rickie, in the window-seat, is about to give some secrets away . . . G. E. Moore was talking . . .

. . . or rather jerking, and he was still lighting matches and dropping their ends upon the carpet. Now and then he would make a motion with his feet as if he were running quickly backward upstairs, and would tread on the edge of the fender, so that the fire-irons went flying and the buttered-bun dishes crashed against each other in the hearth. The other philosophers were crouched in odd shapes on the sofa and table and chairs, and one, who was a little bored, had crawled to the piano and was timidly trying the Prelude to Rheingold with his knee on the soft pedal.

The expensive tobacco smoke and warmth of the tea is soporific; our hero finds the events of his day floating past him . . .

. . . he had read Theocritus . . . lunched with a merry don and had tasted Zweiback biscuits; then he had walked with people he liked, and had walked just long enough; and now his room was full of other people whom he liked and when they left he would go and have supper with

[Ansell] whom he liked as well as any one . . . in one year he had made many friends and learnt much, and might learn even more if he could but concentrate his attention on that cow.[21]

Morgan Forster left Cambridge in 1901; on May mornings now, 100 years on, the brown cows, or their descendants, still roam knee-deep in buttercups in the meadows, attesting to their realities. He had chosen not to remain in their company, feeling himself unfitted to any of the professions that courted his Apostle friends, most sadly knowing that he could not follow his lost father's footsteps into architecture, and so he returned to his mother. Aunt Marianne Thornton's money allowed them an extended continental tour of nearly two years; perhaps Lily Forster hoped the architectural fervour might be awakened, but from the outset he seemed to regard it as a sophistication – 'I had got ready all the appropriate sentiments for the New Sacristy,' he wrote to Edward Dent from Florence on sightseeing at San Lorenzo, and 'they answered very well' to Michelangelo's setting and Medici tombs: 'More spontaneous perhaps were my feelings at seeing the cloisterful of starved and maimed cats.'[22] He found Assisi 'most wonderful' (and wished they were staying there, instead of Perugia), realizing the impact of a painted interior 'and not merely patches of colour' in the lower church of the Sacred Convent of St Francis, but the weather was bad and it was too dark 'and the Giotto allegories were almost invisible'.[23] Forster's Italy never lifts out of architectural disappointment; an enthusiast would by now be writing of nothing but Brunelleschi domes, pendentives and lunettes, of porphyry and *pietra serena*, but he admitted 'though I do love Italy she has had no such awakening power on me . . .' and he blamed the weather: 'When the sun is in she is uninteresting and even ugly.'[24] No architect could ever sustain such pallid passions; he seems permanently to be as Lucy Honeychurch was to be 'in Santa Croce with no Baedeker', feeling under the weather and accident-prone (he fell down the steps of St Peter's in Rome and broke his arm), finding great doors shut against his entry or baulked in his view – 'I wish I didn't see everything with this horrible foreground of enthusiastic ladies, but it is impossible to get away from it.'[25] Italy finally slayed the would-be architect in Forster, if ever there was one, and destined him to write for a living. His novelist's heart sparkled on those same ladies in *pensione* 'brawls', at having an Arno view, on fleas and a spider in the soap bowl, and the raffish behaviour of waiters, and the occasional scented gem:

I went to Nemi the other day, and got right down to the temple of Diana. The place is covered now with lilac and blue violets, pale blue and mauve anemones, cyclamen, and grape hyacinths. It's a glorious place.[26]

The Forsters returned through middle Europe in a series of leaps and recuperations; from Cortina d'Ampezzo came a letter with a paragraph so superb that it might be the shortest of the Forster short stories:

We had a splendid but strange journey from Belluno to the Cadore, with some ladies from Dalmatia, a drunken coachman and a young man travelling in spectacles for a Pieve firm, very amiable, afflicted with the tape worm, and also drunk. He sang long excerpts from Verdi and then remarked 'English poetry, I know it too', proceeding to declaim with the most exquisite taste 'I hard a leetle poney its name was Darple Gree'. He loved England, on account of its Bath Oliver biscuits. Up the hill into the Cadore the drunken coachman got down and left the horses to themselves and they began to stroll towards the precipice for the sake of the view. Loud screams from the Dalmatian ladies, who together with my mother bounded out like acrobats on to the road.[27]

Forster had missed his Cambridge of easy friendships and his letters had pleaded for gossip, but once returned home in the late summer of 1903 he did not attempt to seek them out, rather storing all those useful Darwins, Stephens, Symondses, Vaughans and Stracheys, and even teatime encounters with Girtonians, away. His life was falling into a pattern of leavings, and findings, and he had stories to write: he had left Rooksnest and Cambridge, he had found his first story while taking a walk near Ravello in May, it 'was as if it had waited for me there',[28] and we know full well of *Angels* conspiring in San Gimignano.★ Another story 'hung ready in a hollow tree not far from Olympia',[29] and surely the wild journeying of 'The Celestial Omnibus' owes much to the drunken coachman *di Cadore* in the Dolomites? There was to be no going back; he settled his mother into a villa in Weybridge, so that he could write. He had become so sensitized to stories that he must have felt like a magnet: the one Cambridge friend he did keep was Bob Trevy, Robert Trevelyan, a younger son of the Cambo enclave at Wallington in Cumberland, who was (against family wishes) determinedly poetical, married to a moneyed and musical Dutchwoman, Elizabeth des Amorie van der Hoeven, and living in the south country. They were having a house built, The Shiffolds, gazing southwards from the greensand ridge of Holmbury Hill in Surrey: 'I wish you would quickly inhabit your new house,' wrote Forster, 'I want it for some people of mine. They are living there at present in the greatest discomfort not knowing which way the front door opens or what the view is like, and till I go there to tell them they will never get it straight.'[30]

★ *Where Angels Fear to Tread* is set in San Gimignano, where Forster stayed overnight on this trip: the title may owe something to Alexander Pope, the originator of 'Fools rush in where angels fear to tread'; also lapsed Apostles are 'fallen angels'.

The Trevelyans obliged with a home for the Honeychurches, and the *pensione* view of the Arno (for Lily Forster) and Bessie Trevelyan's piano playing coagulated into *A Room with a View*.★

Forster's early output was nothing short of manic: his first published work, 'The Story of a Panic' (the Ravello story), was published in G. M. Trevelyan's *Independent Review* in 1904, and then four novels – two 'Italian', one Cambridge and one *Howards End* tumbled out in the ensuing five years, to be rounded off with 'The Celestial Omnibus' and its five companion stories in 1911.

The boy who rides in the Omnibus lives in Agathox Lodge, No. 28 Buckingham Park Road, Surbiton – it was the right end:

After No. 39 the quality of the houses dropped very suddenly, and 64 had not even a separate servants' entrance. But at the present moment the whole road looked rather pretty, for the sun had just set in splendour, and the inequalities of rent were drowned in a saffron afterglow. Small birds twittered, and the breadwinners' train shrieked musically down through the cutting – that wonderful cutting which has drawn to itself the whole beauty out of Surbiton, and clad itself, like any Alpine valley, with the glory of the fir and the silver birch and the primrose. It was this cutting that had first stirred desires within the boy . . .[31]

It is down the alley between the garden walls of villas 'Ivanhoe' and 'Belle Vista' that the boy, who lives with unimaginative people, finds the Omnibus waiting, the horses with smoking sides, the driver Sir Thomas Browne.† That Sir Thomas had been dead

★ The Honeychurches' home village, Summer Street, fits every detail of Holmbury St Mary.

† The mystical power of 'The Celestial Omnibus' is in the unexpected; Sir Thomas Browne appears, unintroduced, as does 'Dan . . . some one', presumably Dante Alighieri. In many ways it is the most intriguing and revealing of all Forster's works.

for something like two and a quarter centuries, that he was most famous for his treatise on *Hydriotaphia* or *Urn Burial*, both qualified him for his job and ejected Forster's reader into the required quixotic state. Agathox Lodge stood for the villas of petty convenience that he had lived in, both in Tonbridge and Tunbridge Wells, and most closely, because it was in the same county, for his Weybridge home, a villa on Monument Green which he had found named Glendore, and changed to Harnham, in honour of the picturesque hamlet beside the river Avon outside Salisbury, which he knew and loved. Harnham, a villa for Lily Forster's life's desires, detached (by the narrowest alley from one neighbour) and bay-windowed, and distinguished by 'a beautiful brass bound door step'[32] which they took on from the previous residents, was to be his home for twenty years, and the house where he wrote everything that made him famous. It was as if, every morning that he sat down to write, he took his own metaphorical omnibus, being carried beyond the commonplace villa, the domestic regime and the demands of the local literary society, into places that he wished to inhabit, Cambridge, Rooksnest, Italy and the Surrey hills, these safely beyond the North Downs which protected Abinger and Holmbury from suburban contagion.

Forster was himself the boy who boarded the Celestial Omnibus, which makes that rather rarely read story the key to so much of his life. It might be suggested that he dismissed the charms of Weybridge too hastily, and ignored material with possibilities. Monument Green is a triangularish space where Thames Street becomes Monument Hill; the Monument is a Doric column with blue and gold sundials, which originally marked the seventeenth-century development of Seven Dials, close to Covent Garden, but was turned out of London and re-sited at Weybridge in 1820. It commemorated Frederika of Prussia, Duchess of York: the Duchess, discarded by one of Queen Victoria's rakish uncles, had ended her days at Oatlands Park close by – reputedly spending most of her time in the dim chambers of the fantastic grotto there, amid stalactites of shells and satin spars, embroidering seats for the Chinese bamboo chairs and playing with her pet dogs and monkeys. The grotto had been made by the eighteenth century's master of such arts, Josiah Lane, for the fabulously rich and dissolute 9th Earl of Lincoln, the object of Horace Walpole's great passion. It had survived intact into Forster's day.[33]

Beyond Oatlands Park, where Henry VIII had married Catherine Howard and Queen Elizabeth I had hunted stags, were the watery meadows beside the winding Thames, with Shepperton Lock – noisy with punters on holiday afternoons – and pleasure steamers plying from Chertsey to Hampton Court. To the south Monument Hill rose to the Surrey pines, through which Forster walked to Weybridge station, and beyond were the heathy heights of St George's Hill. Forster existed among all this, even advertising the delights to his friends: '. . . and perhaps you will at all events pay week end visits to Weybridge River, pine woods, spare bedroom with [Birket Foster's] "The Stepping Stones" on the wall, Literary society, Tom cat who sneezes to come in . . .'[34] But just as Birket Foster's stepping stones were in the Surrey hills, so Forster seemed elsewhere, and neither the grotto nor the river Thames tempted his pen: he simply dressed and undressed, cleaned his teeth, read his newspapers, did a little gardening, was nice to his mother, their friends and relations, for the greater part of twenty-five years without his 'home' making the slightest mark on his sensibilities or his work (except for 'The Celestial Omnibus'). For a writer so sensitive to the spirit of a place, how did he accomplish this? It might be argued, and fairly, that his feelings were elsewhere, that he had simply fallen for his well-connected Indian pupil, Syed Ross Masood, which he certainly had in about 1910, and was consumed with interest in all things Indian, until he actually arrived there in October 1912. But that is to pursue him into far regions, and rush past the rather negative observation about the insubstantiality of the villa on Monument Green. To find out why Weybridge was so cheated of Forsterian fame might reveal more than suburban disappointment.

In his very first story, set in the chestnut woods above Ravello, 'The Story of a Panic', he is dealing not with a thunderstorm on the picnic or a runaway horse but with the seduction of an English boy by the great god Pan. The deity asserted himself through the beauties of the countryside and via the medium of Gennaro, 'a clumsy, impertinent fisher-lad', the stop-gap waiter at the hotel: the boy, Eustace, was first made wild, and mad, and he sang and shouted: 'Never have I listened to such an extraordinary speech,' intones our prosaic narrator. 'At any other time it would have been ludicrous, for here was a boy, with no sense of beauty and a puerile command of words, attempting to tackle themes which the greatest poets have found almost beyond their power. Eustace Robinson, aged fourteen, was standing in his nightshirt saluting, praising, and blessing, the great forces and manifestations of Nature.'[35] It is Gennaro who is sacrificed and Eustace who escapes, laughing, much to the consternation of cousins, aunts and distinguished travellers.

On the second trip in the Celestial Omnibus, this time driven by 'Dan . . . some one', it is the pretentious Mr Bons, President of the Literary Society, who is sacrificed to his unbelief: the boy – 'when the blind flew up at a chance touch of his head' – saw the fabled land . . . 'and there was the chasm, and there, across it, stood the old precipices, dreaming, with their feet in the everlasting river. He exclaimed, "The mountain! Listen to the new tune in the water! Look at the camp fires in the ravines," and Mr Bons, after a hasty glance, retorted, "Water? Camp fires? Ridiculous rubbish. Hold your tongue. There is nothing at all."'' The body of Mr Bons which 'had apparently been hurled from a considerable height' was later found near Bermondsey gasworks.[36]

Thirdly, there is 'Other Kingdom', the most evocative story of all, and with many echoes of *Howards End*: Other Kingdom is a beech copse, bought by the wealthy Harcourt Worters as a minor addition to his acres, and in an expansive moment given, as a second engagement ring, to his fiancée, the green-butterfly-like Evelyn Beaumont. Evelyn is delighted, unbelievingly a woman of property, ecstatic with joy in the possession of something that she does not wish to spoil or change, leaving the copse open for the traditional 'Fourth Time of Asking' when local couples cut their names together in the bark of a tree – 'They cut their names and go away, and when the first child is born they come again and deepen the cuts. So for each child.' Her paternalistic fiancé, very much a Henry Willcox, is amused at her knowing such things, but perfectly convinced that the copse must have an asphalt path, a bridge and a fence, and though Evelyn pleads that that is not what she, the owner, wants, he laughs, calls her a silly girl and has his way. 'The bridge is built, the fence finished, and Other Kingdom lies tethered by a ribbon of asphalt to our front door', Evelyn is imprisoned 'neither reading nor laughing, and dressing no longer in green, but in brown', but there is a terrible storm, and she too escapes.[37]

The snatches from these three stories show Forster's journey: at Rooksnest, when he was young, he had an inviolable belief in the beauty and goodness of nature, and even more so in the beauty of England, and in the native wisdom of the country people who had guarded her for centuries. In Italy he found it to be likewise, though as the Italian landscape has stronger lights and shadows, so its guardians were more vivid characters, still hand in hand with ancient gods, and disdainful of the bloodless curiosities of tourists. So Gennaro, the clumsy waiter, extracts Eustace from his English phlegm, so most brilliantly Phaethon, 'all irresponsibility and fire', and Persephone triumph over the Tuscan tour taken by Lucy Honeychurch, Miss Bartlett (to whom Forster likened himself), the Emersons, Miss Lavish and the Reverends Eager and Beebe.[38]

In England, he knew, the forces of nature were in retreat, their most sacred places dissected – invariably by archaeological clerics – and laid bare for the tramplings of curious unbelievers. Forster's nature beliefs made him lightly druidical – a mystical experience at Stonehenge decreed Rickie's fate in *The Longest Journey* – and it was part of the opacity of Weybridge that he took to walking. Like Lytton Strachey and Rupert Brooke, he used the comforts of Hilton Young's cottage, The Lacket, 'replete with hot baths and the novels of Arnold Bennett', at Lockeridge, for walking the Wiltshire downland: in October 1909 he returned to Stonehenge, walking through a black night and torrential rain with Young, who steered them by compass and a cycle lamp – 'We broke into Stone Henge at midnight, and ate on the altar stone, which may have been sacrilege but was more probably the other thing. Poor Stone Henge has been ruined these 5 years, but it got its own back that time. I don't ever want to see it again.' The 'other wonder' he noted, was the glare of Salisbury, spreading through the southern sky.[39]

Characteristically Forster felt that Nature, the English country-side, in her waning powers, was letting him down. This was the legacy – it seems in retrospect – of his four months at Nassenheide in Germany, in the summer of 1905, tutoring the daughters of Elizabeth von Arnim and her 'Man of Wrath', the Count. He had been recommended to the Countess by his Cambridge friend Sydney Waterlow, and it promised to be one of the more bizarre experiences of his life. Elizabeth, who was born Mary Annette Beauchamp, was nearly forty; she had been a vivacious and musi-cally talented butterfly of a girl, courted and netted by the sad, middle-aged widower Count, and pinned to childbearing and suffocated by Berlin social life. Rather as the fictional Evelyn Beaumont delighted in Other Kingdom copse, so Elizabeth von Arnim had fallen in love at first sight of the wilderness beauty of the neglected garden and schloss of the Count's Pomeranian estate. She had insisted on spending her time there, in her garden-paradise of lilacs and silver-pink peonies (two plants with a talent for surviving when feebler species have long disappeared) – and was famous for her story, *Elizabeth and her German Garden*, which had been published and reprinted eleven times in 1898, and continued to amass editions. Forster arrived at Nassenheide in chilly April, into a bucolic and domestic chaos, under a leaden sky, the bleakness enhanced by the flight of the cranes and the deer galloping across immense ploughed expanses. He could find no garden.

When the Countess got over her prickliness at discovering that her daughters' tutor was correcting the proofs of his *own* novel, *Where Angels Fear to Tread*, the two of them developed a bond of understanding and sympathy. Forster discovered for himself the beauty of the place she loved; how the spring came slowly but with the warmth of a few days in May 'an unimagined radiance' broke over the land, revealing magical groves. One of his favourite places was where 'the birches lined the dykes and strayed into the fields, mistletoe hung from them, some of them formed an islet in the midst of the field of rye', and there he would spend warm afternoons, with his German grammar.[40] Elizabeth had been misunderstood about her 'German garden', for hers was not an horticultural exercise but a retreat, a place to be herself and find serenity – not least for the sake of her children. Forster's pupils came to love him; all in all he had a marvellous taste of paradise, full of jaunts, games, dancing and flowers, but the overbearing Man of Wrath – 'though he was a pupil of Liszt, and wonderfully good'[41] – denies everyone's enjoyment of the piano, as of the flowers, and rules as a tyrant of experimental potato and lupin growing: the jackboots of philistinism on the march. The Count destroys Forster's belief in Nature, or perhaps frightens it out of him: 'Nature, whom I used to be so keen on, is too unfair . . .' he admits to Arthur Cole in the July of his Nassenheide summer. 'She evokes plenty of high and exhausting feelings, and offers nothing in return. To quote the Man of Wrath: "You will never be able to talk of Beethoven to a crayfish. Even if he hears you, you will never know it, for his bones are outside, and this prevents any intelligent facial expression." But the Man of Wrath prefers the crayfish to Beethoven and me.'[42] In Germany – perhaps it was no accident – in 1905, Forster had discovered that wrath and crayfish were planning to take over the world!

The Count, Harcourt Worters and Henry Willcox were the coming men.* While one scenario might be that Forster's homo-sexuality made him identify with the subjugated Elizabeth, Evelyn Beaumont and Margaret Schlegel, that is to miss the point of the argument. In the last pages of *Howards End* the sisters are standing in the garden discussing the world to come; Helen points to the 'red rust' of creeping suburbia coming across the fields:

'And London is only part of something else, I'm afraid. Life's going to be melted down, all over the world.' Margaret knew that her sister spoke truly. Howards End, Oniton,† the Purbeck downs, the Oderberge, were all survivals, and the melting pot was being prepared for them. Logically,

---

* The real Count, the fictional Worters and Willcox all protested sensitivity while being utterly ruthless in pursuit of their aims; they are entrepreneurial bullies.

† 'Oniton' was the location of Henry Willcox's country house in Shropshire, which Margaret Schlegel found druidical and mystical – A. E. Housman's 'land of lost content', which appealed to Forster. *A Shropshire Lad* was first published in 1896.

they had no right to be alive. One's hope was in the weakness of logic. Were they possibly the earth beating time?

'Because a thing is going strong now, it need not go strong for ever,' she said. 'This craze for motion has only set in during the last hundred years. It may be followed by a civilization that won't be a movement, because it will rest on the earth. All the signs are against it now, but I can't help hoping, and very early in the morning in the garden I feel that our house is the future as well as the past.'[43]

The widowed Margaret, had her story continued, would have been generous to the National Trust; Helen, on the other hand, would have searched out something more militant. Forster, relieved of Howards End, leaving Rooksnest to its fate, having discovered that his Thornton view of Clapham had gone, that Weybridge was beyond saving anyway, climbed aboard his own oriental omnibus. The accident of Weybridge, that Sir Theodore Morison had retired there from India (and was undoubtedly a member of the Literary Society), brought his ward, Syed Ross Masood, into Forster's acquaintance by the most respectable means, and allowed him to escape. But 'sweetest Morgan' – a name he would soon revel in – or his antennae, had divined the heart of the English infection that was to become an epidemic; sweet Morgan loved the English countryside for its own sake, not as social cachet, intellectual prize, desirable residence, a possession (for he had never possessed any of it), but as a product of the centuries which worked well, where the nation's heart was beating time.

A war would have to be fought over it, of course, but in one way the war was lost well before it started: a love so close to the heart of things should never be politicized, but it was fast being so, and in a corner of Surrey – the opposite corner to Morgan's Abinger to which he would return – this was the case.

In the summer of 1891, when he was still an innocent boy at Rooksnest, and the felicitous family of Stephen were intact and happy by the sea, a handsome civil servant was settling his wife and daughters into that corner of Surrey, which he already thought of affectionately as 'the holy land'. His name was Sydney Haldane Olivier, he was aged thirty-two, of splendid stature, and with an interior streak of rebellion spliced from generations of Huguenot preachers who had bearded Catholic France before finally settling in England. Many of his childhood summers had been spent with French relatives, and his handsomeness was enhanced by a Mediterranean sun-browned physique; his attractiveness cannot be over-estimated. He was unhappy at prep school but resolved to play the game and wait for better things: these he found at Tonbridge School (from where Forster crept friendless and ignorant), where he announced himself a liberal and became an authoritative head boy. His conformity was ballasted by his love of walking, and at every opportunity when set free he would take the train west to Chiddingstone or Penshurst and wander in the valley of the Eden and up into the wooded canyons of Crockham and Ide Hills, with the attainable views of Kent and Sussex melting into the blue. Olivier's walking map, which he treasured, was marked 'The map of the Holy Land'.[44]

Oxford polished him and there he met Graham Wallas: together they read J. S. Mill and Herbert Spencer, and *Punch*; he pondered architecture but opted for the Colonial Office, which was 'better than schoolmastering'.[45] Once in London his heart led him to Canon Barnett's Toynbee Hall, where his voluntary duties included inspecting latrines in Lisson Grove, and his attention was caught by the American land reformer, author of *Progress and Poverty*, Henry George, then on a lecture tour. Olivier joined the new Land Reform Union in 1883 and helped edit their journal *The Christian Socialist*. In the Colonial Office he found Sidney

Webb, and at the Hampstead Historical Society he met Edward Pease and George Bernard Shaw; the natural progression – or predictable outcome as it seems at this remove – was that Olivier was one of these pioneers who questioned the Fellowship of New Life founded in 1884 but joined the Fabian Society, as it became the following year. Olivier, the least well-known, or almost forgotten, Fabian, was closer to William Morris than to Sidney Webb: he believed in the goodness of human nature, that free will was the only honourable human condition, that capitalism had its uses but that competitive materialism had none. By means of his magnificent presence and personality he was to carry off a distinguished diplomatic career, but, as Leonard Woolf his sometime colleague was to contend, he became 'an eccentric combination' and a bundle of paradoxes – socialist and high Tory, pro-Empire and anti-Imperialist, practical agnostic and yet believer in immortality (at least his own) and a 'bureaucratic collectivist and libertarian individualist'.[46] He was first knighted and then made Lord Olivier, and in splendid court dress his glamour matched that of his nephew, another Lord Olivier, playing in Rattigan's *The Sleeping Prince*, or in *The School for Scandal*, in his prime.

This dazzling bundle of paradoxes and his wife Margaret, the sister of the Cambridge radical Harold Cox, wanted to bring up their daughters in the simple country life of his favourite upland, at Limpsfield Chart just across the Surrey border, west of Westerham. Harold Cox (1859–1936) was an extremist of socialist circles and a follower of Edward Carpenter, whom both Roger Fry and his friend C. R. Ashbee (as well as Forster) had admired while they were at Cambridge. (It was Cox who sent a pair of Indian sandals, with a thong that curled up from the sole over the toes to the ankle fastening in a Genie of the Lamp way, which became Carpenter's pattern for those he made for himself and friends –

the origins of the 'brown bread and sandals' of the simple life.)
Carpenter (1844–1929), poet, prophet and priest, hovered over
life at Limpsfield Chart – as a result of a vision he had bought a
smallholding at Millthorpe near Sheffield, where he immersed
himself in the toil, grit and grime of the labouring life, selling his
own produce, sandal-making and advocating the sacred rite of
male love and beauty. The spectre of Carpenter's extremism was
always in the background.

The Chart – or Common – had the soil of freedom, unruly
greensand hills with steep, water-washed tracks and valleys with
beechwoods, pines, birches, heather and gorse, far removed from
the sedate and ancient village of Limpsfield, and a vigorous walk
from Oxted station, where the railway had arrived in 1884. The
Chart still honoured the yeoman landholdings of medieval independence, it was a scattered settlement of eccentrics – ripe for
conversion to a Fabian society. The Fabian secretary Edward Pease
settled at The Pendicle in Pastens Lane – his wife, Marjorie Pease,
was to be a redoubtable chairman of the Godstone rural district
council: the Oliviers took over the Sanders family farm (poor
farming soil had meant the Sanders men had worked on the Oxted
railway viaduct) and converted it into their tile-hung cottage
home, Champions. There they raised – running wild and free –
four (naturally) beautiful and highly intelligent daughters:
Margery, Brynhild, Daphne and Noel.

Equally formidable in her way was their neighbour Constance
Garnett: Constance Black, as she was born (1861), was one of the
children of a solicitor, Town Clerk and later coroner of Brighton,
brought up in Ship Street. She was short-sighted, of uncertain
health, but had what was called 'a fine mind', and aged seventeen
she had gone up to Cambridge, to the early Newnham of Jane
Harrison, Ellen Crofts and Anne Jemima Clough. One of her best
friends was Florence Brown (later to be the mother of John

Maynard Keynes). Constance was poor and had to earn her living: in London she became a governess and a Fabian follower, and met the mop-headed – like 'a kitten on the top of the maypole' – Edward Garnett, son of the great doyen of the British Museum reading room, and poet, Dr Richard Garnett. Constance had a passion for the countryside, which she had only ever seen on rare holidays; they went walking to 'such places as Heathfield and Burwash' . . . 'small quiet villages and one could walk all day on the Sussex roads meeting nothing but an occasional wagon or farmer's gig', staying at old inns, in perfect summer weather – 'a happy time for people of small means and simple tastes'.[47] Edward Garnett and Constance were married in 1889, and they found a tiny gothic lodge on the Broome Hall estate at the foot of Leith Hill, with a small garden and orchard, where Constance became a keen gardener. The garden and the countryside were to be passionately half of her life: the other half was her involvement with the Russian émigrés she met while working at the People's Palace Library in Whitechapel. Six months after the difficult birth of her only son, David, on 9 March 1892, she went to Russia to learn about the country and its people: on her return she was elected to the Fabians, and having taught herself Russian she began her marathon translations of Russian literature. Her father David Black died, leaving her a legacy of £1,000 which she decided to spend on a house in the country. The Peases and Oliviers – the girls would be ideal playmates for David – made the Fabian air of Limpsfield Chart a natural attraction; the Garnetts' brother-in-law, the mystic and scholarly William Harrison Cowlishaw (married to Edward's sister Lucy Garnett), who was a disciple of Morris and the Arts and Crafts life, was to be their architect. Their house of stone, left rough as it was cut from the nearby hillside quarry, was built in a buttercup meadow, close to the medieval boundary, the Scearn Bank: they named it The Cearne. The Cearne grew out of its site in an earthborn way, L-shaped, hand-finished, with hand-wrought iron latches and catches made by the local blacksmith, and Cowlishaw plastered the main bedroom ceiling with hoops of briar roses in a Burne-Jones style. The front door was massive, 'studded and hinged with heavy iron as if for a castle'.[48]

The more serious advantages of the simple life on the fresh and sandy Chart came into play immediately, when three weeks after they moved in – and the curtains not up – Edward Garnett fell ill with typhoid fever. Constance nursed him tirelessly, keeping him alive on liquids and dosing him with quinine, and he recovered: the good water from their new deep well, and the free-draining sand, which meant their drains were 'beyond reproach' (there was no bathroom and the privy was outside the back door, 'with the basic necessities provided by a bucket of ashes and an old copy of the fat illustrated catalogue of the Civil Service Stores'), were critical.

After this all three Garnetts, Constance, Edward and four-year-old David, slipped into life at 'the dear little Cearne' as if it was a favourite garment: Constance had her study, with easy chairs with peacock blue covers either side of an inglenook fire, and Edward Garnett read manuscripts in his long wicker chair in the porch, with interludes of two or three days a week in London. There were four bedrooms, one each, and the big one with briar roses for visitors. They were a perfect cottage industry, David – he had already earned his nickname, 'Bunny', from a rabbitskin cap that Constance had made for him after Randolph Caldecott's 'Baby Bunting' – had benign companions in helpers and neighbours, so encouraging and spoiling him that at four years old he had already assumed the confidence that would sweep him into Bloomsbury company: he remembered 'strutting up to the stable in a new long coachman's coat, talking to our new man, Bert Hedgecock, while

Nettle, a pretty red bitch, played about us – my dog. Bert was grooming Shagpat – my pony. The sense of property was intensely developed, and I was conscious of being monarch of all I surveyed.'[49] The 'coach' was a governess cart, the Welsh pony a pony of all work, and Bert Hedgecock the garden and stable lad – it would have been typical of Constance to give him one of Edward's cast-off coats which he draped around the little boy while he groomed the pony! This was already the little 'Buck Bunny' who was to haunt Vanessa Bell with his assuming charm and what we would call 'sticking power'. He was reared on the sunny slopes of Scearn Bank, in the earthly paradise of unstained oak, bare floors and deep window-seats, in the 'delicious aroma of woodsmoke, apples and country-sweetness' that Constance's discovery of beauty allied to Fabianism had made. In 1901 Edward Garnett became reader and adviser to Gerald Duckworth's publishing house – the 'lethargic alligator' as Virginia Stephen called her stepbrother. In complete contrast Garnett was this bespectacled, rather startled, mop-headed figure, so bookish that he can only be imagined as bound in well-rubbed calfskin, this shuffling Svengali of literature who ushered so many into fame, Wells, Conrad, Belloc, Galsworthy, D. H. Lawrence, W. H. Davies, W. H. Hudson and Edward Thomas, and many more, and they all came drifting to The Cearne at some point or another.[50] They seem a list of legends now but in reality they were not so grand, usually tired and shabby, often truculent or sad (Wells the notorious Lothario had to be kept well away from the lovely Olivier girls) and the good life of The Cearne soothed and sheltered them, and many of Constance's Russian friends and their relations as well. The locals called the Chart 'Dostoevsky's Corner'. Through all the toil – plodding through *The Brothers Karamazov* and *War and Peace* – her garden was her respite: it was not merely flowers, though she was very fond of old-fashioned scented things, she grew all the vegetables and fruit they ate, and she harvested the hedgerows, and bottled and preserved to the full.

The Olivier girls were the dryads of the Chart woods, spending much of their time roaming fearlessly, and out in all weathers: 'this freedom, coupled with a certain sense of pride inherited from their father, combined to produce four self-confident, independent girls, whose clannish arrogance often led rather too swiftly to contempt of others . . .'[51] In David Garnett's memory, Margery the eldest was 'handsome with the impulsive warmth and sudden chilliness of her father'; Brynhild 'grew into the most beautiful young woman I have ever known'; Daphne, 'crowned with flowers, was exactly as I have always imagined several of Shakespeare's heroines'; and Noel, the youngest, born on Christmas Day 1892, 'was quiet and the least conspicuous'.[52] Noel had many advantages from being the youngest, she was carelessly beautiful and seemed infinitely wise: her passion for nature and wild animals was shared with Bunny Garnett, to whom she was closest in age. Together they made midnight explorations to catch moles and rabbits, to skin them and tan their skins, they stuffed birds and collected skeletons: as it turned out, their adventures informed their career-choices, Bunny to botany and Noel to medicine.

For all the freedoms of the Chart and four years in Jamaica, the girls' educations had always had the highest priority, the best tutors and some months in Lausanne to learn French; the intellectual Margery and musical Daphne went up to Newnham. Noel was the only one to go to school, as her parents returned to help Jamaica in the aftermath of the Kingston earthquake of 1907, and felt that she, at fifteen, needed to settle to her studies at boarding school.

The school they chose was John Haden Badley's Bedales, with its curriculum of 'co-education, the simple life, disciplinary rigours, the open air, hygiene, Ruskin and Morris, arts and crafts . . .

folk dancing' and the isms – 'vegetarianism, teetotalism, pacifism, intellectual liberalism, pink middle class socialism' – all wrapped up in moral earnestness and determined on votes for women.[53] Bedales had been set up in 1893, but in 1900 had moved to its spiritual home at Steephurst, a big brick Victorian house in 150 acres of enchanted countryside at Steep, just north of Petersfield, on the Hampshire border with Sussex. Steep, aptly named and not a countryside for the slothful, nestles below the contorted chalk cliff that edges the Weald, which creates the chain of hanging beechwoods, or hangers, that stretch from Langrish for a dozen miles northwards to Gilbert White's Selborne hanger. The unconventional school was both protected and adorned by its setting, combes so densely wooded as to appear remnants of the ancient Wealden forest, their sides so deep that clouds of foliage billowed from their craters as russet and purple fires. The Bedales community had nestled itself in among the tiny fields and paddocks and narrow lanes of this garrison home of charcoal burners and woodsmen, and in accordance with Badley's philosophy had assumed the ancient traditions as a forcing ground for modern lives. The poet Edward Thomas was already claiming this benign country for his own, having come to live in Berryfield Cottage, a mile by footpath from Bedales, where his wife Helen was an enthusiastic believer and helper, and their son Mervyn a pupil. An Old Bedalian and 'ardent young Yorkshireman', Geoffrey Lupton, had abandoned his family's engineering business and apprenticed himself to Ernest Gimson's Cotswold furniture workshops: in 1908 Lupton had established his building and furniture-making back at Steep. If Edward Thomas was the poet in residence, so Lupton became craft-builder by appointment, with a stream of school buildings beginning with the Lupton Hall, which he gave to Bedales (and eventually the stunning Gimson-designed Memorial Library, 1920–21), as well as cottages and houses for schoolmasters in the Arts and Crafts style, which have further enhanced the character of the area. The Lupton furniture business was to be taken over by Edward Barnsley, so that ladder-back rush-seated chairs and plain unvarnished oak tables became the Bedales 'style'.

Another witness to the Bedales that was to nurture Noel Olivier, Jacques Raverat and Ferenc Bekassy, all close friends of Rupert Brooke, was Marjory Gill, the niece of Eric Gill, who arrived in Noel's last year. Marjory Gill's rather distrait energies and unhappy previous school experiences were grounded in the social responsibilities she found – being part of the team levelling their own tennis courts, digging the swimming-pool. She discovered her own talent for book-binding, and enjoyed gardening, design and planting sessions with the legendary Oswald Byrom Powell, 'Osbos' to forty years of Bedalians: Marjory became a landscape architect and married Clifford Allen, the pioneering Fabian and socialist.[54]

Bedales suited boys from abroad for whom an English public school was too much of a culture shock; in return, the educational establishment found Badley's 'experiment' both and at once 'ridiculous and alarming'. Girls seemed admirably equipped to face the shark-infested waters of the modern young woman's life, if Noel Olivier and Marjory Gill are examples to go by. Old-fashioned men thought that in their Janey Morris-style dresses in duns and dark greens, their sandals and hair banded in block-printed scarves of their own making, they were making themselves ugly – others found them as intriguing as emerging butterflies. All these attitudes are evident in this letter of 28 May 1909 from Rupert Brooke to the young Noel Olivier, pulling Rugby rank to storm the Bedales enclave: 'On next Monday I am going to stay with my Uncle,' he announced . . . '(a prophet called Cotterill) at Godalming . . . my uncle is writing a book on Brotherhood, Universal Love, Humanity etc.[55] . . . I am going on one of those days . . . to see Jacques . . . he is an old Bedalian . . . who lives at Froxfield, near Petersfield. He will take me to see Bedales; and talk, maybe, with Badley (or however your man calls himself) who is an old school-fellow of mine, and we have mutual friends, and long to meet each other.'[56]

Noel was well able to withstand his joshing: John Haden Badley had been at Rugby, but he could hardly be longing to meet the offspring of a dimly remembered assistant housemaster whom he had probably only known in his pram. However, before this narrative becomes engulfed in the fancies of Rupert Chawner Brooke, it is worth a pause to note the difference that a few miles of southern England made. While Morgan Forster in suburbia was easing his fictional Schlegel sisters of *Howards End* (metaphorically) out of their Victorian corsets, and Lucy Honeychurch in *A Room with a View* was attempting to live as she played her Beethoven, on Limpsfield Chart, with a little help from Bedales, the new women had been reared.

3

Rupert Chawner Brooke

M rs William Parker Brooke liked to remark that her second son Rupert and Rugby's golden jubilee Memorial Clock Tower came together, in the summer of 1887. The clock, a golden sandstone, free-standing Big Ben, quickly became Rugby's symbol of merriment, swagged and flagged for the jubilee of 1897, dressed like a maypole for King Edward VII's visit in 1909, a truly floral clock for George V's Jubilee in 1935 and magnificently crowned and cloaked in red, white and blue for the Coronation of 1953. Rupert Brooke would have been sixty-six, middle-aged, in that Coronation year, had he not succumbed to blood poisoning on the French hospital ship *Duguay-Trouin* in Skyros in April 1915:[1] his clock, with its round and rather cheerful face, has lived on, through sombre remembrances and town celebrations, a constant bystander at every big event, the unblurred presence in every photograph of the Market Place, the hub of all Rugby life, down the twentieth century.

Rupert Brooke spent eighteen of his twenty-eight years in Rugby, that most ordinary Midlands market town known for its railway junction and famous boys' school. The English public school system has profited enormously from this common juxta-position of a classical education grounded in the timeless routines of good people going about their daily business, of institutional prowess cheek by jowl with entrepreneurial pride. For this was the combination that produced 'the handsomest young man in England' – when 'handsome' implied he had style and manners too – and in Rupert's case he seemed to owe a great deal of himself and his characteristics to the place of his nurturing, rather than to his genes. Rugby was his birthplace, his first outings were to the new recreation ground along the Hillmorton Road, his worldly tastes were formed in the respectable High Street, trailing into shops behind his mother, his pocket money clutched in his small hot hand – and his first remembered escapade was to follow the marching town band. He was only five when his father became a Rugby housemaster, and Mrs Brooke assumed responsibility for the domestic welfare of fifty boys besides her own three: Rupert's brother Dick was six years his senior and always in another phase of life, and his baby brother Alfred, known as Podge, was only one, so Rupert was either on his own or given seniority over Podge. Privilege and neglect were equally his lot; whatever insouciance and passions were in the gift of Rugby school, Rupert had them in double-dosage, for he hardly knew anywhere else. But he had such early exposure to institutional living, to the life of a pack animal, that his sense of his own individuality was fragile, and as the middle of three, let alone one of fifty-three, he longed for his parents' attention. There is a story that when he was just fourteen and a new boy in his father's house, he presented himself sitting cross-legged on a shelf of the dumb-waiter – when Mrs Brooke went to open the hatch for lunch she found Rupert with a notice pinned on his chest, 'Mother, behold thy son.'[2] His not overly robust constitution also suffered from school life – he once blamed his conjunctivitis, recurrent 'pink eye', on 'gazing too often on Butterfield's architecture', the predominant 'streaky bacon' brickwork of Rugby's buildings.[3] The doctors blamed the dust in the corridors of the Brooke house, School Field, which stands open to all the westerly winds blowing across the playing fields, the Close; with windows opened front and back, every cranny and corner must have been 'swept' daily, a swirl of dust, down and papers filling the air. How the Brookes came to School Field, when the Butterfield buildings were vividly new, but Rugby school was already three and a quarter centuries old, forms the essential prelude to Rupert's story.

The school is the foundation of a prosperous Tudor grocer, Lawrence Sheriffe, for the benefit of his home town; Henry Holyoake was first accoladed as a 'great' schoolmaster, and he 'lived among his boys and his books' for forty-three years, dying in 1731 'full of years and honour'.[4] In 1750 the school moved to the site of the local manor house, establishing its bond with the town; the architect Henry Hakewill, a favourite with the Warwickshire gentry, designed the present stony, squat and castellated buildings, which were completed by 1813, with the main entrance facing down Rugby's High Street. On the opposite side, to the south, the headmaster's house and School House faced on to the wide green expanses of the Close; despite the existence of some magnificent elm trees, the sheer space of these accumulated green acres contributed to the Rugby passion for football as a fast, running game. In 1823 a boy named William Webb Ellis, so the school historian Mr M. H. Bloxham recorded, picked up a ball and, instead of backing to take his kick, ran with it towards the opposing goal − and by the mysterious processes of boys' lore and legend this obscure action on a grey November afternoon invented the game of Rugby Union football.*[5] It also catapulted

---

* Writing in 1900, H. C. Bradby noted that a tablet to commemorate Ellis's exploit had been placed on the wall of the headmaster's garden.[6] There is a new statue of W. W. Ellis by Graham Beeson outside the school, facing down Warwick Street.

the school into fame, although it was headed there already with the advent of Dr Thomas Arnold as headmaster in 1828. Dr Arnold found a nest of bullying, flogging and all the nastier barbarities of the schoolboy mind, and transformed the whole ethos of education: his reign was only of fourteen years – when he died suddenly in June 1842 he had already become known as 'the greatest Headmaster in the country'.[7] He was succeeded first by Dr (later Archbishop) Tait, then in 1850 by Dr Edward Goulbourn: Goulbourn paid for the building of a new boarding house, designed by George Gilbert Scott, a rising church architect, in 1851, on an acre of ground at the south-east corner of the Close. It was first known as Mr Arnold's, after the great Doctor's son, C. T. Arnold, housemaster from 1853 until 1878. The postal address was 2 Barby Road. Dr Goulbourn had also given the rest of the field – a rectangle across to the Dunchurch Road which enlarged the Close – to the school; the boys – who else could call a field 'New Bigside'? – made it playable for cricket by their own labours. No. 2 Barby Road became School Field, the only house, apart from School House itself, on the sacred green Close – all the other school houses, with their private histories, appearing as suburban villas set in leafy Horton Crescent or along the Hillmorton Road.

After Goulbourn came another great headmaster, Dr Frederick (later Archbishop) Temple, a keen walker (who, while at Balliol, walked the forty-eight miles from Oxford to Rugby in a day to meet Dr Arnold, and back again)[8] and a tree climber – he is reputed to have climbed each of the giant elms then in the Close within a short time of his arrival at Rugby in the new year, 1858, when he was thirty-six. Presumably 'achieving' trees was rather like netting butterflies, a bonding with the natural world, for Dr Temple was a radical headmaster, believing in all-roundedness, the almost equal status of studies, sport and worship, and he

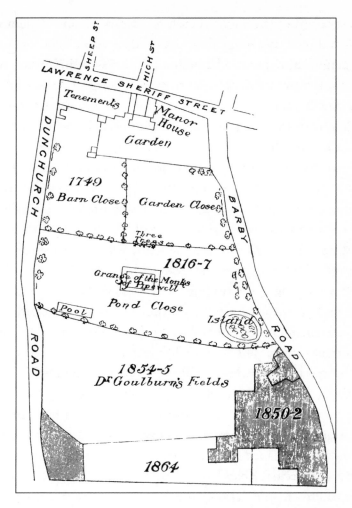

Rugby School, the layout of The Close with School Field in the lower right-hand corner.

introduced the natural sciences to the curriculum. 'A boy ought not to be ignorant of this earth, on which God has placed him,' he informed the Public Schools' Commission, '. . . and ought, therefore, to be well acquainted with geography. He ought not to walk in the fields in total ignorance of what is growing under his very eyes, and he ought, therefore, to learn botany.' Chemistry, he added, was useful in almost every occupation.[9] The energetic Dr Temple also launched a building spree, with his own money and funds from the masters, so that the school's trustees could do little but hrrumph! and tut-tut! at the *gros gâteaux* layerings of brickwork introduced by William Butterfield, freshly conjured from the new chapel at Balliol College. Butterfield's ecclesiological earnestness, devotion to his work and his God (perhaps in that order) made him the Church's favourite architect, but only the 'granite on fire' of Dr Temple could have foisted brick stripes and diapers on provincial Rugby, and made them stick. Butterfield's buildings were to rise around the Close for the next quarter of a century – the New Quad, the rebuilt Chapel, the New Bigschool, the 'fever cottage', the reading room and Art Museum and gymnasium: 'the streaky bacon' style they called it in Oxford,[10] and one imagines endless schoolboy epithets at Rugby. The most important thing about Butterfield's architecture was that it could not be ignored. Nor, in schoolboys' everydays, avoided.

Rugby School loved Dr Temple and was sad to lose him in 1869: it sank into four years of scandal, decline, a bad press and litigation over the misappointment of the next headmaster, who was finally persuaded to 'retire' to a remote rectory in Lancashire. Recovery was in the hands of the expansive Dr Thomas Jex-Blake, who had to enlarge School House to accommodate his family of two sons and nine daughters (one of whom was to be Mistress of Girton College). Dr Jex-Blake oversaw the progress of Butterfield's Rugby – though New Bigschool was 'one of the ugliest buildings of its kind' in Rugby's own opinions; he introduced art, archaeology and antiquities with the opening of the Art Museum – 'a delightful form of culture often too little thought of at home and school'.[11] He also appointed William Parker Brooke from Fettes College in Edinburgh as an assistant master in School House.

The Brookes hailed from Norfolk (as did Dr Jex-Blake); generations of farmers with a variety of subsidiary talents from around
Great Walsingham, near the north Norfolk coast, had produced a
son, Richard England Brooke, who went to Cambridge and into
the Church. He became the incumbent at Bath Abbey; something
of a figure in a fashionable city, he married Harriet Hopkins from
Lincolnshire and they produced two daughters and four sons: the
daughters were to be Rupert Brooke's spinster aunts, living at their
father's retirement villa in Bournemouth, Grantchester Dene; one
son, Alan England Brooke, was Dean of King's College when
Rupert arrived there and, rather more essentially, another son,
William Parker Brooke, was to be his father. W. P. Brooke went
up to Cambridge, exchanging Trinity for King's, then to Fettes
College as a joint-housemaster with the Revd Charles Cotterill,
whose sister Mary Ruth he married on 18 December 1879. There
was no place for a married housemaster at Fettes, but the head,
Dr Potts, had come from Rugby, so he put in a good word for
W. P. Brooke there, and the Brookes duly arrived, at a comfortable
but ordinary villa on the corner of Church Walk and Hillmorton
Road, conveniently a few yards from School House, in January
1880. Their first boy, Richard England Brooke – Dick – was born
the following year, then came a daughter who died; then – though
Mrs Brooke hoped for another daughter – Rupert Chawner
Brooke on 3 August 1887. Their third boy, Alfred, was born
in 1891 and the family was complete. The following year the
headmaster, John Percival, offered W. P. Brooke the 'plum' of
School Field – now handed over completely into the school's
ownership by Dr Goulbourn, but still like the other houses an
independent fiefdom, where the housemaster (on a salary of £500
a year) was running a kind of academic hotel and profits were
made. Headmaster Percival, who had taken over in the year of
Rupert's birth, 1887, was the son of a Westmoreland farmer and

champion wrestler, and something of a whirlwind – he found the school full of idleness and 'with a good deal of evil',[12] and set about removing both with vigour.

So the Brookes took their young family along the Barby Road to School Field, into the gravel drive and up the steep stone steps into the front door of the housemaster's house. It was a big, impressive Victorian pile of dark red and blue bricks, high-gabled, high-ceilinged and breathing Rugby's high moral tone, which engulfed them. For five-year-old Rupert it was life on senior-school scale assumed before he had even begun his formal lessons, both adventurous and intimidating. Mrs Brooke's drawing-room was to the left of the door, with a big bay window overlooking the lawn and protecting hedge, then across the expanse of New Bigside to the glories of sunsets in the west. Mr Brooke's study was opposite, connecting with the boys' quarters, the seniors' cells, the barn-like dining-hall for fifty boys and the family, and an equally barn-like dormitory above, with some rooms in the attics for senior boys.

School Field had a large though undistinguished private garden, with a tennis lawn, flower-beds beside the drive and under the windows, and a proud young Cedar of Lebanon which was most likely moved from a site near the chapel, where one appears in a photograph of 1870, to make way for Butterfield's rebuilding works. (The cedar is still there.) Rugby tradition favoured spring gardening (cricket sweeping all other activities aside during the summer): this originated in the dressing of the Island – a tumulus mound next to School Field, moated by Cistercian monks for fish-keeping, and sacred to the Great Rebellion of 1797 when the boys had fortified it against their hated headmaster, Dr Ingles. For years afterwards the Island had been turfed and flowered for ceremonial inspection on Speech Day, then the Wednesday in Easter week: the headmaster and his guests solemnly admired the daffodils, violets, anemones and primroses that had been pillaged by armies of small boys, overseen by the Sixth Form, from neighbouring fields and gardens, probably the guests' own. This smart schoolboy enterprise had been spoiled when Speech Day was changed to the summer term, but Rugby's pride in spring flowers hung on, and in Rupert's days the garden of School Field was bright with daffodils and huge clumps of *Primula vulgaris* (and the primroses are still there; clumps so large as if to allow for the pilferings of long dead boys, and with some to spare).

The flat Rugby horizons continued to fill the Brookes' lives, with a summer break at Bournemouth, and aunts Lizzie and Fanny at Grantchester Dene, or a Brighton hotel. In the late March when Rupert was eight a terrific storm felled seventeen of the great elms in the Close, opening up the view from School Field to School House and the 'streaky bacon' effect all round. Butterfield's long era of rebuilding Rugby came to an end that summer (and his long partnership with Rugby's craftsmen builders, Parnells, who were to divert to the coming man, Edwin Lutyens) when the scaffolding came down on the tower of St Andrew's church, another landmark, the parish not to be out-towered by the school.

Just after his tenth birthday Rupert started at his prep school, Hillbrow – 'another of those solid institutional buildings erected with alternate layers of red and blue brick, without heating of any kind, and the inevitable boring draught in stone passages that smelt of dust and the leather of down-at-heel shoes'.[13] After someone had seen him across the road, he walked the 100 yards into yet another version of Rugby life: at Hillbrow he was contemporary with Duncan Grant and James Strachey, small apostles of his own future. And the Bournemouth or Brighton routine was broken in the summer of 1899 when the Brookes went on holiday to St Ives, and Rupert played beach cricket with the Stephens – Virginia was long known as a demon bowler.

Rupert Brooke entered his father's house, in the School Field sense, in the autumn of 1901 when he was just fourteen; with his August birthday he might have been the youngest but was actually the oldest (and tallest) in the class. He walked down the corridor of his own home into schoolboy dualities, being one of them, and being the housemaster's – 'Tooler' they called W. P. Brooke – and more particularly 'Ma Tooler's' son. Rugby's traditions and timetable engulfed him – the timetable so immutable that it was printed in H. C. Bradby's *Rugby* in Bell's Great Public School series in 1900 (Bradby was to succeed W. P. Brooke at School Field) – with lessons starting at 7.15 through till 6 p.m. with the break from 1.15 until 3. He threw himself into every aspect of school life, but he was constantly brought down by ailments, allergies, influenza, toothache or the perennial pink-eye and dis-patched to the Butterfield fever cottage across the road in Horton Crescent, while his mother maintained routines at School Field. He was different from the other boys, and learnt to diffuse the differences in dramatizations. But he adored Rugby and every-thing about it – in the spring of 1904 after some illness or other his hard-pressed mother sent him and thirteen-year-old Podge to friends in Italy: Rupert was blasé about Pisa and Florence, the latter's 'indefinable quiet sadness' accorded with his mood, but he looked forward to leaving 'as though I were being freed from prison'.[14] His spirits were too low, and he was too young yet for Italy; besides, people died there – very particular people: Shelley, Browning and Arthur Hugh Clough – and he had yet to live.

Speech Day 1899 confirmed Rugby traditions with the unveiling of a statue of Thomas Hughes, whose *Tom Brown's Schooldays*, first published in 1857, had carried Dr Arnold's virtues and Rugby's fame all over the English-speaking world. Hughes, in white marble by Thomas Brock RA, on his granite pedestal outside the Temple Reading Room in the Barby Road, exhorted passers-by: 'Watch ye: Stand fast in the faith; Quit you like men: Be strong.'[15] Tom Brown was lauded as 'the incarnation of the highest form of the British schoolboy' – and his presence, with Dr Arnold's, was still very real in Rupert's day, especially as he haunted the Temple Reading Room for daily snatches of Chaucer or Dryden, which fascinated him, but which as a junior he was not allowed to borrow. Dr Arnold's name, so Bradby reliably informs us, was still on everyone's lips, prompted by a stream of pilgrims to his study and his grave.[16] Rupert Brooke, with no insistent ancestry of his own, could not help but absorb some of the intensity of the Arnold zeal, the self-criticism, abhorrence of hurting others and disregard of pain to himself, that were to be characteristic of him: he also assumed, somewhere at the corner of his mind, the Arnoldian view of the 'temptation' of natural beauty. Dr Arnold had always loved wild country – he found Warwickshire boring and flat – and justified his holiday house, Fox How, between Ambleside and Rydal Water (and in easy reach of the Wordsworths), by taking his children on 'arduous cross-country rambles . . .' to analyse 'the characteristic features of a country and its marked positions, or the most beautiful points of a prospect' to correct 'the seductive overtures of nature'.[17] The good doctor's prayers that 'the sense of Moral Evil be as strong in us as my delight in Natural Beauty' – or their sensations – were strongly evident in Brooke (who assiduously avoided the Lake District in his own wanderings).

But for all the 'streaky bacon' buildings, pink-eye and the ghost of Tom Brown, Rupert's Rugby career was something of a triumph. He survived the tortuous 'runs', across the soggy meadows to Bilton, Barby and Crick; he played an enthusiastic half-back for his house XV, and his cricket was best of all (as it was for Rugby) – he played for his house and the School, with a climax in the prestigious Marlborough match at Lord's at the end of his last summer term (his tasselled and fading cricket cap is perhaps his most poignant memorial, amid the paraphernalia of the great game in the Rugby school museum). And he won prizes for poetry and prose (an essay on William of Orange) and a Greek scholarship to Cambridge.

As he made the first momentous transition of his life he appears very much in the scholar gypsy tradition of Clough and Matthew Arnold: Arthur Hugh Clough was virtually adopted by the Arnolds, so all three had that unrestrained diet of Rugby in early life. Rupert, like Clough, was marked by a stressfully overloaded conscience; Clough at the same stage was 'manifestly destined for great things . . .' but 'perhaps already at the limit', the 'Too quick despairer' of Matthew Arnold's lament, *Thyrsis*, after Clough's too early death in 1861, aged forty-two.[18] Was Rupert, too, destined for the realms of 'gold-dusted snapdragon' and 'stocks in fragrant blow'?

> Roses that down the alleys shine afar,
> And open jasmine-muffled lattices,
> And groups under the dreaming garden-trees,
> And the full moon, and the white evening star.[19]

Sometimes Rupert's young life seems interchangeable with Matthew Arnold's; Arnold at twenty-three was to be echoed by Brooke at nineteen: 'a perplexing figure, poised between dandyism and melancholia, between a burgeoning aestheticism and declining faith in God'.[20] Ian Hamilton's study of Arnold proposes an all too chilling prophecy for Brooke – 'a son in mourning who made everybody laugh; a youth marked for early death who appeared to have all the time in the world'.[21] Brooke would turn to the Puritans, Arnold had won the Newdigate Prize in 1843 for his epic poem *Cromwell*; both were temporary assistant masters at Rugby in the way of duty; Brooke's dandyism was already turning heads in the streets of Rugby as he would in King's Parade, Cambridge – he was almost six feet tall, with blue eyes, his head

poised well on a rather long neck. The slight upward turn of the nose, as delicately moulded as his other features, seemed to give his whole lithe frame an attitude of eagerness that matched his facial expression. The very fair hair with a reddish tinge in it looked ready to grow luxuriantly if allowed. It seemed a shame to cut it, so it wasn't, and a toss of the head from right to left, to shift the hair from his forehead, became a characteristic gesture.[22]

Brooke followed the poetic pathway of Arnold and Clough, but of James Thomson, Byron, Shelley and Browning too – particularly the young Browning, atheistic and vegetarian – and in a fateful early friendship with another famous Rugbeian, the actor William Charles Macready. Poetry and the drama were his natural goals; and in the early 1900s aestheticism, Swinburne, Aubrey Beardsley and Oscar Wilde were highly fashionable: a picture he painted of himself forms a fitting farewell to his schooldays:

[*Scene*. The Close on a purple evening in June. The air is full of the sound of cricket and the odour of sunset. On a green bank *Rupert* is lying. There is a mauve cushion beneath his head, and in his hand E. Dowson's collected poems, bound in pale sorrowful green. He is clothed in indolences and flannels.]
[Enter Arthur.]
Arthur. 'Good morrow. What a tremulous sunset!'
Rupert: 'Ernest Dowson is one of the seven geniuses of this age. I am the other six . . .'[23]

This superb youth actually went away by himself for the first time in the summer he left school, 1906, to the Russell-Smiths, who had two sons at Rugby, in their comfortable holiday home at Brockenhurst in the New Forest. He was delighted to discover, as Virginia Stephen had done, that the general waiting-room of the down platform at Brockenhurst station had signed photos of Tennyson, Browning, Longfellow, Bishop Wilberforce and G. F. Watts among others, all a gift from Julia Margaret Cameron, in gratitude because she had a reunion with one of her sons there after his long absence abroad. The Russell-Smiths, whom he called 'ordinary and merry' one minute and 'ridiculous and gross' the other, introduced him to walking, and to the beauties of the Forest, which was the first crack in the Rugby aura.

Of the five poetic memorials on the south wall of Rugby school chapel, four – Landor, Matthew Arnold, A. H. Clough and Lewis Carroll – went to Oxford; Brooke is the odd one out. It was a critical difference: instead of the vale of dreaming spires there was the bitter wind from the fens, instead of Puseyism there was to be Fabianism, instead of sentimental indulgence there was the austere dappling of the puritan tradition, touching everything as sure as Milton's pansies were 'freak't with jet'.* Cambridge, the city of the Darwins, woke Rupert Brooke up, it gave him brilliant and difficult friends, it gave him his life-enhancing river landscapes of the Cam and the Ouse – and last, but hardly least, the society of rather remarkably radical young women. He arrived beneath the grey cupolas and pinnacles of King's College in the October of 1906, newly fledged into freedom but uncertain as to how to start. He was quiet and rather lonely. Tragedy struck just after the

---

* There was not one Butterfield building in Cambridge, though Butterfield had restored the church at Trumpington, the next village to Grantchester, but sombrely in stone.

Christmas holidays, when his elder brother Dick became sick and died of pneumonia; he was twenty-five. Rupert, 'ill with age' at home, broke out in the Easter vacation, on a walking tour with the obliging Russell-Smiths:

Then my sad heart sang over Kent and Sussex . . . We slew a million dragons and wandered on unknown hills. We met many knights and I made indelicate songs about them. We passed Amberley and Arundel, and Dunton and 'Petworth, a little town' as Belloc somewhere finely says . . .[24]

He caught the mood of Belloc's 'April' and it cheered him:

Come then with me, I'll take you, for I know
Where the first hedgethorns and white windflowers blow[25]

– and back in Cambridge joyously walked back to his lodgings with Belloc 'wonderfully drunk' after a good dinner and discussion at the Pembroke Society. He wrote to a friend at Rugby: 'you can tell Ma if you see her; but for God's sake don't say he was drunk, or she'll never read him again.'[26] He was struggling to be a dutiful, Christian and sober son to his grieving parents, and loyal to old friends, but becoming quite a different young man – 'terribly Fabian' under the influence of his most forceful Cambridge friends Ben Keeling and Hugh Dalton. The young Fabians – neo-Pagans as Virginia Stephen called them – were constructing their own map of approved places for living: 'Tomorrow I am going to the most beautiful place in England to work,' Brooke boasted to a Rugbeian, Andrew Gow. 'I have made seven poems on it, some very fine, and all resting on the fact that Lulworth Cove rhymes with love: a very notable discovery.'[27]

From our age of hackneyed images it needs some effort to

understand quite how much Lulworth Cove – visually, emotionally and socially – was to mean to this young man whose life was
so short of dramatically beautiful places and so full of the featureless
Midlands plain. How he came to choose Lulworth he does not
say, but it was already famous, the illustration in the geography
book come to life – of an exquisite limestone bowl broken by the
sea; Keats had loved it, Hardy too (Rupert was convinced he
would meet Tess D'Urbeville there), and he could very well have
visited it, at least visually, from a Bournemouth paddle steamer,
which was the most usual way to go. A few cottages with neat
gardens, where teas could be taken in summer, made up the Cove
community of his day. Most rewardingly, it was a place *he* chose
to go, making the arrangements with Mrs Chaffey at the West
Lulworth post office himself, with his own friends, who included
Hugh Russell-Smith and Dudley Ward. They cycled from Wool
station, packs – mainly of books – on their backs, for independence
at Lulworth was at first a reading party, and only later, with the
advent of the Fabian young women, the Oliviers, and Katharine
Cox, and some Stracheys and Keyneses, did it come to mean
camping parties and love and laughter upon the soft, green downs.
When Rupert called Lulworth 'the most beautiful place in
England' he meant it, at least as far as he was concerned himself:
he gave notice that from now on his was to be a diet of lovely
places. He was in the van of the changing perceptions, that natural
beauty was virtuous, rather than the temptation that Dr Arnold
had imagined.

The triumvirate Keeling, Brooke and Dalton wanted to change
the world; all they were allowed was lively eccentricity. The
galvanizing influence was that of Frederic 'Ben' Keeling, the
senior of the three, who had arrived at Trinity College in October
1904, feeling he had found his true home. Keeling's father had
been a comfortable Colchester solicitor who was in his mid-sixties

when he took a very young third wife of twenty-something. Both parents had died while Ben and his brother Guy were at Winchester, a school which had already marked Ben for a rebel against the stultifying routines of his home life – 'a lanky youth, with big brown eyes and ineffective chin',[28] blundering, head-strong, absurdly egotistical and yet full of public spiritness and ready for self-sacrifice.[29] Keeling was the ideal Fabian placeman at Cambridge. He did not flinch at running battles with the bloods and rowing men who made the Fabians their target because it was the first university society to give equal opportunity to women members, and for its importing controversial speakers. Keeling masterminded Keir Hardie's visit, fooling the enemy while the speaker was spirited out of back doors and down alleys to his audience, and returned safely to King's; liveliness was never a bar to popularity, and boosted by the Liberal landslide victory of 1906, for which Brooke had worked in Rugby, the Fabian membership soared to sixty that autumn.

It was at the same time, in making his way to his 'courtesy' visit to his uncle, the Dean of King's, that Brooke had met a fellow freshman, Hugh Dalton. Dalton came from an even more rigid background than Rugby – his childhood divided between a place that inculcated within him 'a certain irreverence towards auth-ority', Windsor Castle, and the beloved gardens, tennis and fives courts, shrubberies and woodland walks around his grandmother's lavish home, The Gnoll, at Neath, in what was then Glamorgan. (As a child, he recalled, he told his grandmother that The Gnoll was too large for her and should belong to the people of Neath: today, it does.)★ But surviving the impact of the 'massive personal-ity' of his father affected Dalton most – his father was Canon John

---

★ Hugh Dalton's memoirs, *Call Back Yesterday*,[30] recall his childhood memories and his affection for Brooke.

Neale Dalton, who had so effectively cowed the personalities of the royal princes, the ill-fated Eddy and George, soon to be George V.★

Dalton – 'very tall, loose jointed with cold grey eyes contradicted by a humorous mouth and the loudest voice one could possibly imagine'[32] was a Tory when he arrived, but his affection for Brooke, and their exuberant idealism, converted him to the Fabians, as it did others, including George Mallory,† the mountaineer, at Magdalene, Gerald Shove, the Stephens' cousin, teaching economics with John Maynard Keynes, Geoffrey Keynes,‡ his younger brother, Francis Birrell§ – the son of Asquith's Secretary for Education – and Arthur Schloss, the orientalist who changed his name to Arthur Waley;★★ variations

★ See Ben Pimlott's biography of Hugh Dalton for Canon Dalton's effect on his son.[31]

† George Mallory was very much a part of the Brooke circle, admired by Lytton Strachey and painted in the nude by Duncan Grant; he left Cambridge to teach at Charterhouse, where he married Ruth Thackeray Turner, the daughter of the architect.

‡ Geoffrey Keynes (1887–1982), a surgeon as well as a scholar, knew Brooke from the age of fourteen until the last year of his life and was to become one of the four literary trustees appointed by Mrs Brooke's will in 1931; he was to prove a loyal and faithful servant to Rupert Brooke's memory, collecting and editing his poems and letters, and seeing the Hassall biography into print after the author's sudden death in 1963.[33]

§ Francis Birrell (1889–1935) was to move from the Cambridge Fabians into Bloomsbury, opening a bookshop in Taviton Place with David Garnett in 1919.

★★ Arthur Waley (1889–1966) went to work at the British Museum, where he taught himself Chinese and Japanese, becoming the famed translator of *The Tale of Genji* and other volumes. He was devastated by Brooke's death – and the outcome, his loyalty to Beryl de Zoete through her mind-distorting illness and his love for the Australian girl Alison Grant, is movingly told in *A Half of Two Lives* by Alison Waley.[34]

of these composed parties for walking, along the Cam to Ely, punting to Grantchester, and camping weekends in the water-meadows.

In 1908, on Sunday, 10 May, the Fabians were addressed by Sir Sydney Olivier, newly returned from Jamaica; Rupert Brooke reported this significant evening to his mother the next morning,[35] – the dinner afterwards had been in Keeling's rooms at Trinity – 'very Socialist' of one course and fruit, for twenty-five people who included Katharine Cox from Newnham College:*

Wells also was there, Lady Olivier, and the two youngest Olivier girls. Brynhild Olivier is left behind to run Jamaica! It was great fun. Amber Reeves and Wells were perched up behind on a window-sill. They came in late and couldn't find a seat . . .

He didn't elaborate on Wells and Amber Reeves, the Cambridge Fabian treasurer from Newnham – of whom Beatrice Webb noted: 'the double first Moral Science tripos, an amazingly vital person and I suppose very clever, but a terrible little pagan'.[36] Rupert found himself next to Margery Olivier, who was also at Newnham and a member of the Fabians; the two youngest Oliviers, Daphne and Noel, fifteen and a Bedales's schoolgirl, had come with their mother. He also did not tell Mrs Brooke that in a kerfuffle over a dropped teacup, somewhere at the end of the evening, he came face to face with Noel and tumbled into obsessional love. After almost everyone had gone Brooke and Keeling were left to argue with Wells, which they enjoyed.

* Katharine Cox (1887–1938) was the daughter of a Fabian stockbroker, orphaned by the time she arrived at Newnham College, and of independent means. She refused Jacques Raverat (who married Gwen Darwin) and eventually fell in love with Rupert, becoming pregnant by him, but miscarrying. In 1918 she married Will Arnold-Forster.

When he wrote his duty letter home two weeks later, he reported that John Milton's tercentenary was to be celebrated on 10 July at Milton's old college, Christ's – 'they have asked some of us to get up a performance of *Comus*'.[37] The 'us' was yet another of the Cambridge societies that burst like buds in May (Brooke and Dalton set up the Carbonari, named, like the pasta sauce, for the early-nineteenth-century Italian revolutionaries with whom Byron plotted): the Marlowe Society, born the previous New Year to produce Elizabethan plays, had Rupert as President, Geoffrey Keynes as Secretary and Francis M. Cornford as Treasurer.* Rupert was enchanted by the whole romantic idea of *Comus* in Christ's garden, where Hobson's Conduit is a burbling presence – handmaiden of 'Sabrina fair' the river goddess – with the hoary, many-tentacled 'Milton's' mulberry on its mound and green curtains of box and yew; but the practical stage manager in him asserted – what if it rained? *Comus* was removed to the New Theatre, where it was a legendary success, with celebrities and critics as for a major theatrical occasion. Lytton Strachey wrote a sympathetic but not uncritical review in the *Spectator*, Thomas Hardy, Robert Bridges, the poet laureate Alfred Austin, Laurence Binyon and a not totally impressed Edmund Gosse were present.[39] Margery Olivier and Katharine Cox were dancers, Noel helped backstage, Sybil Pye, also at Newnham and from the Chart, helped with scenery and costumes, as did the cousins Frances and Gwen Darwin.

Milton's fantastic ruralism, the currently fashionable Edward

---

* Francis M. Cornford was a classics fellow at Trinity College, Jane Harrison's star pupil, brilliant and unorthodox, described by A. C. Benson as 'the great agnostic, with a fine sturdy pale face and crimped black hair', and by Virginia Woolf as 'like something carved in green marble' and just as silent. He married Frances Darwin in 1909, and they became Rupert's most staunch and supportive friends.[38]

Carpenter's *New Life*, and Shaw, Wells and Fabianism were a potent mixture, taken in deep draughts. *Comus* had inspired them:

> What hath night to do with sleep?
> Night hath better sweets to prove,
> Venus now wakes, and wakens Love . . .
> Come, knit hands, and beat the ground,
> In a light fantastic round.[40]

Keeling and Brooke had been involved in a Fabian reading of *Man and Superman*; they had adopted the doctrine that sex was a serious matter of procreation and that opposite temperaments produced the 'most desirable' children. This led them into a series of tortuous relationships, especially for the young women involved, and broken hearts; though what did they matter? Their first reaction to this puzzle – Brooke already suspected that Katharine Cox was his earth-woman and the unattainable schoolgirl Noel Olivier was his muse – was to go mad in the springtime: 'picture to yourself,' he asked Jacques Raverat,

> what a strange place was our England for four days about Eastertide. For I went dancing and leaping through the New Forest, with £3 and a satchel full of books, talking to everyone I met, mocking and laughing at them, sleeping and eating anywhere, singing to the birds, tumbling in the flowers, bathing in the rivers, and in general, behaving naturally. And all in England, at Eastertide![41]

Such an England gave birth to his ideal woman, all the genetic characteristics impossibly in one body –

> . . . and, in the end of the days, came to a Woman who was more glorious than the Sun and stronger than the sea, and kinder than the

earth, who is a flower made out of fire, a star that laughs all day, whose brain is clean and clear like a man's and her heart is full of courage and kindness; and whom I love.[42]

In the absence of such a paragon, at least in his arms, it was cold baths and solitude, both much vaunted by Ben Keeling, who certainly infected him with the desire for solitude: in the same frenetic spring of 1909 as these junketings Rupert was in Devon, lodging at Becky Falls beside the Becka Brook, a tributary of the Dovey on the eastern fringes of Dartmoor – 'returning to nature', rising early and entangling himself in a chest expander (which didn't) and a strict regime: 'eat no meat, wear very little, do not part my hair, take frequent cold baths, work ten hours a day and rush madly about the mountains in flannels and rainstorms for hours'.[43] The result was, inevitably, a chill, poisoned ankle or other ailment, and consequent imprisonment in yet another family vicarage or stuffy hotel with his parents.

Few people saw the serious side of him, he hardly wished to see it himself; perhaps he was only ever lost for words once (apart from in his letters to Noel) – in a long confessional to Ben Keeling. Keeling had gone from Cambridge to work for socialism in the East End of London and was extremely depressed but all the more determined for the fight: Brooke had to tell him that though he was working hard to establish the Fabian foothold for the rising generations in Cambridge, he could not join him. Between Rugby and Grantchester, and his other limited visions of the earth, he had discovered himself to be 'in love with the Universe', 'or with certain spots and moments of it' . . .

Half an hour's roaming about a street or village or railway station shows so much beauty that it is impossible to be anything but wild with suppressed exhilaration. And it's not only beauty, and beautiful things.

In a flicker of sunlight on a blank wall, or a reach of muddy pavement, or smoke from an engine at night there's a sudden significance and importance and inspiration that makes the breath stop with a gulp of certainty and happiness.[44]

He felt intensely that he was part of a changing society – he could not be disgusted with it nor the people within it, most of all with them, nor have time for pessimism, for he had to influence what that change might be. He had come upon, as if by accident, the Achilles heel of Fabianism and socialism (though of course he did not say this to Keeling), as practised by the intellectuals – that it was all very well suffering from nine till five on weekdays in some city squalor, if one had a retreat in an unspoiled corner of paradise for weekends and holidays. This duality, which Brooke could not stomach, seeing some beauty and self-respect in everything, was to mark the face of twentieth-century Britain more deeply than any other belief.★

Ben Keeling had first rowed with him along the Cam to camp in Grantchester's dreaming meadows and taste the delights of Mrs Stevenson's teas in her orchard, where the undergraduates liked to go at blossom time. It was in search of solitude, needing to work for his finals, and also tactfully to avoid his promise to share a house with Hugh Dalton, that Brooke took lodgings at The Orchard in the summer of 1909:

a small house, a sort of cottage, with a dear plump weather-beaten kindly old lady in control. I have a perfectly glorious time seeing nobody

★ Keeling moved to Leeds to manage the labour exchange; he married Rachael Townshend but found it impossible to live with her and their daughter; he enlisted in the ranks and was killed in the war. If he and Brooke had lived, Britain, one feels, would have become a very different place.

I know day after day. The room I have opens straight on to a stone
verandah covered with creepers, and a little old garden full of old-
fashioned flowers and crammed with roses.[45]

He worked at the Elizabethan poets, read and wrote, wandered
by the river, bathed every morning and sometimes by moonlight
in Byron's Pool, took his meals of fruit (mostly) out of doors in a
world that smelt of roses. He may not have been entirely this
pure, but at moments he found himself in harmony with his
hopes and ideals, and for these moments rose-scented Grantchester
slipped into his heart.

His merely second-class degree came as a shock; only wanting
to be a poet, unfit for any worldly occupation, he needed a
fellowship at King's and would now have to work doubly hard
for some essay prize to catch up. He went skiing in Switzerland
in the New Year and came home with food poisoning and flu, to
find his father suffering from headaches so bad that it was decided
that Rupert would have to stay and help at School Field. W. P.
Brooke died on 24 January 1910 and was buried the day 'his' boys
returned for the new term. Rupert got up from his own sick-bed
to find himself stand-in housemaster, an alarming position for a
twenty-one-year-old: Rugby had let him go, as on a long leash,
but now he was looped back, and could see his Cambridge life
and friends only in the distance. His predilection for feeling
old was aggravated by this leap into his father's shoes, his vivid
imagination gave him warped, oedipal nightmares, which frac-
tured his relationship with Mary Brooke. Rugby School was
not a benevolent institution, and with almost indecent haste the
Brookes were turned out of School Field at term's end: Rupert,
to his disgust, found himself living at a number, 24 Bilton Road.
There was no denying it was a demotion, actually out of sight of
the sacred Close, on the non-school side of town: he was torn

between feeling that he gave inadequate help to his mother, and, on the other hand, that he just could not grasp hold of his own life. He took refuge in poetic parody: a little of Belloc, some of Hardy and Matthew Arnold, the merest speck of Milton, but not much Brooke, was the first product of Bilton Road:

> Oh, soon
> The little white flowers whose names I never knew
> Will wake at Cranborne. They've forgotten you.
> Robin, who ran the hedge a year ago,
> Runs still, by Shaston. Does he remember? No.
> This year the ways of Fordingbridge won't see
> So meaty and so swift a poet as me
> Mouthing undying lines. Down Lyndhurst way
> The woods will rub along without us.
> Say,
> Do you remember the motors on the down?
> The stream we washed our feet in? Cranborne Town
> By night? and the two inns? the men we met?
> The jolly things we said? the food we ate?
> The last high toast in shandy-gaff we drank,
> And – certain people, under the trees, at Bank? . . .[46]

The stanzas rolled in this vein, all extremely angry and rather lewd. He was struggling for life and fresh air: 'You are a devil to tell me about the smell of peat,' he accused Dalton, who was writing in from somewhere leafy. 'I dream of it and wake sobbing.'[47]

April brought relief when, finally released from his mother's settling in at Bilton Road, he achieved Cove Cottage at Lulworth. 'I roam the cliffs and try to forget my bleeding soul,' he wrote to Geoffrey Keynes, using School Field notepaper, marked Nevermore, for the last time. Lulworth asserted healing powers: 'This is heaven – Downs, Hens, Cottages and the Sun,'[48] he teased Edward Marsh, who he knew would have him for an opera-going dandy, with fine and intimate dinner afterwards and old brandy talk till dawn. Marsh was an unfailing talent-spotter for handsome young men; he had noted Brooke in the Greek play when he was first at King's – radiant 'like a Page in the Riccardi Chapel'[49] (and for his variation on Mark Gertler see page 168) – and he was notably difficult to resist. His role as private secretary to Winston Churchill gave him influence; as the inventor and editor of *Georgian Poetry* volumes he was an important patron; his bachelor apartment in Raymond Buildings in discreet and quiet Gray's Inn was a *pied-à-terre* for many, as it was to become for Rupert.

Rugby had receded, for Bilton Road, where he joked that he wore shoes and there was no garden, had no power; it was merely a changing-room for his deep affection and sense of duty to his mother, younger brother Alfred ('Podge', who shadowed him to King's, the Carbonari and the Fabians) and his other lives. His summer was to be barefoot in The Orchard, where May Day invitations were issued for breakfast 7.30 for 7.45 a.m., and he was ensnared with happiness. With some glee he declined Marsh's invitation to somewhere more exotic: 'The apple blossom and the river and the sunsets have combined to make me relapse into a more than Wordsworthian communion with nature, which prevents me from reading more than 100 lines in a day, or thinking at all.'[50] He was working on Puritanism in English drama through the Elizabethans and up to the Civil War, immersing himself in dangerous realms for an impassioned young man – the extremes of viciousness and horror, bawdiness and high farce, that he found in the plays of Middleton, Fletcher and John Webster (on whom he was to write his King's fellowship-winning dissertation). Brooke's puritanical contempt for 'things corrupt and unclean' invoked his scorn and the worst of his temper, and was deeply

1. Virginia Stephen at twenty, studio portrait by George Charles Beresford, 1902.

2. 'Sweet Morgan': E.M. Forster in 1915, aged thirty-six, four of his six famous novels already written.

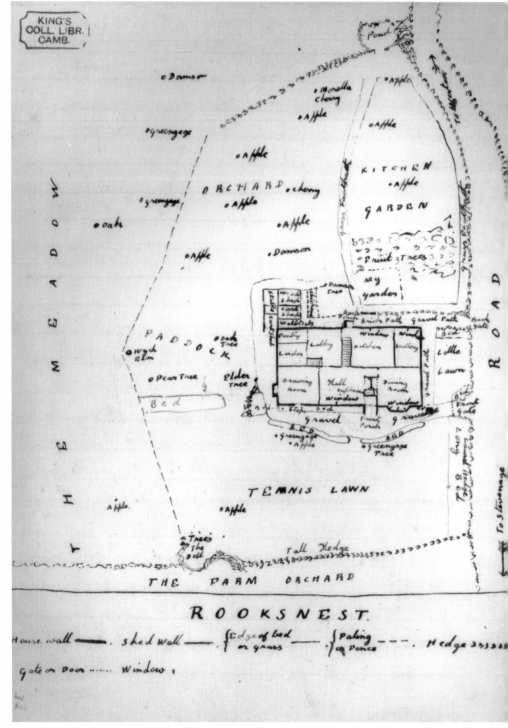

3. Rooksnest, the real-life Howards End, a considered plan of the house and garden, drawn by Forster when he was fifteen.

4. Netherhampton House, Wiltshire, the gate bearing the Gauntlett arms, from a drawing by Alys Fane Trotter.

5. St Ives, Cornwall, as it was when Virginia spent childhood holidays there; the figure second from the right is the painter Alfred Wallis.

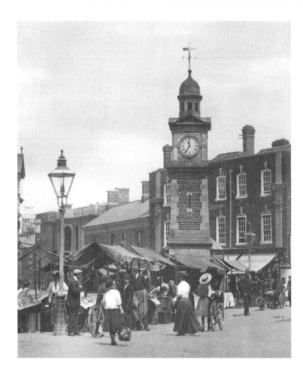

6. Rugby, the Golden Jubilee Clock Tower of 1887, the year of Rupert Brooke's birth.

7. Rugby, *Cricket on The Close*, from a painting of 1889 by Jarmyn Brooks, showing School Field, the house which became Rupert Brooke's home in 1902.

8. Theatricals at Limpsfield Chart. Left to right, Margery Olivier, David Garnett with goblet to his face, Dora Cox in background, Daphne Olivier kneeling in foreground, Edward Garnett in dark jacket, Speedwell Black sitting in foreground, Mabel Hobson wearing beard, Brynhild Olivier, Noel Olivier, Harold Hobson wielding axe.

9. L.P. Hartley as a Harrow schoolboy, with his father, Harry Hartley, and his sisters Enid (right) and Norah (left). Enid in part inspired the character of Hilda Cherrington.

10. The Orchard, Grantchester, with tables and deckchairs set out beneath the apple trees, *c.*1910.

11. Rupert Brooke, reading in the Old Vicarage garden at Grantchester, summer 1911.

. 'May Races' on the river Cam, *c.*1908. Rupert, in his Old Rugbeian blazer, right of the 1sthead, reads a letter as he leans against the stair; to his left Virginia Stephen awaits a light r her cigarette from (?) Dudley Ward. The photograph was taken by Florence Keynes, so Geoffrey and possibly Maynard are there too.

13. Carrington: *Hill in Snow, Hurstbourne Tarrant,*
the view from Ibthorpe House, watercolour, 1916.

14. Carrington on the high hedge ladder at Ibthorpe in Hampshire, *c*.1913.

15. Carrington, *Hoeing Vegetables*, fresco panel at Ashridge House, Hertfordshire, 1912.

ingrained from generations of his own Puritan ancestors,[51] – and he was to be 'living' with these puppeteers of God and the Devil, in the thrall of Merrie England, for over two years. His 'dateless' quality, 'which makes it easy to picture him in other centuries, yet always in England',[52] which charmed his friends, was the key to his discovery of his writer's soul, and his needful baptism by drowning in this past. It was almost as if the young Milton had returned from retreat in the meadows at Horton, intoxicated by the beauties of earth and sky, but tortured by odes on moralities and carnal lusts.* A common enough complaint, this Miltonic quandary was to mark Brooke's existence; it is the key to him and especially to his love affairs and stormy relationships with young women. All of inconsequence, except that at moments he, Rupert Brooke, could match Milton on the heights: for Milton's stanza, from his 'Ode on the Nativity of Our Lord', written just after his twenty-first birthday in the early days of 1630 –

> And the yellow-skirted fays
> Fly after the night-steeds, leaving their moon-loved maze

– there is Brooke's closing to 'The Jolly Company', written in November 1908, when he was also twenty-one:[54]

> . . . For, all the night,
> I heard the thin gnat voices cry,
> Star to faint star, across the sky.

Brooke in Arcady dates from that summer of 1910 when England moved from being Edwardian to the new Georgian age. He

---

* The parallels between Brooke and the young Milton, especially as in Belloc's biography of Milton,[53] are very strong.

Fabianized on a caravan campaign to Hampshire and Dorset speaking on Poor Law reform (the Minority Report),* to Llanbedr in north Wales for the summer school; he schemed and cultivated shamelessly, trekking to Petersfield to see Geoffrey Lupton and the 'gloomy' Edward Thomas, and to Limpsfield Chart to David Garnett and the Pye family, all in usually frustrated efforts to spend time with Noel Olivier. His haunts are predictable because he is loyal to his favourite places, Mrs Primmer's at Bank – in the footsteps of Ben Keeling, Virginia Stephen and the Oliviers – Lulworth Cove, the Devon beauty spots and the Wiltshire downs (using Hilton Young's cottage at Lockeridge). At Lulworth Lytton Strachey's reading parties were at a rented house, Churchfields, in West Lulworth, but Rupert had opted to be nearer the sea, right down in the Cove with the fishing boats, in the last house, Cove Cottage, built of clunch and warmly roofed in coral-coloured tiles. From Cove Cottage he could sprint barefoot across the narrow track and up the steep, green cliffside to plunge into the pools in Stair Hole, their waters warmed from washing over the sun-baked rocks. (Every local knew that the Cove itself offered an icy bathe.) These places, and his returns to Bilton Road, all fell into a pattern, radiating like the spokes of a jagged wheel, from the hub of Grantchester.†

---

* The Fabian Society's amendments to Poor Law reform, known as the Minority Report, advocated removing the stigma from state aid, and separated children's welfare, unemployment, and old age into separate categories; Brooke was intensely involved, with the Cambridge Fabians, in this campaign for at least two years.

† Rupert was ousted from Cove Cottage in 1911 by the arrival of the London surgeon Alfred Fripp and his family, who rented it permanently until Fripp inherited a legacy which enabled him to build Weston House on the cliffs opposite Cove Cottage, in the late 1920s. Rupert and his friends resorted to camping.

In the middle of August, returning for some Cambridge theatricals with Francis and Frances Cornford (who had married in 1909), Gwen Darwin, Justin Brooke and others they could muster, he was shocked to find 'horrible' people in his house at the Orchard (there had been talk in the village, and a row with the Stevensons over bare feet, and especially young ladies' bare feet), so he took himself next door to the Old Vicarage, a lodging house he had once commended to Lytton Strachey. Its advantages were aired many times to many people: 'a deserted, lonely, dank, ruined, overgrown, gloomy, lovely house: with a garden to match. It is all five hundred years old, and fusty with the ghosts of generations of mouldering clergymen.'[55] The reality was perhaps even better. Grantchester was – well before Brooke – the most romantic of the Cambridge villages, isolated in the flood meadows of the Cam, away from any main road – unlike its sister village, Trumpington, across the river and on the high road into Cambridge. Grantchester's walled street winds narrowly, keeping secrets: the young Queen Elizabeth had once ridden this way, dressed in black velvet, her red hair caught in a jewel-spattered caul and topped by a feathered cap[56] – a beckoning ghost for Rupert. The church is ancient and architecturally distinguished, with 'nodding ogee arches' in the chancel, and a yew-shaded churchyard promising ivy-draped urns; the clock is on the north face of the tower, facing the majority of villagers scurrying to church – it has stopped many times but opinions differ as to whether it was ever at 'ten to three'.[57] The Old Vicarage had been a 'good, new built Vicaridge' the year Charles II died, in 1685, so has the look of the prettiest of English buildings, red brick with a hipped roof, tall chimneys and pretty dormers. By the early nineteenth century it was abandoned by vicars, spurned by the sensible as too damp, but ripe for romance. The romantic arrived in the person of Samuel Page Widnall, who bought the house in 1853: his father had been a tenant, and a nurseryman, famous for the Widnall dahlia grounds which had displayed their vibrant colours across the Old Vicarage gardens and into the Orchard tea garden grounds, some six acres, and were exported all over Europe and to America.[58] The younger Widnall was a keen naturalist, an interpreter of birdsong, and an obsessive builder of follies in the Old Vicarage garden, mostly in the ornamental gothic style; he made models in wood and plaster (his model of Grantchester Mill is in Cambridge Folk Museum and that of the church in the church vestry), and wrote and illustrated the products of his own hand-built private press.[59] Samuel Widnall had died in 1894, something of a local celebrity, to be succeeded by another, his sister-in-law, Miss Lallie Smith, 'the little Fairy Godmother of Grantchester', who taught the local children their Milton and Spenser. Miss Smith died in 1908, and the house was let to Henry Neeve, a carpenter, and his wife Florence, who loved old houses, and took in lodgers. Into this empathetic history stepped Brooke, its natural heir: the gentle Henry Neeve's habitual sitting out near his beehives with a hand-kerchief over his head, reading 'advanced newspapers', was soon immortalized, and he and Brooke conversed on botany. This unkempt, untidy but once distinguished house, with friendly ghosts, suited him so well. The garden was a 'great glory', with a soft lawn and antique flowers and Widnall's gothic ruin, which he liked to fancy was once a nunnery. The lawn disappeared into the shade of the great chestnut trees that lined the mill stream, the 'immortal river' laughing as it disappears under the mill; at night the laughing turned to whispering . . .

> And spectral dance, before the dawn,
> A hundred Vicars down the lawn;
> Curates, long dust, will come and go
> On lissom, clerical, printless toe . . .[60]

Thank goodness the Neeves were easy-going, and Henry Neeve sat reading rather than tidy up the gothic gloom, and Mrs Neeve, loving old houses, clearly loved flowers too . . .

> And in my flower-beds, I think,
> Smile the carnation and the pink;
> And down the borders, well I know,
> The poppy and the pansy blow . . .[61]

It was a perfectly poetic garden, almost a stage set for poetic intonations by a partnership of the river goddess and the talented Samuel Widnall: one of the garden's ornaments, the sundial, had a pedestal made from an old cross from the church, with an open book on which Widnall had carved the inscription himself: 'From the rising of the Sun until the going down of the same, the Lord's name is to be praised.'[62]

Gradually the number of friends that would drop by, calling his name from the lane outside, dwindled to fewer, more appreciative guests: David Garnett – *en route* to sailing on the Broads with the Oliviers – noticed first that there was a photograph of Noel in a silver frame on Rupert's table, but neither mentioned this. They bathed about midnight:

We walked out of the garden . . . into the lane full of thick white dust, which slipped under our weight as we walked noiselessly in our sand-shoes, and then through the dew-soaked grass of the meadow over the mill-wall leading to the pool, to bathe naked in the unseen water, smelling of wild peppermint and mud.[63]

This ritualistic and repeated cleansing brought him into a poetic harmony with the river that hinted at danger, for drowning was an 'easeful death' of temptation to romantic young men. Rupert, however, had a practical side to him: he could spend hours in a canoe with his books, steering with one hand and managing the books with the other, testing the Elizabethan cadences on the willows, shouting them across the water-meadows, with no one (evidently) to call him mad or laugh or even fling their arms around him.★ His greatest skill was to navigate at night, the three miles from Silver Street steps home to Grantchester, even when 'every possible landmark seemed merged in a soft blackness . . . [and] even the water surface had ceased to show the faintest gleam and met its muffled banks invisibly'. Sybil Pye was a not unapprehensive passenger – feeling (like Virginia and the walkers in the dark) disembodied:

floating in some new medium, without boundaries and out of reach of light – of time, too . . . But Rupert kept a steady course: he would know, he said, when we were nearing home, by the sound of a certain poplar tree that grew there: its leaves rustled faintly even on such nights as this, when not a breath seemed stirring. We only half believed him; there were so many poplar trees . . . But he was right; and he landed us without hesitation, and moored his boat as easily, it seemed, as if he had all the light of day to help him.[64]

This unusually healthy and robust vision of Rupert of the river reveals the underlying truth of the cacophony of his legendary life, perhaps the one certainty, that he had found where he belonged, a home. His 'little room' was about seventeen feet square, rather dark, with a big old fireplace and Georgian french window of square bland panes, the nursery gate on the stairs, all

---

★ There are also parallels between Brooke and the young Byron, not only swimming in the river at Grantchester, but in Byron's drifting in his boat with his books on the lake at Newstead Abbey. Brooke, only too aware of the poetry of youth, consciously moved in these ways.

low-ceilinged and small-scale; with the imagined ghosts of Victorian children, the verandah with the sagging roof, 'Pudsey Dawson' the bull-terrier that ate frogs, and the need to rescue the frogs, with Mr Neeve's honey for breakfast and tea and unlimited supply of Mrs Neeve's apple pies, the Old Vicarage suited him well. In autumn 1910 Morgan Forster stayed for two nights, and the following summer Virginia Stephen came, and she must have understood what it meant to him, for they bathed naked in the river.

'The Old Vicarage, Grantchester', which carries the dateline 'Café des Westens, Berlin, May 1912' – and was apparently scribbled in the back of an account book – is a glorious rant, directed at a love he knew he was losing. It is a tirade of passion, exciting to read because it is aimed (harmlessly) at a place rather than a person: his accusations –

> Here am I, sweating, sick, and hot,
> And there the shadowed waters fresh
> Lean up to embrace the naked flesh . . .

– and his love-lilts –

> And sunset still a golden sea
> From Haslingfield to Madingley?[65]

– are much in the same vein as his contemporary letters – those to Ka Cox at the ending of their long and deeply physical affair, to Noel Olivier, whom he had hardly kissed, as she determinedly pursued her own life through University College medical school, and to Phyllis Gardner, after their brief and lusty passion.* The trouble is that it is almost impossible to see Brooke after 'The Old Vicarage', penned whilst he was staying with Dudley Ward (who was working for the *Economist* in Berlin), through the welter of his published passions. His heartbreaks never had time to heal, his literary reputation no chance to grow creatively. Apart from his love-and-hate affairs, the Puritan not easily consigned to history, he worked incredibly hard to complete his Webster dissertation. He was never without his Hazlitt 1856 edition of Webster's plays, reading it in cafés and on trains – the unrestrained diet of the Duchess of Malfi's gratuitous violence might well have over-burdened his sentient soul – and though success was his, so was a nervous breakdown. He is only reliably seen in the consoling company of settled friends, such as Jacques and Gwen Raverat, and especially the Cornfords, Francis and Frances, at their new house out on the Madingley Road at Conduit Head, named for the source of the old Trinity College water supply, which still fed the fountain in the Great Court: along the watery way between Conduit Head and Grantchester, as a Fellow of King's, there was a momentary glimpse of a future.

But under stress, and losing grip on Grantchester, he began his Icarus-flight to doom, unnervingly forecasting his own fate over and over again. He streaked through Bloomsbury, literary and theatrical society, partying with everyone and everywhere in the space of a few short months: flying so high sealed his fate. The resourceful Edward Marsh, who was making him a Georgian poet, also introduced him to the London theatre world, and to the actress Cathleen Nesbitt, who would become Rupert's next love. Marsh, having the most charismatic political master of the day in Winston Churchill, opened the door to Downing Street, the Asquith set and Liberal political society; society and Brooke were

---

* The letters and manuscript from Phyllis Gardner were deposited by her family at the British Library in 1948, sealed for fifty years. They have been opened and some exhibited for the first time, revealing the Brooke-Gardner romance of 1912, in the exhibition *Chapter and Verse, One Thousand Years of English Literature*, at the British Library, 2000.

mutually enchanted, but it could not last. Rupert could not sustain the pace of his own life, he was exhausted from his dissertation and the unresolved tangles of his head and heart. He was admitted to his King's fellowship on 20 March 1913, dining in the company of old men (or so they seemed to him); he had long talked of travelling to North America and now there was nothing for him but to make a dramatic exit, stage left, which he did from Euston on the Liverpool-bound boat train two months later. His farewells had been elaborate, with many notes of last possible sightings and long, cruelly reasoned letters to Cathleen Nesbitt advising her – rather in the tone of an 'agony aunt' – that her career would not be forwarded by a season in New York. His letters to the distraught Katharine Cox – whom he persistently addressed as 'dear child' – were equally callous, and the state of his mental health must be seriously questioned. Frances Cornford had already divined that he just wanted to get away from them all, for a 'deep sleep'.

Certainly the purposes of his half-way round the world trip were obscure; he had a bundle of introductory letters, which he managed to leave behind (and which though they reached him in America he could have hardly used), and some intention to find a New York publisher for *Georgian Poetry* and his own future projects as well as to send back pieces to the *Westminster Gazette*: these tasks were conspicuous failures. He was a bad sailor and it was an uncomfortable crossing, but even that cannot excuse his failure to register any excitement at his first taste of New York: his reactions to both America and Americans were those of the most boorish English racist snob – or those of a seriously dulled mind. Granted Edward Marsh and the Asquith circle were not likely to be in touch with New York culture, but Rupert seemed unaware that he had arrived in the city that had been so recently galvanized into a passion over modern art by the massive Armory Show of over 1,000 post-Impressionist and Cubist works, including those of Van Gogh, Gauguin, Picasso, Matisse and Cézanne, and that the intellectual and artistic quarter, Greenwich Village, was still buzzing from this revolutionary event. Brooke, who professed himself both a modernist and a Fabian (at heart), was actually in New York the day the intellectuals and artists led the great Paterson Silk-workers Strike Pageant down Fifth Avenue, an event which virtually launched the liberal left in American politics.[66] Had his Fabian connections not told him of Herbert Croly's *The Promise of American Life*, a counterpart to Graham Wallas's *The Great Society*, which fostered his own beliefs, and how Croly and America's golden couple Willard and Dorothy Straight were working towards launching *New Republic*, the liberal weekly that would fight for a better world?* He did meet Ellery Sedgwick of *Atlantic Monthly*, and went to Boston to see Sedgwick's cousin, the poet and dramatist Amy Lowell (great-niece of Virginia Stephen's godfather James Russell Lowell) – and though she gave him a glimpse of Harvard, where was his *alter ego*, Walter Lippman?†Nothing of this exciting world, this world of Emerson and Thoreau (Robert Frost had just left for England) and of the lyrical golden ponds and purple woods of New England, a melding of poetry and landscape just as at his own Cambridge and Grant-chester, nothing of this reached him. He must have been very ill indeed.

In a somewhat uncomprehending daze, Brooke the 'traveller' crossed Canada – which he found comfortingly British but rather pointless all the same – with bouts of homesickness: he sent Edward Marsh the following regrets:

* With Croly and *New Republic* he might have found a job for life!
† Walter Lippman, friend of Amy Lowell, was leading the Harvard liberals 'to build a citadel of human joy upon the slum of misery to give the words "brotherhood of man" a meaning.'

Would God I were eating plover's eggs,
And drinking dry champagne,
With the Bernard Shaws, Mr and Mrs Masefield,
Lady Horner, Neil Primrose, Raleigh, the Right
Honourable Augustine Birrell, Eddie, six or
seven Asquiths, and Felicity Tree,
In Downing Street again.[67]

In Toronto he was pleased to discover that the Arts Club had heard of him: his comments on Niagara Falls matched those of the usual tourist. He spent his twenty-sixth birthday at a hunting lodge on Lake George, some sixty miles from Winnipeg, surrounded by bears, caribou and Indians: he was beginning to appreciate the wonders of the North American continent at last. By way of Vancouver (no comment!) he arrived in San Francisco on 15 September; he had been travelling for almost four months, and at last there seemed to be some benefit accruing. 'There's a sort of goldenness about "Frisco"' was not the most original of observations but at least here he had come to the right quarter, and was staying in Piedmont Avenue in Berkeley with a university professor, Chauncey Wells. The professor and his wife made him very welcome, and Berkeley charmed him; he fraternized both there and at Stanford, and was amused at the 'wide-mouthed awe' that greeted one who knew Goldie Lowes Dickinson and had met John Galsworthy and Belloc.[68] Thank goodness that he seemed to be recovering the semblance of a human being, a fact endorsed by his decision – from the shores of the Pacific – to travel, in the true meaning of the word, and drift to the South Seas as schooner and steamers might take him.

The Pacific was pacific as he left for Honolulu on 7 October

1913, and it brought from him two of his most admired sonnets: 'Clouds' –

> Down the blue night the unending columns press
> In noiseless tumult . . .

– and that known as 'Psychical Research', from the Society of that name founded by Professor Henry Sidgwick and his wife Nora at Cambridge, and Brooke's memories of a lecture, crossed with a little of Marvell's *Dialogue between Soul and Body*[69] – and a little remembered Matthew Arnold –

> Not with vain tears, when we're beyond the sun,
> We'll beat on the substantial doors, nor tread
> Those dusty high roads of the aimless dead
> Plaintive for Earth; but rather turn and run
> Down some close-covered by-way of the air,
> Some low sweet alley between wind and wind,
> Stoop under faint gleams, thread the shadows, find
> Some whispering ghost-forgotten nook, and there
> Spend in pure converse our eternal day . . .[70]

Brooke was healed island-hopping in the South Seas; once again he wrote lyrical descriptions of the places and the people, of memories and adventures and of his dreams and hopes for coming home. He visited Robert Louis Stevenson's grave on Samoa as he had intended, played Fijian cricket, lived on yam and turtle, sailed to Tavuini for the funeral of a young Fijian princess who had died of pneumonia, had a hundred adventures and made many friends, and ended with Christmas in New Zealand – 'a sort of Fabian England'[71] – and, all too characteristically, a poisoned foot. At the end of the first week of January 1914 he sailed for

Tahiti, finding paradise in most of its guises, in a native village called Mataia, where a smiling village girl named Taatamata became his lover. At Mataia he wrote, in February 1914, 'Tiare Tahiti' – to 'Mamua, when our laughter ends . . .' which is her poem; but he was so restored to health that he wrote many others, eventually published, including 'The Great Lover', in many senses an autobiography of his inner self, to that date, in early 1914.[72]

Rupert never forgot Taatamata, but (his foot healed) he was longing for home, as if he could smell the English spring. He left in early April, via San Francisco again and then a transcontinental train to Chicago, Pittsburgh, Washington and New York. Now restored to health, he did seem to appreciate America, but he had no time, he was desperate to get home, filled with an urgent love for his mother and all his friends, longing for the sight of England. He caught the scent of new-mown hay long before the boat reached Plymouth – and at the end of the first week of June 1914 he was in his mother's arms, hugging her and laughing, finding her 'younger and madder' than ever.[73]

His delicious euphoria lasted easily through to his birthday, his twenty-seventh, on 3 August which he was to spend with Podge and his mother at Bilton Road. On the Sunday, the 2nd, they drove out, in Brooke's car, to deepest Warwickshire, to Hampden-in-Arden, north of Stratford, Shakespeare's country, though with 'No holly and horns and shepherds and dukes' nowadays, Rupert wrote:

But it *is* lovely. It's the sort of country I adore. I'm a Warwickshire man. Don't talk to me of Dartmoor or Snowdon or the Thames or the lakes. I know the *heart* of England . . . Here the flowers smell of heaven; there are no such larks as ours, and no such nightingales . . .[74]

He rambled so happily in this vein, knowing it was all nonsense – well, not quite; but knowing he was well and healed and full of hope once more.

That was the tragedy of it all: the day after his birthday Britain went to war. He went to the Cornfords on holiday at Cley-next-the-Sea on the north Norfolk coast, close to the country of his ancestors. In London his destiny was sliding into place: a strong young New Zealander named Bernard Freyberg had accosted Churchill, First Lord of the Admiralty, on Horse Guards and asked for a job; Freyberg had heard of the élite corps, the Royal Naval Division, that Churchill had ordered to be set up and he was soon given his commission. The Division needed the brightest and best young men, and Edward Marsh, ever on hand to advise (though unfit to serve himself), introduced Brooke, his Rugby friend the composer and musician Denis Browne, and the Prime Minister's son Arthur 'Oc' Asquith, all of whom eventually joined the Hood Battalion of the Division under Freyberg's command.[75] Brooke threw himself into battalion life and their rigorous training with all the enthusiasm and efficiency that his old school might have expected of him. While they were at Blandford Camp in Dorset he was alarmed to hear rumours that the Old Vicarage at Grant-chester was to be destroyed, and he wrote to Frances Cornford, his note marked 'IMPORTANT', asking her to find out how it could be saved. He later learned that there was no threat, but by this time the Hood Battalion had left for Gallipoli, and neither Grantchester, nor Rugby, nor England would ever see him again.

4

Virginia Woolf and Orlando

Virginia Stephen's comparative happiness at Netherhampton in that summer of 1903, the last of her father's life, prompted the future geography of her own. She found the old house – older than any she had experienced – to be full of friendly ghosts with stories to tell, and the Wiltshire downs, the mysterious 'rise and swell and fall' of the land . . . 'like some vast living thing' . . . became her green sea. Settled in Bloomsbury, she still needed frequent escapes, often on her own, and a mix of memories and visits to friends (including searching out Henry James at Lamb House in Rye) had shown her that the train to Lewes landed her conveniently between seas, both green and blue. For Christmas and New Year of 1910–11 she and Adrian had retreated to an inn, the Pelham Arms at Lewes, from where she wrote to Lady Ottoline Morrell (with congratulations on Philip's election to the House of Commons) of being 'very much tempted to buy a house here. One has the most lovely downs at one's door, and there are beautiful 18th century houses.' From her seat by the fire, 'listening to the creaking of an enormous sign, painted with your family arms', it is to the aristocratic Ottoline that she reveals her atavistic fancies, which she hopes will not be swept away with the Liberals' reform of the House of Lords, for 'there are merits in the aristocracy which don't appear to you – and manners, and freedom'.[1]

Then, with one of her characteristic visual blips, she rented the ugliest of all her houses, a semi-detached red brick villa in Firle, not the pretty part, which she called Little Talland House. She knew it was ugly, but it was to bring two touches of serendipity into her life. Leonard Woolf had returned on leave from Ceylon, into the bosoms of his Apostle friends, weather-beaten and slow-speaking, said Lytton Strachey, 'like one risen from the tomb – or rather on the other side of it'.[2] Fresh air and ruralizing with Brooke, Stracheys and Keyneses and supping in Bloomsbury eventually brought him to Little Talland villa for weekend walking in the September of 1911: he fell in love with Virginia on her downs, seeing her face 'no less clear and fresh than the wind'.[3] Together they discovered – on walking west from Firle to the lip of the Ouse's meandering plain, tucked under Asheham Down (where there were mushrooms in profusion),[4] a deserted house that was much more like the ghost of Talland House, St Ives. Within a few weeks Virginia had persuaded Vanessa that they should take a joint lease on Asheham House: it had been built in the 1820s, and had two sitting-rooms, four main bedrooms, a big attic and two single-storey wings – and looked rather like a Regency hunting pavilion, which it was in some sense, having been built as a holiday house by a wealthy solicitor from Rugby (who probably had a long-term interest in chalk-quarrying and cement). Between the promise of romantic Asheham and the green downs, and during the winter and spring of 1912, Virginia and Leonard Woolf found their trust in each other, and Virginia, with many waverings and collapses on the way, at last happily agreed to marry him, gleefully introducing him as a 'penniless Jew'; they were engaged in June and the deed was announced in *The Times* on 13 August. Leonard, the lugubrious, the parsimonious, fanatically absorbed in anything he did, became the rock on which her fluttering soul rested. While Virginia 'identified

Asheham (as she identified London) with her deepest feelings for England and Englishness' – quoting Matthew Arnold's 'Thyrsis': 'I know these slopes; who knows them, if not I?'[5] – Leonard got on with reviving the derelict walled garden. Her pedigree and genius, her need to write and to be nurtured in the travails of her writing, were – surprising as it may seem – his security, too.*

Asheham sustained Virginia (she and Leonard spent the first night of their marriage there) for seven years:

In winter it could be ferociously cold; in summer it was shady and damp indoors, and rotted all their books. It could be a little 'shut in and dismal', as well as 'dim and mysterious'. It had an underwater feeling: 'the window-panes reflected apples, reflected roses; all the leaves were green in the glass'. It was quiet, except when the new-born lambs were making a racket all night: outside in summer you could hear 'the wood-pigeons bubbling with content and the hum of the threshing machine sounding from the farm.'[7]

Asheham brought the annual hunt for a holiday house to an end; it was there for Christmas and Easter and long weekends, the first settled outpost of Bloomsbury in the countryside. Virginia had a garden of her own, to potter in, but it was Leonard who grew vegetables and flowers for her – and there was nothing more soothing than garden talk at lunchtime. When they were alone, or with visitors, she renewed the rituals of tramping over the downs, toiling up the green shoulders of the majestic heights of

* Leonard was the fourth of nine children of a brilliantly successful liberal Jewish QC who had died suddenly at the age of forty-eight, leaving his family to penury and a certain amount of paranoia. He won scholarships to school and university and passed brilliantly into the civil service, which he hated – feeling 'as if I were playing the buffoon in a vast comic opera' in Ceylon. In contrast, life with Virginia was the sanest of propositions.[6]

Itford or Beddingham hills or Firle Beacon, finding the burial mounds and settlement sites of those who had come this way via the land bridge from Europe, or in Roman times. They could be alone on the heights, looking down on life in the river valley, out across the sunlit sea, inland to point out the string of little flint churches: Piddinghoe the most southerly, round-towered, right at the river's edge, Southease in the hamlet by the river crossing to Itford Halt, Rodmell's St Peter's at the end of the village almost on the marsh and – and where the valley was widest – Itford. All were Norman, ambassadors from a more recent civilization but still full of ghosts: Asheham gave Virginia constantly broader and deeper perspectives than London allowed, and she settled into ancient rhythms, finding comforts there: in 1916, the summer of the Somme bombardment, the guns sounded 'like the beating of gigantic carpets by gigantic women', sometimes faintly as 'the ghost of an echo' but sometimes as though rising from the next fold of green: 'at all times strange volumes of sound roll across the bare uplands', and when walking alone 'you turn sharp to see who it is that gallops behind you'. The phantom horseman passes . . . the sound lapses . . . 'and you only hear the grasshoppers and the larks in the sky'. She felt that the very forms of the downs magnified these strange effects, as they had always done: the guns prompted the remembrance of the ridges along the valley sides, remnants of defences against Napoleon's expected invasion – now the Kaiser would surely come this way, a terrifying but gratifying feature of gossip. Other portents too were the stuff of conversations, the vibrations addled the eggs, the awful July weather was the curse of the guns . . . but by August the sun was blazing, the eggs were wholesome, the locals were no longer downcast and the dreadful guns had been absorbed as another mystery of the earth.[8]

As a writer, Virginia needed to rationalize things that worried her in this way, for it was impossible to commit herself to words without feeling herself in command, the smallest pebble of missing or unexplained information so easily damming the stream. Her life at Asheham brought her notebooks on St Ives and her other places back to life; notebooks in themselves were rarely enough – she needed the sunlit sea in the distance to direct her characters, to sort out the snags in their existences as well as her own . . . and she needed the violets, orchids and harebells on the downs to pinpoint lights and colours. These props, which enabled her most consistent stream of writing to start, she had confirmed by identifying them in Charlotte Brontë's 'long toil with brush and pencil' that gave her scenes 'a curious brilliance and solidity' – quoting from *Jane Eyre*: 'a lane noted for wild roses in summer, for nuts and blackberries in autumn, and even now possessing a few coral treasures in hips and haws, but whose best winter delight lay in its utter solitude and leafless repose'.[9] Virginia found a great deal of ammunition for both richness and repose in her sojourn at Asheham: her first novels, *The Voyage Out* (1915) and *Night and Day* (1919), as well as the early excitements of the Hogarth Press, were fruits of the Asheham years.

Ostensibly Bloomsbury pacifism was influenced by Bertrand Russell and the Morrells, but it was the strand emanating from Limpsfield Chart which actually devolved them to the Sussex countryside, where Virginia seemed to rest, awaiting the gathering flight to her corner of the world.

The young David 'Bunny' Garnett, fond of wild flowers from his Chart upbringing, and rather regretting that his parents could not afford to send him to Cambridge, had studied botany and medical biochemistry in London, finishing in the summer of 1914. By then the Olivier girls had ushered him into Bloomsbury circles and many meetings, including the one with his future wife, Rachel

Marshall, the sister of Frances, but also another of particular significance: Garnett remembered, forty years on, an afternoon of 'temperament and warfare' over croquet and tennis in a Limpsfield garden, interrupted by 'two strange figures' who marched around the corner of the house; one was Adrian Stephen, the other – 'who gave the impression of being slightly made, though he was really five foot ten' . . . with 'very clear grey-blue eyes and a beautiful expressive mouth and held himself with unconscious pride . . .

> Here come the Grants O'Rothiemurchus
> Ilka ane as proud as a Turk is' . . .[10]

– was Duncan Grant. Asked about his homosexuality in later years, Garnett replied that he was 'more leant upon than leaning' – the impact of the young Grant, and undoubtedly his status as the Bloomsbury intimates' most seductively, mischievously homosexual treasure, meant that the leaning was about to begin.

Back at The Cearne on the Chart, in that summer of 1914, Bunny Garnett discussed the war with his mother, Constance. Constance Garnett was profoundly pacifist: it was her nature and politics, apart from her fears that militarism would bring untold suffering to her friends in Russia and Germany, and she utterly deplored the killing of any mother's sons, whosoever they were. She wanted Bunny to do ambulance work and save lives, and – after a short time in Germany on a Quaker relief mission with Francis Birrell (who was unfit for military service) – she won over her precious Bunny, who was inclined to enlist. Constance, whose war was taken up with self-sufficiency in her garden and her publication of seven fat volumes of translations of Dostoevsky, did not perhaps see any ulterior motive – for Bunny was by now in Duncan Grant's thrall: Duncan had been given a commission for designing a production of *Pelléas et Mélisande* in Paris, so off they went, Bunny as a medical volunteer. The French authorities, however, gave Duncan the notoriety of a pacifist anarchist, and ordered him home, Bunny in tow, and in England in early 1916 the Military Service Act brought in conscription: John Maynard Keynes advised Duncan and Bunny that they should do agricultural work, and Major Bartle Grant, Duncan's father, suggested that they take over the house, gardens and orchards at Wissett in Suffolk, which had been the home of a Miss Florence Ewebank, a relative of Duncan's mother. Garnett candidly admitted that Major Grant took all his dislike of the whole situation out on him, calling him 'Your friend Garbage': 'I liked Major Grant, but he did not like me.'[11]

So it was arranged that they should rent Wissett and set up as fruit farmers, an enterprise close enough to Bunny Garnett's heart for him to 'fall in love' with working on the land, and also to become fond of the shade of Miss Ewebank, a countrywoman who kept bees and cultivated the arts of kitchen, garden and orchard with a traditional flourish, rather in his mother's way. They walked into Wissett Lodge as Miss Ewebank had left it: they found it dark and poky, low-ceilinged, with the windows draped with roses and wisteria – everything, wisteria, an 'enormous' ilex, 'huge' fig, outgrown as old ladies' gardens are wont to be. The Lodge itself (actually an enormously pretty Suffolk house of timbering and deep bargeboards) was half a mile up a lane out of the village, with airy views over an agricultural landscape of mute unchangingness. Miss Ewebank's orchards were down the lane, sloping towards the single street of clapboard or brick houses alongside a stream, a tributary of the Blyth, which flowed for about nine miles through Halesworth to Blythburgh and the sea at Walberswick.

They told their friends to turn by the church, St Andrew's,

with its distinctive round flint tower, into a lane that ran with mud in winter, rivulets in spring, and then flowered into a thicket of Queen Anne's lace. The fields still exude fecundity, richness, earthiness, shoulders of browns and greens that lean and roll into thick coppices of trees; in 1916 it was a countryside still fit for Fielding or a Restoration country comedy (indeed, if poor Rupert had been alive to see it, he would have made a sprightly farce of life at Wissett). For it was pure comedy: the orchards were badly in need of pruning and the blackcurrants were diseased. Bunny Garnett dug into his store of memories of Constance at work in her garden, as he had watched and helped her from childhood; he wrote for advice, and he found and studied Miss Ewebank's 'Bee Journal' and collected bees for her deserted hives. They bought chicks, ducklings and goslings from Halesworth market, and when some turned out to be pedigree white Leghorns Duncan suggested they dye their tails to set them apart; so they mixed a bucket of blue dye, and 'dipped' the birds: 'The effect was lovely. With their bright scarlet combs, white bodies and blue tails they looked like French tricolour flags as they sped about their run on the green paddock.'[12] When Miss Ewebank's lawn sprouted early daffodils, Duncan suggested they should take them to Norwich market; they picked and bundled twelve dozen bunches, packed them in hampers tied to the handlebars of their bicycles, and set off at dawn to ride the twenty-five miles (at least) to Norwich. Only their sense of the picturesque overtook them: they enjoyed 'new beauties' at every turn – 'old cottages with early spring flowers in their gardens, cart-horses with jingling brasses drawing the sacks of seed barley to the field. And then empty pastures and pighties and the birds nesting and the first leaves breaking along the hawthorn hedges.'[13] When Norwich came into view they rested, so that Duncan could contemplate the painted landscape of Crome: consequently they got there far too late, the flower stalls and shops were well supplied. They got only a third of the expected price, blew more than that on their lunch, and retired to inspect the cathedral and picture galleries, which took so long that they had to return – very much out of pocket – by train. It must have been blind affection that made Bunny feel that they had done the right thing, and in admiration of Duncan's 'business instincts'.[14]

The Wissett arcadia – the enchantingly pretty house with its view across the Blyth valley, the extensive gardens and orchards in this exquisite countryside – would have made a delicious Bloomsbury legacy; but it was not to be. Vanessa Bell, by now in love with Duncan too, with her sons Julian and Quentin, aged eight and five years, arrived at Easter to spend the summer helping and housekeeping. They had many and curious visitors, including Lady Ottoline, making one of her most striking entries looking like a Bakst design for a Russian ballet, in an embroidered coat over blue silk tunic, with red leather boots, Astrakhan fez and her Portland family pearls.

In the village some of Miss Ewebank's ousted retainers had stirred up suspicions at the Lodge's ménage, and they would unnervingly advance up the lane on Sunday afternoons, to stand and stare over the gate. The tricoloured Leghorns were the last straw, an affront to bucolic dignities, and the hostilities increased. By now the law had also intervened, and both Bunny and Duncan had to submit to tribunals of stalwart Suffolk farmers to justify their objectors' consciences. Their appeals were allowed, but with the proviso that they could not be self-employed. Vanessa did not like Wissett and wanted to be back in Sussex, but the sharing of Asheham with Virginia had not worked well, and now clearly they needed separate houses; it was Leonard who first found Charleston Farmhouse to let, about four miles to the east of Asheham as the crow flies along the ridge to Firle Beacon. Vanessa visited the farmhouse, arranged the lease, and found a brisk young tenant farmer on the Firle estate who was in need of labourers. Her decorations for the Lodge's interior were hastily whitewashed over, to leave all in order before they left.

Vanessa and the Wissett entourage moved to Charleston Farmhouse in October 1916, and, according to her daughter Angelica – Duncan's child, who was born there on Christmas Day 1918 – from her first sight of it Vanessa knew 'it would be the perfect place in which to live'.[15] Constance Garnett, too, liked the idea of Charleston, within visiting range from Limpsfield, and she was soon there, making the best of things:

Yesterday I spent pruning the plums and pears on the walls of the garden – such jolly flint walls . . . We live in a very big kitchen . . . where the central table is always laid for a meal and never cleared – and there are books and writing materials on another table – and washing up at a sink goes on in another corner – and there is yet no . . . feeling of squalor but space for everything and everyone – 3 huge armchairs and a big dresser don't seem a bit in the way.

The pride glows in her words: 'David looks a perfect picture of a young farmer – in his velveteen coat and his gaiters and his mild sunburnt face.'[16]

Bunny Garnett, however, was not so happy, and wrote a wistful poem, 'What is the matter with this house', trying to rationalize to himself the strains of the *ménage à trois*, his own feelings cooled to Duncan's sexual and emotional demands, Vanessa's love for Duncan making her jealous of the 'Buck Bunny' as she called him,[17] and his own love affairs pursued well away from Charleston. For the rest of the war he flung himself into the farming, getting on well with Mr Hecks their employer and being allowed to drive the new tractor; in his memoir, *Flowers of the Forest* (1955), he left a detailed portrait of the sheer hard work and not entirely foul humour of First World War agriculture.

Virginia had warned that the farmhouse had cold water only and awful wallpapers: it had not one jot of architectural pretension or style of any kind – it was square, grey-rendered, with good-sized plain rooms right and left of the front door, and above, and the big farm kitchen that Constance enjoyed at the back, with an endless ramble of outhouses and sheds. The passages were narrow, the stairs mean, and upstairs it was a warren of boxy rooms and attics. Because of the wartime situation they had no means to do anything to rearrange the rooms, renew rotting floors and battered cupboards and doors, install water and heating systems and electric lighting, and by the time Vanessa had secured a longer lease, after the war was over, they seemed to have got used to the house as it was, and gave many of those essentials (to us) rather low priorities. Early Charleston, in the gloom of those war years, isolated down its half-mile lane from the road, a three-mile walk from Berwick station, the house seemingly set at the point where the north-east wind recoiled from the shock of meeting Firle Beacon, in the mud and mizzle was not a cheerful proposition: visitors likened it to approaching Wuthering Heights.

But when Vanessa and Duncan Grant returned in the sunlight of 1920s summers it became quite a different place. The house nestled among blossoms, neatly gated from the farm road, the garden protected from the cows coming in for milking: Angelica Bell remembered her playground amid the picturesque farming of horse-wagons, stooks of corn, hayricks, hand-milking and farmworkers 'with their pale blue Sussex eyes and solid leather boots' and the shepherd and his sheepdogs.[18] Safe inside the gate, the front of the house, bathed in morning sunlight, looked out over a neatly mown lawn which sloped to a willow-fringed pond, just big enough for a rowing boat. Beyond the pond, the orchard of apples, quince, bullace plum, walnut and pear trees was where lessons were taken outdoors for Angelica and her brothers, and Quentin Bell always remembered the spot favoured by the only begetter of Keynesian economics for his afternoon nap with a newspaper: Keynes loved staying at Charleston, weeding the gravel paths with a broken dinner knife for relaxation, and he was there often until 1925, when he married the ballerina Lydia Lopokova and bought Tilton Manor across the fields. The flint-walled garden that Constance Garnett enjoyed made a square on the north side of the farmhouse; this too flowered in the twenties, as gardening became Vanessa's third means of self-expression in addition to her painting and her care of her children. Her flowers filled the house, both painted and in bowls and vases; the garden's story is in dozens of her paintings and in a thousand photographs of smiling visitors and children. It too has little pretension to design: direct paths from the house divide it into big rectangular flower-beds and an oblong lawn, for about two-thirds of the area. The path vistas are closed with ornaments in niches in a box hedge, which divides off a vegetable plot and what (but not until the late 1940s) became a family effort at a mosaic piazza, largely of broken china of their own. Vanessa does not seem to have fussed over colour schemes or contrasting textures or other design notions in her gardening (she could always adjust the colours in her paintings anyway), but she grew and tended, as an enduring pleasure until the end of her days, old-fashioned flowers – red hot pokers, pinks, delphiniums, peonies, lavenders, a santolina hedge, daisies of all kinds, phlox, stocks, alchemilla, columbines, golden-rod, Michaelmas daisies, chrysanthemums and masses of roses.

Just as the garden flowered, so too did the house: gradually over the years doors, overmantels, chests and boxes, some of the walls and window frames acquired their painted decorations by Vanessa or Duncan Grant – their painting together, from each other's

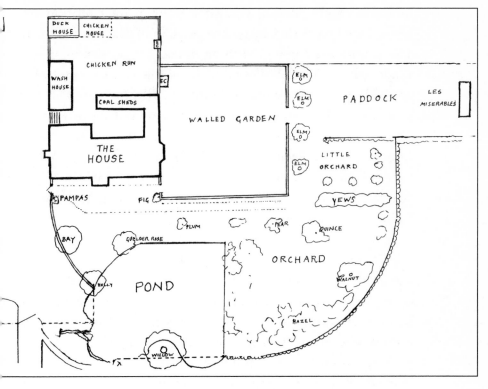

A plan of Charleston Farmhouse gardens drawn by Quentin Bell from his memories of it in the 1920s.

inspiration and criticism, being the heart of their relationship, which lasted more than forty-five years, until death parted them. The comings and goings, drifting in and out of friendships and relationships, the celebrities who visited, the children who grew up and had artistic talents and children of their own, were all part of a story told in the paintings, furniture and decorations of Charleston Farmhouse: some of the most beautiful objects are the embroidered cushions and stools worked by Duncan's mother, Ethel Grant, who came to stay with her portmanteau full of beautiful and expensive wools and silks. The painted house became a house of healing too.

The Woolf marriage was managed by Leonard as a convivial habitat for Virginia's butterfly persona, but she still had 'breakdowns' and her complete immersion of her total self into the business of writing left her fluttering with nervous exhaustion. Musical houses in Bloomsbury had devolved them to 38 Brunswick Square, with – at various moments – Morgan Forster, John Maynard Keynes, Duncan Grant and Virginia's brother Adrian, who married Karin Costelloe, in 1913. In that autumn the Woolfs moved out to Richmond, to a house of their own at 17 The Green, named for William Hogarth. Between the congenialities of Richmond and Asheham Virginia achieved the publication of her first novel, *The Voyage Out*, in 1915: her doctors probably recommended that she give up writing, but as that was akin to giving up eating, some kind of repetitive manual task, more physically demanding than knitting or embroidery, was suggested. One day in March 1917 (Leonard noted the date as the 23rd) they happened to be walking along Farringdon Street and both their attentions were caught by a display of printing machinery and materials – they stared 'like two hungry children gazing at buns and cakes in a baker's shop window'.[19] Inside the shop 'a very sympathetic man in a brown overall' did his sales pitch well, and they became the proud owners of a hand-press, some Old Face type and all the necessary extras, which was delivered and set up in the dining-room at Hogarth House; and instruction book in one hand, they taught themselves to print. Thus the Hogarth Press was born, for a layout of about twenty pounds: it was a brilliant investment, not only for the publishing house itself, but because it removed the major worry of any writer's life, that of finding and dealing with a publisher, and allowed Virginia to see all her friends, relatives and acquaintances from a new perspective, as that of their possible? or would be? or might be? publisher. This role amused her; it dictated much of her voluminous correspondence of the twenties and was the carrot and stick of many of her relationships, including that with Vita Sackville-West. The Press revealed Virginia as an astute and talented publisher – and though some may have sneeringly remarked that it was their child, their substitute for a family, one might add that it was all the more brilliant and useful for that! In May 1919 came two very happy Hogarth Press débuts, that of T. S. Eliot's first published *Poems*, and Virginia's *Kew Gardens*, both printed and bound by the Woolfs, the latter with Vanessa's illustrations;★ of these two, and Katharine Mansfield's *Prelude*, they sent out review copies, and after a week at Asheham they returned at the beginning of June to find the hall carpeted with orders from booksellers. Their 'buns and cakes in a baker's shop window' had taken wing and taken over.

Living on Richmond Green put Virginia back into a similar geography to her childhood Kensington, only now she took her

★ A delightful facsimile edition of Virginia Woolf, *Kew Gardens*, decorated by Vanessa Bell, from the Hogarth Press edition of 1927, was published in 1999 by Chatto & Windus who now own the Hogarth Press imprint. A page from this edition is included as illustration 17.

daily walks around the Royal Botanic Gardens at Kew. She had to walk barely half a mile along the Kew Road to the Lion Gate entrance, at the south end of the Gardens near the Pagoda, to enjoy hours of musings along green paths. Her 'essayette' *Kew Gardens* was both a tribute to the individual character of Kew and a project for the Hogarth Press, with her words and Vanessa's woodblock illustrations woven together on each page. She wrote of July (and presumably July of 1918) and the token cheerfulness of a few beds of flowers kept going through wartime difficulties, eye-catchers on the lawn near the main Kew Green gate: her flowers, 'a hundred stalks spreading into heart-shaped or tongue-shaped leaves half way up and unfurling at the tip red or blue or yellow petals marked with spots of colour raised upon the surface', are exotic and fanciful (though Vanessa's illustrations hint at gloxinias and *Salvia patens*, both favourites of the period). Virginia is teasing; she concentrates on the 'straight bar, rough with gold dust and slightly clubbed at the end', the voluminous petals and the passage of silvery droplets from rain shower or watering can. She lifts the layers of life, to the blue and white butterflies, and to the faces of the people who are attracted by the flowers – the family man musing on how he had long ago proposed to another woman by the lake, 'how clearly I see the dragon-fly and her shoe with the square silver buckle'; widows in black, men philosophizing, women gabbling, the young couple, his hand over hers on the parasol handle which they pressed into the soil before going off to find their tea. Lower down is the alternative world of the snail and the question as to whether it will be caught by a foraging thrush. *Kew Gardens* is a portrait miniature of a London landmark on a hot afternoon, each sensation placed with a pointillist accuracy in time and place – 'Aren't they one's past, all that remains of it, those men and women, those ghosts lying under the trees . . .' and the lethargy that the heat brings. Virginia was clearly happy here, sitting in the shade, contemplating her shoe-buckle, and listening to the wordless voices, the shrills of children, the hum of an aeroplane and the droning and clanking of the motor omnibuses along the Kew Road.

Happiness at the Hogarth Press unfortunately coincided with the end of their lease on Asheham House, and despite Virginia's pleas for renewal they were told they had to leave. The excuse was that it was wanted for the farm bailiff, Frank Gunn, but it seems more likely that the chalk-quarrying agenda was already under way, and clever intellectual tenants like the Woolfs were seen as potential trouble-makers.*

Virginia, desperate at losing her hold on Sussex, and perhaps thinking of all the praises heaped upon Gilbert Cannan's mill at Cholesbury by Carrington, Lytton Strachey and Ottoline Morrell, made an impulsive purchase of the Round House in Pipe Passage, the old sentry walk within Lewes's defensive walls. The original windmill was built in 1800, proved unprofitable and had been converted into a house for 100 years; it was not everyone's desirable residence, but she made an offer of £300 on the spot, and was accepted.[21] Two weeks later, taking Leonard to see it, they were stopped at the sight of a poster advertising the auction of several old properties belonging to the Verrall family, descendants of the eighteenth-century landlord of the White Hart in Lewes (something of a local legend and a friend of Tom Paine), which included 'Monks House, an old fashioned residence and three quarters of an acre of garden, all with possession'.[22] The auction was to be at 3.30 in the afternoon, surely hot and sticky, of 1 July, a Tuesday, at the White Hart Hotel, an event, Virginia remembered, as 'close packed with sensation' as any in her life.[23] Rodmell was, of course, in their westwards view, directly across

---

* Asheham was sold to a cement company five years later, in 1924, and a photograph shows it as the quarry manager's house.[20]

the river and the watery meadows from Asheham: so it was theirs already in a way – a house with 'little ceremony or precision . . . an unpretending house, long and low, a house of many doors; on one side fronting the street of Rodmell, and wood boarded on that side, though the street of Rodmell is at our end little more than a cart track running out on to the flat of the water meadows'. Inside the rooms were small; she discounted 'the value of that old chimney piece and the niches for holy water. Monks are nothing out of the way' . . . the kitchen bad, an oil stove and no grate, no hot water nor bath and 'as for the EC I was never shown it' . . . all these came under the agent's umbrella 'old fashioned'. But the garden, oh, the garden was quite a different matter: she knew at once that Leonard would become 'a fanatical lover of that garden'.

These prudent objections were forced to yield place to a profound pleasure at the size and shape and fertility and wildness of the garden. There seemed an infinity of fruit bearing trees; the plums crowded so as to weigh the tip of the branch down; unexpected flowers sprouted among cabbages. There were well kept rows of peas, artichokes, potatoes; raspberry bushes had pale little pyramids of fruit; and I could fancy a very pleasant walk in the orchard . . .[24]

They paid £700 for Monk's House at auction, and sold the Round House at a £20 profit two weeks later.[25] On 1 September 1919, Frank Gunn the bailiff sent two wagons to Asheham and all their furniture and books were carted two miles, down the lane to Southease Halt, across the river, and up the road to Rodmell, and the rest of their lives.

It may be another semantic fantasy (but then what are writers made of but words?) that just as Virginia collected both St Ives in Cornwall and St Ives in Huntingdonshire, so she recognized a benign presence in the Sussex Ouse, from a faint but happy memory. Her August weeks of 1906, when she was twenty-four, had been spent at the early sixteenth-century hall house of Blo' Norton, on the borders of Norfolk and Suffolk, between Garboldisham and Diss: some of her most delightful journal entries record her experiences as, on foot and on bicycle, she explored this flat land, where

. . . the landmarks resolve themselves into churches and windmills. The river, the Little Ouse deserves its diminutive; you may leap it – fall in as I did this afternoon – but all the same it is not a hazard jump. You are sure of the mud at any rate. And there radiate various minor tributaries, ditches I should call them, did not I know of their relationship with the river, and these are sometimes fenced with barbed wire. Altogether, though a walk . . . has a singular charm, it is not to be undertaken as a way of getting to places. Windmills have a way of staying absolutely still, or receding, to one who approaches them thus.

However, after leaping and circumnavigating, and brushing through reeds, and scrambling beneath barbed wire, it is pleasant to lie on the turf and try steering by windmills and towers . . . today I found the twin sources of the Waveney and the Little Ouse.[26]

This lush land, in that Edwardian summer, seemed shut off from the real world:

We seem to be in the middle of what in geography is called an 'undulating plain' well cultivated, but, apparently, almost deserted. The corn brims the fields; but no one is there to cut it; the churches hold up broad gray fingers all over the landscape, but no one, save perhaps the dead at their feet, attend to their commands; the windmills sail round and round, but no one trims their sails; it is very characteristic that the only sign of life in the land should be that produced by the wind of Heaven. How sleepy and ancient a people must be, who rely on the free gifts of Heaven still.[27]

She found, and loved, Blo' Norton locked in the peace of the ages: the apricot-washed and timbered house, twin-gabled, wearing its roof like a milkmaid's cap, stood much as it had been built 400 years before: 'so modest, and sound, and solid all through; as tho' the centuries only confirmed its original virtues. As you were made honestly, they seemed to say, so all time to come shall but prove and establish your virtue.' Inside, the flagged floors, the screens passage intact, there was an immediate glimpse of the garden, a brick-paved knot-garden held within the arms of the house, bathed in afternoon sunshine, with a lawn and apple trees falling away to the moat, the meadows and the Little Ouse that marked the Suffolk border. 'Such domestic beauty' – combined with her memories of Netherhampton – inspired her taste for Elizabethan England, when 'beauty and splendour were then not for the surface alone, but they sank down and down, till all layers of the state were well steeped in them. A self respecting decorous place England must have been then!'[28]

The path to *Orlando* thus led by way of Netherhampton and Blo' Norton, to Rupert Brooke calling Elizabethan cadences across the river, via Virginia's fascination with Lady Ottoline Morrell, to her fellow-feeling for Charlotte Brontë, for her mastery of prose 'both variable and splendid' – for rendering colours and textures in words:

Yet it was merely a very pretty drawing room, and within it a boudoir, both spread with white carpets, on which seemed laid brilliant garlands of flowers; both ceiled with snowy moulding of white grapes and vine leaves, beneath which glowed in rich contrast crimson couches and ottomans; while the ornaments on the pale Parian mantelpiece were of sparkling Bohemia glass, ruby red; and between the windows large mirrors repeated the general blending of snow and fire.[29]

A Tudor revival in *Jane Eyre* maybe, but the richness, the 'blending of snow and fire', became her literary goal. These traditional riches, the splendours that had seeped down to all layers of society, were perhaps what she had in mind when writing to Lady Ottoline that there were some virtues in aristocracies. They were perhaps the nub of the attractions of Lady Ottoline herself – who carefully and deliberately set herself off as a rare object, at one of her dazzling pre-war evenings in Bedford Square, as Virginia remembered in 1922:

. . . that drawing room full of people, the pale yellow and pinks of the brocades, the Italian chairs, the Persian rugs, the embroideries, the tassels, the scent, the pomegranates, the pugs, the pot pourri and Ottoline bearing down upon one from afar in her white shawl with great scarlet flowers on it . . .[30]

It was Ottoline, mistress of 'lustre and illusion', who made Bloomsbury feel they glittered like Hampton Court in days of yore: and like other national treasures, her style was spirited to the countryside for safety, in 1915, when the Morrells moved into Garsington Manor in Oxfordshire. Garsington, a little younger and a little larger than Blo' Norton, and built of Cotswold stone, was the manor of 'a richly traditional community of the kind which welcomes benevolent patronage and which believed that the aristocracy had as good a right to be eccentric as any of themselves'.[31] In Garsington the Morrells were squire and lady, building a village hall for dances, Philip reading the lesson in church on Sundays, Ottoline providing jellies, cakes and a

Christmas tree and visiting each cottage with presents for the family, and delighting the whole school with her visits and prize-giving, exuding a gorgeous scent and wearing bright red, high-heeled shoes.

If Lady Ottoline had not existed, surely Bloomsbury would have had to invent her, for, purple empress butterfly that she was, she was the cohesive force that brought together unlikely meetings such as Carrington and Rupert Brooke, Bertrand Russell and Mark Gertler, at her pre-war parties in the most grand of Blooms-bury houses, 44 Bedford Square. She was tall and well-built, a conscious largeness she dramatized in her dressing: she was effus-ively welcoming and embarrassingly intimate with those artists and writers who took her fancy, but she bestowed an acceptance not to be had elsewhere. She was ten years older than Virginia, born in 1872 – as her biographer Miranda Seymour calls her, almost a cuckoo in the nest of a philistine aristocracy at Welbeck Abbey, in the hunting and coal-rich shire of Nottingham; at Welbeck, where fifty footmen were chosen for their looks, the young Ottoline had given them lectures in religion. Her father had died when she was five; her mother, it was said, walked out of Welbeck in disgust at Ottoline's elder stepbrother's marriage to Winifred Dallas-Yorke – her stepbrother became the 6th Duke of Portland, in a convoluted Anglo-Dutch Bentinck family suc-cession, from a page who had come over with William of Orange. Her growing up, in Surrey and Italy, was marred by illness and being of a faintly discarded company of women; she was captivated by ancient Italy and the villa gardens of friends and aunts, and in the autumn of 1899, when she was twenty-seven, had enrolled at Somerville College at Oxford to study Roman history and political economy. Philip Morrell, walking home from his father's solici-tors' office, had seen her first on her bicycle – after a courtship and Ottoline's mental collapse, not unlike Virginia's, they were married in 1902. Both had been secret liberals in Tory families; their marriage and the birth of their daughter, Julian, held them irrevocably together, but Ottoline's crushes on a series of high-profile lovers, the artists Augustus John and Henry Lamb, and that fusion of intellect and aristocracy that was Bertrand Russell, were the nectar of Bloomsbury gossip. Those on the fringe whom she warmed into acceptance, like Carrington and Gertler and Gilbert Cannan, appreciated her generosity and sheer style: Lytton Strachey and Virginia could snipe at her, perhaps in that she – scion of a dying breed – should be so much like themselves.

Thus, as the sun still shone even on wartime afternoons, the parties had continued in the garden at Garsington, the familiar faces caught in Ottoline's snaps, taken with her advanced Planex camera using fine German film.[32] The visitors arrived into the sombre square entrance court flanked by massive dark yew hedges, 200 years old and as high as the eaves. The manor house was also squarish, of stone that might appear any colour from grey through to honey and sunlit cream, under a russet-tiled roof, with bands of twin-light mullion windows: it was often likened to a jewel casket. Inside, against the expected background of dark oak and well-kept stone floors, Persian rugs and paintings by Stanley Spencer, Duncan Grant and Henry Lamb, a collection of blue and white Nanking china and Ottoline's embroidery silks, a pianola with fifty piano-rolls for dancing and a black and gold Coromandel screen all sparkled in unconventional companionship. Most talked about were the Green Room, and the Red Room – with walls 'the colour of vermilion sealing-wax'. Miranda Seymour reconstructed some of the riches of this room (from the 1928 sale catalogue):

Rolled up behind a sofa ready for the evening's work is the magnificent flowered bedspread which Ottoline began embroidering in 1916, a brilliant jungle of silk leaves and blossoms which took ten years to complete. Samarkand rugs spatter the floor with yellow and crimson. There are a mass of occasional tables for ornaments, lacquered cigarette boxes, paperknives for cutting the pages of new books. A big Chinese jar in the corner is filled with an almost overpoweringly rich pot-pourri; card tables and backgammon boards are a reminder of Philip's passion for games. Two Chippendale-design easy chairs with high backs flank the fireplace; Ottoline liked to sit in one of them when she was alone in the evening, sewing or reading by the light of the oil lamps.[33]

Through this house that held all the sentient richness of Charlotte Brontë's prose there was the contrast of the garden, the wide lawn terraces, the spreading ilex tree.

The peacocks flying there to roost, their long tails hanging behind, and the grey statues against the dark yew hedges and the pond where white bodies plunged, swam, and feathery poplars and elms beyond.[34]

On the east side of the house was the flower garden, a score of box-edged boxes filled with spring and summer flowers, tulips and dahlias in jewel colours tumbling around drunken sentinels of Irish yew. This part of the garden was Ottoline's creation – it would be nice to think that she had found a fellow-gardener in Norah Lindsay, another romantic aristocrat given to dressing-up, in her garden a few miles to the south, beside the Thames at Sutton Courtenay. They both called upon the garden gods of ancient Greece and Rome, and the quirky mix of spires and flowers in the east garden at Garsington was closely related to the Lindsay long garden.*

* Lady Ottoline and Norah Lindsay were both aristocratic outcasts in a way, and their gardens had an air of romanticism in common, though no evidence of a friendship seems to survive. See Jane Brown, *Eminent Gardeners*,[35] for Norah Lindsay.

'Did you feel as I often did, this is too beautiful, it cannot last?' Ottoline mourned after they had been forced to sell Garsington in 1928.[36] Life there was immortalized by Aldous Huxley in *Crome Yellow*, but the colours and textures of Garsington also enriched Virginia's Woolf's prose – giving her those visual conjunctions that she found it difficult to imagine, that she culled from all her houses and landscapes. In this respect Garsington certainly opened her eyes, preparing her for the overwhelming impact of Knole.

Virginia Woolf first met Vita Sackville-West at a dinner party given by Vanessa's husband Clive Bell in December 1922. Bell had a mischievous intention to ensnare Virginia's emotions, which he felt were under-engaged, and he apparently followed their subsequent relationship with a prurient interest. That the creative outfall was to be far greater than the sum of its parts, and only polished Virginia's reputation more brightly, was a satisfactory revenge.

But Clive Bell had a point; his choice had lighted upon the one person in England, at least within his reach, who might embody the ingredients required for a passionate historical, fantastical involvement on Virginia's part. Vita was aristocratic, with a dash of Spanish gypsy blood, she was tall, dark and beautiful – in a rich velvets and rubies kind of way – she was both literary and apparently leisured, her husband was a diplomat and abroad a great deal working at the peace conferences at Versailles and Lausanne, and the gossips said that theirs was an open marriage and she had Sapphic tastes. She was thirty, she had been married to Harold Nicolson for almost ten years and they had two small sons; she divided her time between a house in Ebury Street, Belgravia, and Long Barn, a cottage-cum-barn conversion with seven bedrooms and four bathrooms at Sevenoaks Weald, just outside the Knole park wall, where she was making a garden. Most of this background was public knowledge, for Vita was also famous, constantly in the society gossip columns and sometimes in the headlines since she was a sixteen-year-old they called 'Kidlet', the only child of the glamorous and controversial Lord and Lady Sackville, who had fought a High Court action to deprive them of Knole, the largest private house in England, and won.[37]

Vita had been born at Knole, which Queen Elizabeth I had given to her ancestor Sir Thomas Sackville: she had been brought up there, hardly knowing anywhere else, and she loved it with a fierce possessiveness, for it held her past, her ancestors, and her sense of herself, and had proved a better companion to her childhood than either of her parents. The Sackvilles had defeated the challenge to their inheritance, but the judge had decreed an entail to the male line, which meant that it would never be Vita's: she was scarred with this adolescent loss, which gave her her creative energy. She was a published poet and successful novelist, and in that year of 1922 both her family history, *Knole and the Sackvilles*, and a novel, *The Heir*, had been published and acclaimed. Virginia noted 'the lovely aristocratic Sackville West' at that dinner party, and after another meeting and exchange of books, she confided to her journal – 'Snob as I am, I trace her passions 500 years back, and they become romantic to me, like old yellow wine.'[38]

The advance to *Orlando* was slow: they developed a literary friendship, spiced with rivalry, and Virginia won Vita as a Hogarth Press author. Vita, admiring Virginia's mind and judgement, was flattered, for despite her distinguished looks and beautiful clothes and jewels, she was shy of society, and by no means wholly confident about her writing. She found that Virginia's 'sort of spiritual beauty' imposed itself on her, calming her busy and self-confessedly muddled life, and that she was 'both detached and human' – so that neither need fear a truly damaging (to their husbands) involvement with each other. Virginia was enchanted by the textures of Vita's style – how she glided down Rodmell's street 'in her large new blue Austin car, which she manages consummately. She was dressed in ringed yellow jersey, and large hat, and had a dressing case all full of silver and night gowns wrapped in tissue.'[39] Admiration prospered at Vita's splendour – 'she shines in the grocer's shop in Sevenoaks with a candle lit radiance, stalking on legs like beech trees, pink glowing, grape clustered, pearl hung'.[40] Here was *Orlando* gestating. But they both had their own lives; Vita (like Rupert Brooke) was capable of keeping several relationships running like parallel lines, never meeting; she went on two long and emotionally captivating trips to Persia to see Harold, who was in Teheran, in 1926 and 1927[41] and the Nicolsons were thought generally inseparable from Lord Gerald Wellesley and his wife, the poetess Dorothy Wellesley. Virginia's life was at home, with words, memories, and her writing. Hogarth Press published Vita's *Passenger to Teheran* – and reading the proofs Virginia noted: 'Yes – I think its awfully good. I kept saying "How I should like to know this woman" and then thinking "But I do", and then "No, I don't" – not altogether the woman who writes this.'[42]

Virginia's fascination was tinged with submission (which would be harmless with a woman), which gave Vita confidence, and brought out – well, brought out the *Orlando* in her: the combination of Vita, striding masterfully down the corridors of Knole and the splendours of Knole itself – the riches of their personal relationship – dogs, poetry, silks and pearls, gardens, were subsumed into tapestries and portraits, the battlements in the moonlight, and tumbles in gilded, canopied and curtained four-posters by firelight tumbled *them* into the past. Vita was transformed in showing off Knole, she had done it since she was a child; for her the centuries 'meant Thomas, Richard or Edward Sackville, Holbein, Van Dyck or Reynolds, farthingale chairs or love seats', she had played with the jewels that Gainsborough painted, 'paraded down the Brown Gallery saluting Admiral Blake, Thomas More and the dashing Philip Sidney, sitting in one of the fabled Whitehall Palace chairs with dolphins at her feet and held court until the shadows disappeared.'*

At Knole, *Orlando* was born before Virginia's eyes.

On 9 October 1927 Virginia told Vita in a letter: 'Yesterday morning I was in despair . . . I couldn't screw a word from me and at last dropped my head in my hands; dipped my pen in the ink, and wrote these words, as if automatically, on a clean sheet: Orlando A Biography.'[44] After that the words came flooding: 'But listen; suppose Orlando turns out to be Vita; and its all about you and the lusts of your flesh and the lure of your mind (heart you have none.) . . .'[45] Would Vita mind? It probably would have made no difference if she had, but she was both 'thrilled and terrified'. On 5 December, almost five years after their first meeting, Virginia was lying by the fire and working up the final chapter.

Vita knew just how capable Virginia was of a liberating conjuring trick: on reading *Mrs Dalloway* two years before, she had written that it was unnecessary for her ever to go to London again (something Vita increasingly hated as she grew older), for the 'whole of London in June is in your first score of pages. (Couldn't you do a winter London now?)'[46] When the book was finally ready, in October 1928, complete with London in the Great Frost of 1608, it had no indication as to who the subject of the 'biography' was, but everyone soon worked it out: Knole was not easily disguised. *Orlando* was a triumph, for Virginia, for the Hogarth Press, in both critical and financial terms; for its subject it was something more – Vita's father had died at the end of

---

* See the first chapter of Jane Brown, *Vita's Other World*,[43] for Vita's immersion in Knole.

January 1928, and she collapsed at the inevitable double blow, the loss of her beloved father and of Knole, into which her younger cousin Edward Sackville-West walked as its inheritor. Vita's pride, and very mixed feelings over her cousin, meant she felt the house closed to her, and her depression was exaggerated by bitter arguments with her mother, the estranged and temperamental Lady Sackville, over the division of spoils. For Vita 1928 was a miasma of painful partings, regrets and sorrows, dashes to Berlin where Harold was and tensions over his future career: to be so far apart was hardest of all for her that year, and in May she wrote to him from Long Barn:

I allowed myself a torture treat tonight. I went up to Knole after dark and wandered about in the garden. I have a master-key so I could get in without being seen. It was a very queer and poignant experience . . . I had the sensation of having the place so completely to myself that I might have been the only person alive in the world, and not the world of today, mark you, but the world of at least 300 years ago. I might have been the ghost of Lady Anne Clifford. I have long resisted the temptation to get out the motor and drive up there, but tonight it was so strong that I couldn't and wouldn't resist it any longer. Darling Hadji, I may be looney but there is some sort of umbilical cord that ties me to Knole – oh! ghosts, Dada, Knole, [her mother] – but not us, my love, not us, not us . . .[47]

So *Orlando* came as – in Harold's words – a 'lovely and glittering and profound' book, the small and precious embodiment of a ghost that had to be relinquished. It was a wonderful gift, one of the greatest that can be given, and Vita wrote in tears . . . 'Virginia, my dearest, I can only thank you for pouring out such riches.'[48] For Virginia, it was as if all her places, her love of old London, her fascination with old houses, had crystallized into a gift to the future. It gave Vita the rest of her life: the following year Harold Nicolson gave up diplomacy and travelling the world and came home to earn his living by writing; within a short time they had found the ruined Sissinghurst Castle, which they redeemed into one of the most beautiful, and certainly the most loved, gardens in the world.

5

Carrington

The A343 from Andover to Newbury is still an old-fashioned road, climbing gently northwards and up from the Anton river valley, through Enham and the primroses and bluebells in Doles woods, until with an ill-mannered steepness it drops down into Hurstbourne Tarrant. Hurstbourne Hill has a nasty reputation, lingering from the days of skidding, shying horses well into a century of unreliable internal combustion engines and overheating brakes, its steepness being only the first surprise. At the bottom, just when the driver's eye is diverted to the George and Dragon as a tempting-look hostelry, the road – tightly hemmed with buildings – turns sharp left, and then, without drawing breath, sharp right. Easily missed in the thrill of the chicane is the turning to Ibthorpe: while the main road continues its downland way north-eastwards to Highclere and Newbury, the byroad to Ibthorpe follows the Bourne Rivulet north-westwards to Upton, then takes the dry chalk-hill track to Vernham, Buttermere and Ham.

Ibthorpe is a hamlet with charms easily missed by motor-borne eyes, with most of its cottages and houses back from the valley road in an ancient 'square road' system: now the rivulet is a winterbourne, dry in summer, but 100 years ago it was a good trout stream.[1] A. B. Connor's *Highways and Byways in Hampshire*, published in 1908, was an advertisement for Ibthorpe's picturesque cottages: 'some in garden plots, and when the dahlias bend and sway with the weight of their gay blossoms between the dark clipped yews, and the scent from fragrant flower beds is borne on the fresh breeze that flirts the long trails of crimsoning creepers, one is fain to declare that here at last must be the most favoured corner' until one turns another corner and finds more.[2] Ibthorpe remains much like this.

In 1913 a respectable couple from Bedford, Samuel and Charlotte Carrington, rented Ibthorpe House from the local landlord, William John Bound: there is a rarely seen and happy photograph of the Carringtons' younger daughter, who was twenty in 1913, perched high on the ladder used for cutting the gigantic yew hedges that are also a feature of several of the Ibthorpe gardens. Perched up there she could gaze down on the rivulet bubbling through its green watercressy bed, with soft water-meadows, a grazing pony or two, and the fields rising in a smoothly, well-ordered chalk-country way to the near horizon. The perspective is curiously foreshortened – it seems possible almost to touch the skyline, a sweeping rim as of a large dish placed against the western sky, and decorated with trees. Carrington painted this view, in snow, in greens and duns and browns, her homage to Ibthorpe, which she loved, and which released her to the greatest happiness of her short life.

When she was twenty-two, Carrington – who had cut off her hair and her Christian name (Dora) as an art student – fell in love with Lytton Strachey, an intellectual, thirteen years her senior, whose friends and relatives thought he was vastly superior socially as well. Carrington knew at once that she wanted to spend the rest of her life with Lytton, and that they would live in this countryside, among the 'most marvellous downs in the WHOLE WORLD'.[3] How she achieved this, and other things as well, is her story: though for her it may have begun on the top of that ladder at Ibthorpe, for us the beginnings are earlier, and must defer to the elder (if not senior) partner.

Giles Lytton Strachey seemed to have lived a parallel childhood nightmare to the Stephens. He had been born, on 1 March 1880, as number eleven of the thirteen children of Richard Strachey, aged sixty-three, and his wife, Jane Maria Grant, forty, at Stowey House, Clapham. Jane Strachey was a Grant of Rothiemurchus, and within a few years her youngest brother, Major Bartle Grant, and his wife Ethel would present her with a nephew, named Duncan.[4]

The Richard Stracheys moved from Clapham to 69 Lancaster Gate, Bayswater, when Giles Lytton was four; he disliked it from the outset, he was overwhelmed, it was 'size gone wrong, size pathological', he remembered, 'a house afflicted with elephantiasis', with big steps up to the porch (extremely big steps for four-year-old legs in voluminous skirts) to a narrow dark hall, with ochre walls and a floor of magenta and indigo tiles, the staircase spiralling 'into a thin infinitude' to a dome of pink glass.[5] It allowed seven layers of habitation but had no garden, nor even a court, a bad outlook and frosted or pink glass windows that were too large to open: little round vents gave all the fresh air there was, and there was one lavatory on the stairs between the first and second floors, inducing much passing on the stairs and noises-off that were all too audible in the drawing-room. That 'monumental' room, the family meeting-place, the 'extraordinary holy of holies', was to give Lytton nightmares of being imprisoned there well into his adulthood: with all the helplessness of childhood, his small, hot hands would struggle with the big door-knob, he would enter a moving, murmuring forest of drainpipe trews and crinolines, the faces far distant, the feet much nearer . . . all kinds of feet, well-polished shoes, boots with the dust of Empire still on them, spats, worn slippers that came from the age of Palmerston or Little Holland House.[6] The drawing-room seems always to have been crowded – 'thick with aunts and uncles, cousins and connections, with Stracheys, Grants, Rendels, Plowdens, Battens, Ridpaths, Rowes. One saw that it had indeed been built for them – it held them all so nicely, so naturally, with their interminable varieties of age and character and class' – their penetrating voices, love of argument and consequently the tremendous volume of noise: they were 'all very alike, all constantly coming and going', a shifting cavalcade that puzzled and awed visitors from 'outside', who must have wondered if they had strayed 'into an isolated colony of some undiscovered form of civilization'.[7]

No. 69 Lancaster Gate was to be Lytton's home until he was twenty-nine, with breaks for schools and Cambridge. Michael Holroyd's evocation of the house's claustrophobic curiosities, compounded by Strachey eccentricities, goes a long way to explain Lytton: when he was about five his uncle William Strachey died, bequeathing him a collection of unworn and exquisitely pretty underclothes, drawers and pants – Lytton was always dressed the same as his sisters, and soon discovered the joys of dressing to cause comment. His mother, Jane Strachey, having been born on a storm-tossed passage to India, believed in the benefits of sea air, so Lytton was sent to school at Parkstone in Dorset when he was nine, and then, with his sister Dorothy, to Gibraltar to stay with their uncle Charles Grant, a captain in the Black Watch. They moved, with the regiment, to Egypt, Lytton dressed in Highland kit, playing deck quoits with the men, happily the centre of attention! He loved the excitement of Egypt, but after that his schooling degenerated into a series of nightmare episodes and unhappy returns to 69 Lancaster Gate: the tall house with its pale pink-lighted gloom seemed to take the 'absurd' and 'ridiculous' little boy and draw him up, like a plant, etiolated and elongated, into the familiarly lugubrious-looking, absurdly impractical, and myopic young man.

Dora de Houghton Carrington's beginnings could not have been farther from Bloomsbury than if she had been born in the Grand Canyon or the Russian steppe: she was born in Hereford, in a dim villa called Ivy Lodge, on 29 March 1893. Her father, whom she adored, was a gentle person, and at sixty-one old enough to be her grandfather (like Lytton's) when she was born. Samuel Carrington had given nearly thirty years of his life to building railways in India, coming home to the chilly, mono-chrome comforts of provincial England and marriage in 1888 when he was fifty-five. His wife, Charlotte, was twenty years younger and she produced five children within ten years; Dora was fourth out of the five, between her brothers Teddy and Noel. Charlotte Carrington was – at least in her daughter's eyes – a prim, mean, nagging bundle of Victorian small-mindedness, whose horizon was fixed in the shrine of her own front room, whose 'true reward of righteousness' was to lead her family up the aisle for Easter Communion,[8] and who relentlessly pilloried the kindly Samuel, until he took refuge in a stroke and some subsequent paralysis when Dora was fifteen. By that time the family had progressed swiftly through villadom to Belle Vue and Belmont in Berkhamsted, and come to rest in Rothsay Gardens, Bedford, the most minor of country towns, with a memorable bridge spanning the Ouse and the presiding Nonconformist ghosts of John Howard and John Bunyan. In Bedford respectability was as oppressive as a thundercloud that never passed, and the town was so well endowed with churches and chapels that Sundays bore the aspect of a civic funeral. Bedford was, however, redeemed for Dora Carrington and so many other children down the years by its remarkable schools: at ten years old she became a pupil at Bedford High School for Girls in Bromham Road, of emancipated aspects

and 'undeniably a feminine job', says Pevsner⁹ of the delightful
buildings by Basil Champneys (commissioned on the strength of
his showing at Newnham College, Cambridge), which sheltered
an enlightened academic and moral attitude to intelligent girls. As
home life at Rothsay Gardens became steadily more irksome and
difficult, school – and the discovery that she was really good at
drawing and painting, which was much encouraged – gave Dora
the strength to rebel, though not in open warfare with her mother,
for she hated 'rows', but in deceit and intrigue to thwart her
strictures. To be fair to the awesome Charlotte, she had brought
up healthy and sturdily beautiful children – Dora at seventeen,
when she arrived at the Slade, was soon noticed by Paul Nash as
an 'amusing person . . . with such very blue eyes and such incredibly thick pigtails of red–gold hair'.¹⁰ In the pencil portraits of her
brothers she drew in response to Professor Tonks's instructions
that she perfect drawing from life (before painting from it), her
elder brother Teddy shares her strong features and rounded mouth,
and the schoolboy Noel Carrington's more delicate build has been
captured in fine, sombre gaze.¹¹

Lytton, of course, had gone to Cambridge; marked by his
curious home and miserable schooling, Trinity College and the
Apostles were his salvation. He found his role as a literary wit, a
sort of latter-day Horace Walpole, full of gossip and *bons mots*
which were well-founded entertainment value to many friends
and acquaintances. His natural habitat evolved as a quiet study,
with deep armchair by the fireside, a table to write on and plenty
of books – the man of letters, permanently full of promise, he was
a professional Strachey, celebrated for being, visiting, and writing
the most brilliantly quotable thank-you letters. Lytton could also
be immensely kind and loyal, he had a disarming ability to find
his fates ridiculous and was rarely at a loss for good stories and bad
gossip. It wasn't that he disliked women, so much as that he was

overwhelmed by them: when his father, Sir Richard Strachey, died in early 1908 his 'rock of impregnable masculinity' was finally submerged, leaving an 'eternal sea' of females raging round the bed-sitting-room that was Lytton's allotted patch in Lady Strachey's new home at 67 Belsize Park Gardens in intellectual Hampstead.[12] For almost the next ten years, until he settled with Carrington, there was to be 'an air of desperation' about his continuous peregrinations, in order *not* to be in Belsize Park. His movements were lightly motivated by work: he lingered at Cambridge, or announced his arrival in Fitzrovia or Gordon or Brunswick Squares (convenient for the Reading Room of the British Museum), he was loyal to Apostles gatherings, but most usually motivated to move – and he could apparently sometimes move very fast – in pursuit of his *culte* of the moment. Lytton's spontaneously combustible passions were the very substance of the Bloomsbury Group, for one could never tell where they would spark: Virginia and Lady Ottoline both had their moments of flame, but more usually with Lytton it was a beautiful – though invariably fading, or perhaps glimpsed too hastily in a bad light – young man: the mountaineer George Mallory, or Rupert Brooke, some unknown, his long-loved cousin Duncan Grant, or (and here he met his match) the painter Henry Lamb. The saga of Lytton's loves fills Holroyd's biography and they do not belong here – but Henry Lamb is more important than most: Lamb, impervious to Lytton's advances, portrayed that 'most photogenic and preposterous figure'[13] in his magnificent portrait against the backdrop of the Vale of Health outside Lamb's studio window: Lytton was the most determined hypochondriac. But Lamb also made Lytton walk, a rucksack piled on his thin shoulders; mufflered and booted they trudged together across Cumberland, and parts of Scotland, and the Wiltshire downs. Lamb was ferociously heterosexual, disdainful of the 'false aesthetics' of the

Bell–Fry school, another medic turned painter and, like Lytton, endlessly concerned with his own digestion. Lamb persuaded Lytton into the open air and wind and rain, and Lytton found that he rather liked the exhilaration. His Cambridge and London-centric view was opened up just in time for him to enjoy the frenetic ruralizing of the pre-war years. A modest syndicate was formed, including Lytton and his brother Oliver Strachey, John Maynard Keynes and other Cambridge friends, to rent a country house they could all use, and where Lytton could write.

While Lytton was learning to walk, Carrington's artistic talents had won her a place at the Slade School, more correctly the Felix Slade Faculty of Fine Arts of University College, London, which was in between Gower Street and Malet Place, just a few steps from Gordon Square.

The Slade had been a mixed college from its foundation in 1871, and women attended life classes (though segregated), but there is a sense that that was – as with the women's colleges at Cambridge – enough revolution for the first fifty years. The 'equality' of being there, using only surnames – she is Carrington from now on – and wearing one's hair fashionably cropped, was on the surface. Underneath nothing much had changed, and women were not really expected to learn to paint pictures, exhibit and sell them, because of course they did not need to, for they would soon be encased in the cocoon of married life. Art school, and the Slade especially, was very fashionable in Carrington's time – and so even more of a game; there seemed to be frequent charabanc outings, picnics, and parties and balls, with the much-reported enrolment of society belles, Diana Manners, Iris Tree and Violet Charteris, whose beaux lounged at the art school doorway, waiting to take them to lunch. In riposte Gerald Shove (who was merely Virginia Stephen's cousin) put on top hat and tails and escorted Carrington and her friends down Gower Street, to the house which he shared with John Maynard Keynes, for scrambled eggs.[14] Even the serious women students tended to be well-connected (Carrington's best friend, Brett, was the daughter of Lord Esher, royal confidante and courtier) and in their twenties – Brett was ten years older than Carrington; if not 'naturals' in London society, then the women were invariably the daughters of artists – 'in the business' so to speak. Carrington was unique, she had no anchorage or street wisdom, she was absurdly young to be on her own in London (though safely at Byng House in Gordon Square, the women's hostel), she was pretty, and puppy-like in her friendliness and enthusiasm, and little wonder, for entirely on her own merit she had escaped from musty Bedford into the world of her wildest dreams. Her fate was to be a girl of enormous talent – those pencil drawings of her brothers are as good as any of Henry Lamb's, one of her landscapes was for years labelled as by John Nash, and her portraits when painted with love, as of her father or Lytton Strachey, are the revelations of rich secrets – whose young life was to be hoisted as on to one of those glistening brass spirals on roundabouts that she and Mark Gertler loved to paint, ever rising and falling to another's demands, with no stillness for her own art.

It is a common curiosity of the British class system that the biggest pit to dig oneself out of, like Carrington's, is lower-middle-class respectability: the higher society both regards celebrity its due, and adores working-class heroes. So it was that the Bloomsbury intimates loved Mark Gertler at sight, a young man who so embodied the colourful deprivations of the streets of Spitalfields and 'Petticoat Lane' as to appear their very own charitable endeavour. Gertler was born in Gun Street, Spitalfields (on 9 December 1891, though he was unclear about the date), though his father, a struggling furrier, took his family back to Polish Austria, Przemyśl, to return when Mark was six, now a street urchin with a shock of black curls, speaking only Yiddish. Mark's infant memory had latched on to some vague glory, embodied in his own travelling clothes – 'my Hungarian coat of deep-orange coloured leather, decorated with gold and scarlet braid, vermilion tam-o-shanter and top boots to the knees', in which he did 'a sort of dance' that set everyone laughing and applauding.[15] He grew out of his precious coat as he grew into a dull London boyhood, warmed by his mother, Golda's, and his father, Louis Gertler's, love; they would have been happy for him to be a tailor, but his artistic talent took him away, and in some perplexity he arrived at the Slade. William Rothenstein sent him on his first trip outside London, to a farm near Andover in Hampshire in the spring of 1909, and the young painter discovered a beauty he had no idea existed. He expressed a completely naïve wonder at being allowed to paint 'in the meadows near little streams which are beautiful beyond words. I can actually see the fishes swimming in the water . . . everything is very beautiful and ideal-like.'[16]

Gertler enjoyed his friends at the Slade, Nevinson, the Nashes and 'Cookham' Spencer: art school was a melting-pot. As well as Professor Henry Tonks's chilly and forensic view of figure drawing (he had started out as a medic who drew his own cadavers), there was real encouragement to go out and find a countryside to, at first, fall in love with, then paint, the second only being truly satisfactory after the first. Stanley Spencer, whose black hair capped his head as the proverbial pudding-basin, arrived with Gertler in 1908: a village boy from the piano teacher and organist's big family in Cookham-on-Thames. His talent had brought him by way of Maidenhead Technical Institute, an equivalent route to Gertler, but they were opposites in that Spencer, as his nickname shows, was completely integrated, if not obsessed, with his river-country life: he had, as Christopher Neve has written, been born in it, 'he learned it back garden by back garden', slowly, through daily experience in the timelessness of childhood.[17] The young people at the Slade laughed at Cookham Spencer's obsession, but they understood it: the Nash brothers, Paul and John, were hardly less obsessive, but they were older and not to be laughed at – a pair in sleek suits, snazzy jackets and big hats who were so outrageously talented, alternately serious and capricious people, that they naturally led the others. Paul Nash (who left the Slade at the end of 1911 but continued to haunt it) was already speaking of the Kensington Gardens of his childhood, where he found his 'first authentic place' off the beaten pathways which was 'strangely beautiful and excitingly unsafe'; of his (and his brother's) passion for Wittenham Clumps, the rings of trees crowning the Sinodun Hills that brood over the Thames valley like doppelgängers between Wallingford and Abingdon: the sacred clumps, 'the Pyramids' of their art, were much discussed. Equally precious to the Nash brothers was their garden at Wood Lane House, Iver Heath, where visitors were greatly welcomed, and Gertler was positively bowled over: 'What a splendid way to live. What beautiful surroundings. How beautiful the country is. It will be my ultimate aim to live in the country,' he staccatoed to Carrington. April showers and approaching dusk brought about a black-blue sky; a rainbow

with a blaze of different colours from one field, made a complete and most accurate semi-circle and finished up with another blaze in another . . . In the garden there was a little tree full of brilliant white blossoms which stood out strong and light against the sky. The whole effect was divine. They have also in their garden a certain yellow flower with a little brown check pattern on it. The wood, before coming to the lake, was also very beautiful. Some of the trunks of the trees were bright green, whilst others were purple. The ground was orange-brown, with the fallen and faded leaves. Some of the trees had very unusual trunks.

One trunk looked like a bundle of many-coloured snakes. On others, where the rain had fallen, the colour was beautifully spotted, with green, purple and orange. Between the trees and branches the sky could be seen through in brilliant white-light spots and shapes.★[18]

That it was the Nash brothers' garden made it so special, and Carrington was duly smitten. The garden was really the realm of John, the younger brother, self-taught as a painter through Paul's encouragement, and with a passion for botany acquired at school (where he took it up to avoid playing cricket). John Nash had dual ambitions, to be an artist-plantsman, combining painting more domestic landscapes than the probing abstracts of Paul Nash, and doing botanical drawing and gardening. During 1912 Carrington's friendship with John Nash came perilously close to subjugation in her own estimation – perilously because the love of painted gardens and landscapes and of gardening which he inspired in her, seemed like love for him. John Nash was a persistent suitor, arrogantly unable to believe that neither did she want to marry him, nor anyone, but she did hope that their shared abilities were enough to keep them close. In the summer of 1913 she made a pointed play of her views on life and art: Roger Fry and Duncan Grant had been advocating a revival of mural painting as a community art, leading the Slade students on a spree to cover the walls of stations, cafés and schools with paintings – footballers, swimmers, paddlers in the Serpentine and animals at the zoo were the appropriate images for the students' dining-hall at London's Borough Polytechnic. For this summer of 1913 Carrington's

★ Ronald Blythe's *First Friends*, from which this is quoted, is a detailed record of Carrington's friendship with the Nashes, written from the cache of letters which Ronald Blythe found in a tin trunk in a brick bread oven at Bottengoms, John and Christine Nash's home in Suffolk, after their deaths.

friend and fellow student Constance 'Cooie' Lane, who lived with her mother at Nettleden in Hertfordshire, on the edge of the Ashridge estate, had persuaded the estate to let her paint murals on the walls of the servants' hall. The great gothic house, home of the 3rd Earl Brownlow and his artistic wife, Countess Adelaide, was a sympathetic setting, where the artist–craftsman tradition had been treasured for centuries. John Ruskin, George Frederic Watts and Oscar Wilde had all been entertained, and listened to: Carrington was, once again, bowled over by an unfamiliar beauty. The most amazing 'early' Italian garden which she thought she saw was in fact Repton's fading rosary in its hedged circle, with great circular layouts and armorial beds of flowers (all now restored), designed by Earl Brownlow's mother, Lady Marian Alford, an artist–gardener of considerable skills. However, these are but pedantic icicles; the love of Renaissance belief in art was in the air of Ashridge. The two students were given the large bare wall, which entailed drawing cartoons six feet by five feet, with a team of estate workers who put up the scaffold and taught them plastering. For Carrington it was heaven: they outlined the life around them, the landscape and the big elms, Lane doing a sheep-shearing, Carrington doing haymaking and gardening scenes. She felt like Giotto, she loved controlling her army of workmen, who entered into the spirit of the thing: best of all, at the end of the day they trudged wearily home across the fields. Very best of all was when Lane and her mother went away, and Carrington had the murals and the cottage to herself. Each of the mural panels 'was unified with a border of burnt gold and cerulean blue', and in the opinion of Jane Hill,

Carrington's use of colours and forms to create vistas was expert. The meticulously painted companionable planting of larkspur, cabbages, sunflowers and onions in serried ranks creates a foreground. The dusty pink of the woman's simple dress takes us one step back without separating us from the flowering sedum and the silk back of the bewhiskered man's waistcoat, which have the same colour. The larkspur's blue appears again in the withering elms and highlights the cabbage leaves. Golden corn lights up the middle and far distance, glows again in the sunflowers, the young boy's breeches and the wooden handles of the hoes.[19]

Both the technique (Carrington was pleased to find them intact when she took Ralph Partridge to see them in 1925)* and the colours were her own triumph; her inspiration may have been Sir George Clausen's *The Mowers* (1891) and in turn would find an echo in John Nash's *The Allotment* (1914).

Nash married another Slade student, Christine Kuhlenthal, though his first love for Carrington stayed in his heart.[20] For the nubile Carrington another elephant trap awaited: Slade students were in fashion, and the art- and artist-loving patron Edward Marsh had already had a café encounter with Gertler – 'a beautiful little Jew, like a Lippo Lippi cherub'.[21] Gertler had progressed from an elevated euphoria, looking down on Spitalfields men feeling that they had it all wrong 'and that I am really in a way a superman, for in order to be happy they seek unworthy and impossible things whilst I can go out and thrill with happiness over a tree, a blade of grass, a cloud, a child, an onion, any part of nature's innocent work', to an almost fawning appreciation: 'Just one other thing that makes me so happy, that is my nice friends amongst the upper class. They are so much nicer than the rough "East Ends" I am used to', and finally to feeling 'cut off from my own family and class'.[22] Gertler had clung to the comforts of

---

* The murals are in what is now the information centre and library of the Ashridge Management College (see illustration 15).

his mother's warm kitchen, and had painted his mother in her accustomed chair, keeping her past the witching hour of lunch, until 2.30, and the dinner was burnt: father and mother exploded – 'They said I love my art more than them.' This mystifying progress was poured out to the all too sympathetic Carrington, Gertler deciding at some point that she was – and portraying her as – the perfectly comfortable Jewish-looking girl his mother would like him to marry. Their entanglement drifted on, complicated by the upper-class associations of their art: the inevitable invitations to Lady Ottoline's were duly issued and accepted. Gertler oscillated between Garsington, appearing in Lady Ottoline's photographs as an awkwardly-suited faun, at mischief in a garden, and the safety of his Spitalfields roots. In July 1914 he wrote to Carrington from Mrs Cooke's at the Old Coastguard Cottage, Pett Level, near Hastings: 'I am more at home and more happy than I've felt for a long time . . . My place is by these sort of people. I belong to this class. I shall always be unhappy if I try to get away from this class to which I belong.'[23]

Carrington, who was by nature so sympathetic, was also slightly better equipped to cope with the complexities of their new artistic life: *au fond* (while Marsh gave Gertler an allowance) she had to work tremendously hard to keep herself at the Slade. She won an important scholarship and several prestigious prizes, but also took private commissions and gave painting lessons, to pay her way to the end of her course in 1915. Her freedom to paint, to be able to experiment with all kinds of decorative effects, and most importantly ever to strive to improve her painting, was at the very core of her being, and she was (almost) always able to protect this from her importuning male friends. But she had no ambitions to be 'famous' and in that, in other people's eyes, she was vulnerable: she gave up the Slade stricture to sign and date her paintings as soon as she left, and – as Jane Hill writes – she 'had an innate dignity and was much affected by what she felt to be ugly or vulgar; exhibiting, which was like casting pearls before swine, fell into this category'.²⁴ Even though she sold a drawing for £5 8s. through a New English Art Club exhibition in 1914,²⁵ she came to think they were a dull lot, and it was hardly surprising that the celebrity-seeking images of the Omega workshops and Blooms-bury intimates also failed to impress. She and Mark Gertler were deeply united as a pair of brilliantly talented waifs who could tread the starry lawns of Garsington together and not get their feet burned. Gertler wrote to her: 'When you said that the artist's name didn't matter in a picture and you did not want to be a big artist yourself, only a creator, I felt I loved you more than I ever have before.'²⁶

The Carrington family's move to Ibthorpe House in 1913 was tremendously important; why they gave up a lifetime of villas in the south Midlands for a big, square Georgian, chequered brick mansion in a Hampshire valley is unexplained – it could have been a move for the sake of Samuel Carrington's failing health, or perhaps a more fitting home from which Charlotte Carrington might marry her daughters. Carrington's elder sister's marriage was the big event of the spring of 1915 – 'the ridiculous farce, the sham festivity', as Carrington dubbed it, ensured it would not be repeated.²⁷ But even her mother's hated provincial manners could not spoil Ibthorpe: at last she had a real home to return to as her last months at the Slade slipped away, with no other future – but painting – in sight. She was able to set up a studio in one of the outbuildings, and she decorated her own room at the top of the house: 'I painted the cupboard a lovely blue & red & green, & the board round the bottom of the wall, (scurtain board?) green, & the window sill & my bed bright blue & distempered all the walls a creamy white.'²⁸ Her view from her window was that of the great dish of the downs, *Hill in Snow at Hurstbourne Tarrant*, which she painted in watercolour, with the black trees silhouetted against the smooth, white, almost vertical fields which was just one of her impassioned tributes. In warmer weather she found the big square lead-lined valley of the roof, where she could hide in quiet for hours on end; in her reading, of which she did a great deal, she discovered that Ibthorpe House had a Jane Austen connection: in 1792 it had been rented by Mrs Lloyd, the widow of the rector of Deane, with her daughters Mary and Martha, who had been close friends with Cassandra and Jane at Steventon vicarage. Deane and Steventon were to the east, between Overton and Basingstoke and about fifteen miles by carriage or Carrington's bicycle along country roads. She would have smiled to discover that the unsatisfactory Mary Lloyd was married to James Austen from Ibthorpe, and the wedding party had to wade through floods to Hurstbourne church, but that the dear sister Martha, given a home by the Austens, and Jane and Cassandra's lifelong friend, happily married another brother Frank, who rose to be an Admiral.[29]

Living at Ibthorpe convinced Carrington that 'to love the country, the trees and the good hot sun', as she wrote to Gertler on a May evening in 1915, were to be her salvation. Amid the Ibthorpe gardens she became infected by her love of gardening – her pride in producing vegetables and growing tulips of fantastic colours to please her painter's eye – encouraged in lingering, neighbourly conversations over the cottage gateways on warm evenings. She walked and cycled the long, sunny lanes, and in these ways she found, with perfect timing, the life she loved; most important of all, she ventured up to the sudden heights of Hippenscombe, Chute and Combe, breathlessly winning the stupendous views – was it five or seven counties at a glance? – and she fell deeply and permanently in love with this great chalkland heart of southern England.

Carrington also learned a great deal, about life, literature and gardening, all of which interested her, from a home that the Bloomsbury *haute-coterie* rather despised, mostly because it reminded them of how narrow their much prized unconventionalities were. This was Gilbert and Mary Cannan's windmill house at Cholesbury, in the Chilterns between Berkhamsted and Wendover. Cannan was a Manchester Grammar schoolboy from a modest background who won a scholarship to King's College, Cambridge (where he occupied unsung years between Forster and Brooke), and was called to the Bar, but gave up the law to write. His heart had been broken by the sculptress Kathleen Bruce,★ and rather on the rebound he had found his solace with an older woman, the unfortunate Mary Barrie, the neglected wife of the creator of *Peter Pan* – so publicly known to be enamoured of the tragic Sylvia Llewellyn Davies and her four young sons.[31] Cannan was cited in the Barrie divorce, which, despite pleadings to newspaper editors from H. G. Wells that it was a matter that held no public interest, was cruelly screamed from the headlines: Barrie was deeply remorseful and generous, and Mary's settlement included their country house, Black Lake Cottage at Tilford in Surrey, where she had an elaborate garden of rockeries, bowers and ponds, lit by Chinese lanterns on summer nights, as she described in her book, *The Happy Garden*.[32]† Gilbert and Mary had settled at Black Lake, but found it too expensive; they couldn't stand London life, and by way of a rented cottage in Bellingdon Lane, Chesham – a magnificently long lane that slides up its own small Chiltern valley to the open heights of Cholesbury Common – they had found the windmill, with a cottage and outbuildings,

★ Kathleen Bruce rejected Cannan for Robert Falcon Scott. Diana Farr[30] writes of the Edwardian literary scene from the revealing perspective of one whom the Bloomsbury Group knew, but hardly mentioned.

† Diana Farr[33] gives good descriptions of Black Lake Cottage at Tilford and its garden and the Mill House at Cholesbury.

in 1913. Both of them appreciated the place, the 'commons and wheatfields and beechwoods, where the loveliest wild flowers grow', and they made an exciting house, the windmill converted to big, round and comfortable rooms, Gilbert's study looking towards 'the four corners of heaven and earth'.[34] Mary Cannan's taste was rather chintzy and for too many ornaments, and her gardening philosophy would have shocked Carrington, had she found it in *The Happy Garden*: 'If you are a woman, then marry an artist, an author or a clergyman and make it clear to him that your garden is to be the central idea of both your lives, stipulate for an adequate allowance to meet the temptations of the autumn catalogues, select your friends, discard your acquaintances, and set to work.'[35]

Cannan, tall and fair, described by Lady Ottoline as having 'the appearance of a rather vacant Sir Galahad and whose mind was prolific, poetic and romantic',[36] was unused to spoiling and enjoyed his married comforts, but had to work hard to support them. His stream of popular novels and plays have slipped into oblivion now, but Lady Ottoline had noticed his novel *Round the Corner*, put two and two together, felt the couple might be ostracized and issued an invitation to 44 Bedford Square: Lytton Strachey's verdict on Cannan was 'an empty bucket which has been filled to the brim with modern ideas – simply because it happened to be standing near that tap'.[37] But for once Lytton's opinion, tinged with jealousy and coloured by finding Cannan rather attractive, did not matter: Mary Cannan was thrilled that they 'passed the tea test' with Lady Ottoline and progressed to dinner, the Russian Ballet and Garsington Manor.

There was a jaunty air of independence about Cholesbury, where Cannan played village cricket and drank at the Falcon, very different from feudal Garsington; and yet Cholesbury Mill was to become a stepping-stone, an anteroom to Garsington. It was to be a refuge for Mark Gertler and therefore for Carrington, for

Katharine Mansfield and John Middleton Murry, Frieda and D. H. Lawrence, Vladimir and Elizabeth Polunin, and many more: it was to be the house and countryside, above all others, that gave Carrington the idea that she might be an artist and live in the country. In early August 1914, Cannan told Lady Ottoline Morrell that Lytton Strachey had been at the mill, enjoying bowls in the garden, and saying that he too would like to find a country cottage.[38]

Despite having several haunts in common, Lytton Strachey and Carrington never actually met until December 1915: 'God knows why they asked me!'[39] was Carrington's comment on her invitation for three wintry days at Asheham with Clive and Vanessa Bell, Duncan Grant, Mary Hutchinson and Lytton – but perhaps God did know something, apart from the obvious that she made equal numbers. Her mischievous expedition into Lytton's bedroom in order to trim his beard, when with the scissors poised over his face he opened his eyes wide – and she fell in love – rates high among magical moments. The ensuing clandestine relationship transformed them both into actors of delightfully comic parts: she, vivacious, mischievously 'votre grosse bebe', your Mopsa, wanting to whisk him off to Inkpen and Combe and places she loved, on her motorcycle – which she had yet to acquire or learn to ride; he, tall, thin and bearded, setting off with rucksack and this diminutive, boyish-looking companion, her 'uncle' Lytton, amazed that anyone could court his fancies so, and yet playing along in the best of humours. Lytton was perhaps absurdly flattered: she was puzzled for a time, she had never known anyone like Lytton before, he was clearly the antidote to her mother – whom she felt was as bad as Mrs Bennett in *Pride and Prejudice* – and, even though hidden in the mystique of love, there was the ultimate security of his homosexuality. Suffice it to say, for how are we to know, that they fell into, settled into, what Lytton called 'a great deal of a great many kinds of love'.[40]

Needing frequent escapes to Nature while she was at Ibthorpe, Carrington had soon discovered the Netherton valley lane from Hurstbourne that wound lazily up through wide grassy verges and hazel coppices to Combe, a tiny hamlet in the Berkshire downs. A long slow climb on her bicycle through primroses, anemones and bluebells in their seasons, a deep-breathing climb, took her to where the road arrives at a resting-place, a wide space, actually the turning circle for carts and cars to negotiate the hairpin bend that carries the road into Combe village. The lull of this natural resting-place is a blessing upon walker or rider, all the more enchanting for the ancient little church awaiting investigation, and behind it, in the age-old partnership, the manor farmhouse. In the spring of 1916 – the guns from France ever only the lowest of rumbles here – Carrington composed her fantasy of living at Combe with Lytton, up the lane through the woods of primroses and anemones to the empty house, mellow brick with a seventeenth-century look and, as she discovered, Jacobean oak panelling in the dining-room. It was faded and dusty, holding innumerable treasures in its heart, with a walled garden and an orchard, all awaiting her tender hands. She was now familiar with Asheham, which she liked immensely, and Garsington, and knew that Combe would fulfil the requirements of Lytton's Bloomsbury status, and that they would be visitable there. Then, suddenly, one day in June, she went to tea with the owners, farmers named Mackilligan, only to be told that the house had been taken, and the builders were in: 'You can imagine what this meant,' she shrieked in a letter to Lytton. 'Taken! By whom? What repairs? At last I managed to escape and rushed away on my bicycle . . . Never had the landscape appeared more lovely; as if to flaunt, it showed its very best, because it was no more . . . How I cursed myself for being so foolish as to believe that no one but I could ever live there . . .'[41] It was worse when she arrived: the garden had been neatened, 'Little violas with pert yellow faces and geraniums sniggered round the foot of the house in newly made beds', and inside – the painters showed her round – distemper was covering the ghostly decorations of the past, red and yellow patterns in one room, white flowers painted on a black wall in another – 'the spirit has been driven out by distemper, and white paint everywhere. It will never be what it was. A huge chunk of me is cut away, so many dreams. It all seems impossible. What right had they to come and steal it? Oh, Lytton, why is one so small against these creatures.'[42]

During August Carrington and Lytton went on a walking tour of the West Country together; Carrington returned with new resolve, announcing from Ibthorpe that she had 'boldly' been into all the Newbury estate agents and written letters to those in Hungerford and Reading. She told her mother that the house was for a group of women Slade students. Among Lytton's Bloomsbury friends there were plenty of ideas – his country base should be at Garsington, or at Cholesbury, or at Plumpton or Wilmington in Sussex, as the Bell, Grant and Garnett ménage moved from Wissett to Charleston. Carrington had to hold her own, and sent Lytton her map 'of the best land in Europe', the Berkshire downs, to steady his shaky geography.[43]

Nothing happened for almost a year on the housing front. Carrington's favourite brother Teddy was reported missing on the Somme, and early in 1917 they knew that he was dead. Lytton was gentle and consoling, as she painted his portrait through that winter: her *cher grandpère* or *mon oncle* in his most usual pose, in a deep armchair, his head back, his fine but rather furry features concentrated upon a book, held in those long-fingered white hands. The painting symbolized their closeness, but most of the time she was left with the symbol alone. Lytton flitted, as usual, from the Woolfs to the Bells, to Garsington or the Augustus Johns at Fordingbridge; Carrington might appear for a concert or a party – a decorative addition they thought her, but hardly took her seriously. She had a miserable time, with bad dreams and even delusions over Teddy, having no money and needing to work, getting a lecture from Leonard Woolf over her engravings for a Hogarth Press book, not being able to say goodbye to the hurt and needful Mark Gertler, and Ibthorpe, a tearful mother and her beloved father in sad decline. After another walking holiday with Lytton in late August she returned to Ibthorpe, where, surprisingly, it was her mother who produced the details of the Mill House at Tidmarsh, which was to let. An 'old fashioned house', with an acre of ground and a small orchard, three reception rooms, six bedrooms, sixty-five minutes to London on the train and a handy post office, for £52 a year.

Lytton was alerted: 'Mopsa' with her bicycle, and the train, dismissing two other possible houses *en route*, wrote her verdict from a Newbury teashop the same afternoon, Friday 19 October 1917 –

Tidmarsh Mill it is to be. Its very romantic and lovely.
Vast big rooms, 3 in number,
2 Very big bedrooms and 4 others,
Bathroom; water closet;
very good garden and a shady grass lawn
with river running through it.[44]

The Mill House was duly vetted by Oliver Strachey and the lease taken. Tidmarsh was barely a hamlet, beside the river Pang, just over a mile south of Pangbourne, where the Pang flows into one of the loveliest reaches of the Thames. It was sideways on to the mill lane, 'very old, with gables and some lattice windows' looking out on to the garden: all the rooms had electric light. The

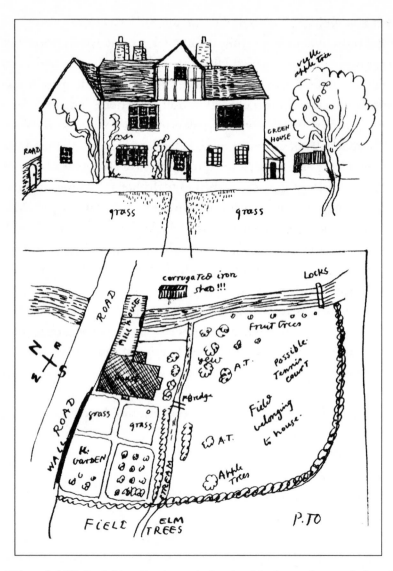

Tidmarsh Mill, Berkshire: Carrington's sketch of the house front and plan of the garden, 1917.

working mill was behind the house, the romantic jumble of buildings with a catslide roof, which Carrington painted in all its russet, watery glory.

All the better furniture for the house came from the Stracheys, and Lytton was to buy himself a four-poster bed at a local sale. Carrington's wholehearted contribution, rather on the lines of a bright shepherdess preparing to live with a prince, was very much in character: her parents were leaving Ibthorpe and turning out, but she could not tell the truth about Tidmarsh and her mother sold the things she really wanted, an old candlestick with Japanese decoration and an eighteenth-century embroidery, so she scoured the outhouses for useful water-cans and jugs and squirrelled away discarded china and utensils that her mother would not miss. She was allowed to raid the Ibthorpe gardens, for plants and cuttings and produce – 'everything is packed with apples artichokes & potatoes' – and jams and chutneys and sacks of nuts from the friendly farmer's copses were triumphantly ready for the new life. (Good walnuts and filberts were to be the noisy finale to many a Tidmarsh lunch.) She was sorry to leave Ibthorpe – 'The view from the window now that the trees are bare, is lovely,' she wrote to Lytton, who was ill in London; 'one can see right up the valley and the ridge of the hill opposite stands up hard and sharp like the back bone of a whale. But one day when we are old, and very rich I shall bring you here to live.'[45]

It was, as Virginia had the good grace to remark, Carrington who had to do all the work getting the Mill House ready: in late November she and her Slade friend Barbara Bagenal moved in and painted walls and floors – she didn't know what Lytton would think, but 'we think it's almost as good as Charleston', though without the wall decorations.[46] Lytton was actually seriously ill at this time, incarcerated in London beyond her reach, except in promises: 'Never again are you going to behave like this! After

November you will start a regular life at Tidmarsh, supported by glasses of milk, and vigorous walks.'[47] She was quite right of course, and she expended great energies to keep up a jocular tone, but Lytton was terrified of what he had let himself in for. *Eminent Victorians* was published in 1918, a timely indictment of the establishment's mindset that had caused the war – svelte and sharp critiques of Dr Arnold of Rugby, Florence Nightingale, Queen Victoria and General Gordon. He was lionized, invited everywhere, and felt he must be free to come and go as he pleased, untethered. Carrington's year was haunted by reminders of Teddy, by accusations from Mark Gertler, who discovered that she *was* living with Lytton, and deceptions to prove to her parents that she *was not*. After her father's death in December 1918 she was so distraught as not to care any more what her mother thought, but soon she admitted to her diary that her fantasy of being chatelaine to Lytton's writer's life had proved a little dull: 'All his adventures and experiences are mental, and only enjoyed by himself. Outwardly it's like the life of one of the hens. Meals dividing up the day, books and reading in the morning, siesta, walk to Pangbourne, more books. A French lesson with me, perhaps dinner. Reading aloud. Bed and hot water bottles, and every day the same apparently.'[48] She comforted herself by imagining that his inner life was full of fantastic doings, great schemes 'and plans for the future which I could never guess', but it probably wasn't; it was inhabiting that region of the past where his subject dwelt, as he was tuning himself into the life of the young Victoria – as Carrington noted: 'A long walk, and talk about the Georges before tea.'[49]

Virginia noted, not too unkindly, that Lytton's influence 'deranges her spiritual balance a good deal' . . . she was ceaselessly active, ever doing things whether at Tidmarsh or staying away at Asheham . . . 'She kisses him & waits on him & gets good advice

& some sort of protection', acting as a sort of valet-cum-housekeeper in Virginia's view – or a wife, of just that suburban kind that she so despised? Summer weather brought scenes of rural peace; she 'read the Young Visitors [*sic*] in the sun in the orchard. I envy that book. How good, firstly to be able to create so detached from this world, and then to live such a life, a life without accounts, parents, and these Russian situations!' Lytton was sitting out on the lawn, cushioned, shaded and comfortably writing, so she 'sent back dinner three times' out of 'reverence', then could resist hers no longer, and he came in and said he was all the time waiting to be called – 'We roared with laughter most of lunch over it.'⁵⁰ She painted during the afternoon, her painting now only ever squeezed in between the gaps of routine, and then: 'Interesting conversation at tea about Peterloo, Trades Unions, and Cooperation. Lytton has promised to read me the first part of Victoria tonight – I am excited.'⁵¹ Entangled in this sycophancy (though she was not entirely serious) and frustrations of a good deal of a good many kinds, the colours and details of life at the Mill House are virtually obscured. Into these rural vacuums stepped a friend of Noel Carrington's, the cheerful, willing and exceedingly nice Ralph Partridge, with whom Carrington began an affair (and Lytton did not). Ralph's generosity of spirit, and labours in the house and garden, made life at Tidmarsh all the more comfortable, and, to regularize the ménage and please Ralph, he and Carrington were married one day in May 1921. It seemed a reckless action, most of all to Carrington; she was secretly fearful that she got on Lytton's nerves and he might ask her to leave Tidmarsh, but knowing that he was fond of Ralph, hoped that all three together they might keep the *status quo*. Her fears wrung from Lytton a long letter of undreamed warmth: addressed to 'My dearest and best,' it continued to:

you angelic creature, whose goodness to me has made me happy for years, and whose presence in my life has been, and always will be, one of the most important things in it . . . We are all helpless in these things – dreadfully helpless. I am lonely and I am all too truly growing old, and if there was a chance that your decision meant that I should somehow or other lose you, I don't think I could bear it. You and Ralph and our life at Tidmarsh are what I care for most in the world – almost (apart from my work and some few people) the *only* things I care for.[52]

Tidmarsh Mill was an apprentice triumph, both for life with Lytton and Carrington's own maturing as an artist: disapproving of the hothouse and gallery-slaving painter, she was becoming a kind of community artist, a troubadour with her varying talents which she dispensed generously wherever she worked. At Tidmarsh she drew likenesses of Lytton; she painted the mill itself magnificently in oils, its red roofs reflected in the mill stream, on which floated some imaginary black swans; she gardened – growing her favourite tulips and dahlias and then painting them; and then – as the opportunity for frescoes seemed missing – she researched and practised other traditional arts. She made exquisite pictures with coloured inks and silver foil on glass and gave many as presents, she engraved book plates and paper headings, and besides the painted furniture for Tidmarsh and other people's houses, she painted signboards for Pangbourne shopkeepers and a series of inn signs.[53] These included the Greyhound at Tidmarsh, the Roebuck at Tilehurst, and the Spreadeagle at Thame in Buckinghamshire. The first two were for the brewery – 'If the Brewery will stump up £10 a sign I'll be content . . . for the rest of my life'[54] – but the Spreadeagle most likely came via the landlord, John Fothergill's, friendship with Tonks and Will and John Rothenstein. Through Fothergill's belligerent enthusiasm for his new role as innkeeper, the famous free-standing Spread-eagle sign, on a heavy post that was also a lamp-post, adorned with much wrought ironwork, became a symbol of his transformation of a shabby and 'exceptionally public' house into one of the most celebrated hostelries in England with a celebrity clientele. The costs of the sign rocketed to £190, an enormous sum for 1924, and then Fothergill stopped counting; he tells a racy tale – and though he says she 'painted it beautifully' one somehow doubts she received the lion's (or eagle's) share.[55]

Though stylistically, in bold image and clarity of line, she was an artist of her own time, Carrington's polymath achievements, always rooted in her strong sense of place, retained the aura of the Arts and Crafts movement. Underlying her evident attractiveness, this characteristic sparked her involvement with Ralph Partridge's friend Gerald Brenan.

Brenan, spoiled, egotistical, rebellious and artistic, was probably the most sympathetic of all Carrington's lovers, the most in tune with her: from infancy in India and boyhood in the Cotswolds, in revolt against his parents' respectability and school regimes, he had conceived an admiration for Ernest Gimson and the Arts and Crafts builders and furniture-makers. He had been through the war, Ypres, Paschendaele and the Marne, and survived to a longing for a primitive and purer life and people 'whose point lay rather in what they were than in what they said or did' – as he wrote of Augustus and Dorelia John, whom he (and Carrington) admired[56] – as opposed to his distrust of most of Bloomsbury. No rural retreat in 'tepid' England could hold him and he had moved to Spain in 1920. It is in Carrington's letters to Brenan that she reveals some of the pleasure of life at Tidmarsh: 'A perfect day' was to take the sluggish train to Newbury and visit a little shop of treasures owned by the eccentric Mr Jarvis, from where her most favourite things had come, 'the delft dishes, my Spanish book of woodcuts,

Lytton's snuff box'; sadly the shop was closed and Mr Jarvis found to be ill. After a 'wretched' lunch at the White Hart Hotel they decided to have another try, to find Mrs Jarvis, in her draper's shop, and she let them into the curiosity room to rummage:

I selected 5 exquisite old coffee cups, of finest china, with saucers, all sprigged and different. Three without handles. Then we found two large decanters square shaped, which cost 6s. each; very old glass. A deep Spanish bowl for salad and 8 very old liqueur glasses of great beauty . . . and 3 very heavy glass drinking tumblers for 4/- each, one which was dated 1720.[57]

Elated at their purchases and the news that Mr Jarvis might recover, they bought sticky buns and set out to walk home along the Kennet and Avon canal.

It was a perfect hot afternoon and the beauty of the long diminishing canal was amazing. We passed locks and mills, groves of willows, old red barns and flat fields of grazing cattle.[58]

At Midgham they caught the train to Theale, from where they were used to the two-and-a-half-mile tramp to Tidmarsh. There the garden was full of sunflowers and talk of sundials; an early autumn storm covered the lawn with apples. The success of Lytton's *Queen Victoria* had enriched their lives, and boxes from Fortnum & Mason, cheeses from Paxton & Whitfield in Jermyn Street, and crates of wines from Soho were arriving for Christmas: Carrington was making Liberty silk dressing-gowns for all, they had bought 'a lovely bedspread, Queen Anne embroidery with a big sun flower in the middle, very pale colours, with flowers embroidered all over it' for Lytton's four-poster, and she was to decorate the bed, paint a dresser yellow and make a lampshade.

She felt the Mill House in winter 'so snug and warm, lined with its walls of coloured books' because in the gloom she couldn't see the rat holes and the dust – 'one curls up in it like a fox in its hole, contented'.[59]

Come the spring, though, and they were off to sunnier climes, to North Africa and Italy; on the last Sunday of May, 1923, Carrington was returned, depressed at the awful cold and flat greenery of the Pang valley. In truth her depression had more to do with a visit to her suddenly 'Dearest Virginia', whom she couldn't wait to see on her return, because the Woolfs had been to Yegen, a remote village in Andalusia, to stay with Gerald Brenan. Virginia, fully up to the situation, fed her stale iced cake and told her that Gerald was going to marry an American girl. It turned out not to be true, but Carrington was furious that every-one but she seemed to be going to Yegen: behind the scenes it was now Lytton who was worried that the Carrington–Brenan affair might frighten off Ralph Partridge, and so destroy his little household. Carrington took her bitterness out on Tidmarsh, now scorning it as flat and provincial – 'I hate these backyard hens and ducks. Ugh! Perhaps we will leave it soon. It is too green and stuffy.'[60] Poor Tidmarsh had had its day, and after a summer trip to France they started house-hunting, Carrington, of course, knowing exactly where to look. On 23 October 1923 she noted in her journal that she was 'in love' with a house:

It is called Ham Spray House. That's a good title to begin with. It is within a mile of the village of Ham and the village of Inkpen and a stone's throw (if one threw well) from the most marvellous downs in the WHOLE WORLD – Inkpen Beacon . . . We saw a ramshackle lodge, a long avenue of limes but all wuthering in appearance, bleak, and the road a grass track. Barns in decay, then the back of a rather forbidding farm house. We walked to the front of it and saw to our amazement in the blazing sun a perfect English country house. But with a view onto downs before it that took our breaths away . . .[61]

Ham Spray House was expensive to lease, and clearly to maintain, but Ralph's father had recently died and left his mother comfortably off, and Ralph and Lytton hoped to afford it between them; they put in their offer but heard nothing. On the strength of this new future, Lytton relented and it was arranged that Carrington and Ralph should go to Spain in the winter. Before she left, in mid-November, they had heard nothing – 'I felt my Ham heart inside give a crack when it found the letter box empty,' she wrote to Lytton; 'There are some griefs too great to speak about and Ham Spray is one.'[62] For a month Brenan and the Andalusian landscape absorbed her, then in the first week of 1924, when she and Ralph arrived in Madrid, they heard that Lytton had bought the lease of Ham Spray for something over £2,000. As she travelled home Carrington happily planned the rooms, painted them in her mind's eye a hundred times and planted the garden of her dreams.

She had soon winkled out the Miss Woodmans, living and gardening in Ham village, who had been born in Ham Spray House; their father had built it, and made the garden, when he was a young man: that seemed to make it early Victorian, which was its appearance, plainly rectangular with five nicely proportioned sash windows in line on the first floor, and doors replacing the downstairs middle window, front and back. The garden side of the house was trimmed with a verandah on a wrought-iron frame, with a roof of corrugated iron, painted. There were plenty of outbuildings, a cottage for the housekeeper and a copse of trees sheltering it from the east wind: the southward view, across lawn and flower-beds, included a big ilex, then gave on to the most stunning expanse of Carrington's beloved scarp ridge of the chalk, at its most majestic from Ham Hill to Inkpen Beacon, Combe Gibbet and Walbury Hill.

A crate of painted Spanish plates and jugs, all very large, and some chintzes from Granada had come back from Spain with Carrington, and Gerald Brenan's arrival had brought more offerings of chintzes; she had written revealingly: 'Lytton thought the chintzes very beautiful. Is it absurd to be in such ecstasies over inanimate objects? Yet it is easier to show it over two tigers in a jungle on a blue background than over one tiger [Brenan] in a Belgravia Hotel . . .'[63]

In tangential ways such as these, Ham Spray House made its entry into persistently tumultuous lives. Carrington and Ralph Partridge moved in during the last week of July 1924 while Lytton was in France, and she was soon absorbed in painting and decorating, dragooning in every willing helper. Lytton managed to buy the freehold of the house, then made his will, leaving it to Ralph, as Carrington's husband, which he felt ensured her security long after he was gone. This imposed the burden of protection on Ralph, who was seemingly willing to bear it, even though he had met and fallen in love with Frances Marshall, ex Bedales and Newnham College, who worked in David Garnett and Francis Birrell's Bloomsbury bookshop.* The internal complexities of life at Ham Spray were thus to obscure the house itself, as if it could only be seen through a shimmering gauze of temperaments and emotions. Noel Carrington thought the house was his sister's 'masterpiece', yet few had the detachment to see this: Ham Spray was never praised or admired like Charleston, it was an essentially

---

* In the serious issues of life, the property, the avant-garde Bloomsbury men were peculiarly old-fashioned, and it seems strange that Lytton did not bother to find a lawyer who would remind him that, by 1924, a woman could inherit property of her own. If Carrington had discovered herself 'worthy' of inheriting Ham Spray one feels she may have clung on to life rather longer.

private house – never splashed across magazine pages as the artistic home of a celebrated author, never even the backdrop of inter-views: it seems only to have been photographed once, in unfor-giving black and white. This, unfortunately, was not merely the attitude to the tangible arrangements of rooms or even the atmosphere that prevailed, it was the attitude of all the Bloomsbury commentators and memorializers to Carrington herself. The electric situation whereby Frances Marshall became so regular a visitor as not to be a visitor at all, and Lytton imported a stream of increasingly rich and aristocratic young men for his own amuse-ment, left Carrington a prey to ceaseless activity, dissipating her emotional energies into long letters to anyone (after Brenan had faded to his own Spanish life) who would read them. She, who had sacrificed her serious painting, was called to sacrifice ever more, inching fragments off her soul; her response was not – as it was of Vanessa Bell at Charleston – to flood her home in colour and floral extravaganzas, it was to create with a sure and delicate touch that has defied imitation.

Ham Spray was a countrified house, with the unpretentious honesty that she had met in the Miss Woodmans: it was one room deep, with a corridor, and had the air of being lived in, prior to their coming, in a well-housekeepered and sober way. Inside the front door was a small sitting-room, the light – as in all the downstairs rooms – steadied and softened by the verandah roof outside the window, hung with an unlined chintz curtain on large rings. It was rather a house rule that curtains were undrawn, even though the windows went dark, until they were needed to keep out the winter's bitterest cold. This sitting-room had an oval cast-iron grate, the oval echoed in arched niches either side of the chimney breast; these niches were rather cunningly filled with low cupboards and five bookshelves, not fitted, but free-standing in gentle proportion to the alcoves, with two big Spanish dishes on the top, shown to advantage against the domed alcove. The walls were plain, but the single boarded beam across the ceiling had a chamfered panel painted in a darker tone, as were the alcoves and the mouldings on the cupboard doors. Rumour has it that the predominant colours of the house were soft olive greens, cloudy yellows and mauves and russets. This room might have been soft greens, for widely striped and floral chintzes covered the sofa and wing armchair beside the fire. There was a standard lamp of plain lightish wood, with a pleated shade: Carrington made many of the lampshades – there was a small pleated shade on the lamp on Lytton's writing table – and it seems likely that as Ralph Partridge set himself up as a professional book-binder, she used some of his papers and buckrams.

The dining-room, with a round pedestal table with lion's feet, was set for four, covered with white cloth over a tapestry, with Regency dining-chairs, their seats loosely covered in chintz. All the covers, for chairs and sofas, were informal and softly fitted, sometimes in plain reps or linens or chintz, and invariably made by Carrington herself. The dining-room roof beam was delicately painted with a flower motif, well spaced, and this continued into a frieze, about ten inches deep, all around the room. The frieze sat on a picture rail, on which hung Duncan Grant's lively duo, the *Juggler and the Tightrope Walker*, which Lytton had bought for sixty guineas in 1920 as a mark of his approval of the end of Grant's Omega phase.[64] The juggler and the tightrope walker offered a wry comment on the ménage: in 1929 Lytton also bought Grant's voluptuous pink *Venus and Adonis*, her disembodied head swivelled to keep an eye on the distantly cavorting god – said to be an allegory for life at Charleston, but relevant enough at Ham Spray too. In the dining-room, the fireplace, cast-iron with some leafy decoration, and a plain mantelpiece supporting a long mirror that reflected the greeny hue from the window opposite: fit companion for the Grant circus acts on the east wall was a painted dresser, perhaps of limey soft green or cloudy yellow base colour with plain double doors, low doors, decorated with huge and explosive vases of flowers. The shelves were crowded with Spanish plates and the motley selection of delicate cups and saucers from Mr Jarvis in Newbury. Carrington loved cooking, and worked in an easy companionship with various housekeepers and maids: crème brûlée was a speciality, and good cheese, cherry brandy and celebratory champagnes were much appreciated. Sherry seemed the tipple of the house, before meals (in that interminable Cambridge way) and drunk far into the evenings. Carrington loved most to serve the produce of her vegetable garden: one meal of triumph was 'Epoch making; grapefruit, then a chicken covered with fennel and tomato sauce, a risotto with almonds, onions, and pimentos, followed by sack cream, supported by Café Royal red wine, *perfectly* warmed.'⁶⁵ This was regaled to Lytton and a repetition promised on his return.

Upstairs, Carrington had lavished labours on Lytton's writing-room: the fireplace wall had wide-striped and hand-blocked wallpaper – one of 'Fanny Fletcher's Papers' – and a painting of Voltaire, seated at a table with his hand raised in benediction upon a group of friends, in a plain giltwood frame.★ Lytton wrote at a Pembroke table, sitting in a rush-seated ladderback armchair with a plump chintz seat cushion; the table was set behind a small sofa which fronted the fire, with his favourite round-backed low chair beside it. A beautiful, fine Aubusson carpet covered the floor, laid over a plain matting. The whole east wall of the room had built-in bookshelves, in bays, each bay topped with a painted panel,

---

★ Michael Holroyd describes Ham Spray interiors, including Fanny Fletcher hand-blocked wallpapers made with carved potatoes (or cut oranges) in mauves, olives and cloudy yellows.⁶⁶

carefully lettered with subjects for the books, and undoubtedly (though not visible in the photograph) finely lined in gilt.★

In the bedrooms, the four-poster beds seemed to multiply; Carrington had painted Lytton's to complement his sunflower and flower-embroidered bedspread, she had one of her own, and Frances Marshall recorded in a piece called 'One day at Ham Spray' how she had woken suddenly on a May morning in 1927, after oversleeping – 'framed by the green and white posts and yellow curtains of my bed' in the 'Pink Room'.[68] Frances gives us no other details of Ham Spray, apart from breakfast being on the verandah and tea on the lawn, and that the wind whipped the pollarded aspens and the tops of the elms in the avenue so that they had to shout to each other. Unseen, the other delights of the house have to be imagined: Carrington painted chairs – one Maples looking Chippendale was given a broad rush seat and soft green frame; she made delicate paintings on glass, mounted on silver paper; she painted tiles for wash-basins and bathrooms – 'passion-flowers, legs of mutton, fishes, abstract shapes and whole orchestras of cats playing cellos';[69] she worked on the biscuit base and sent them for glazing after decoration. (At Ham Spray kittens and cats, chickens and ducks, were an essential part of the ménage.) So many of the things she made, and small pictures and objects she painted, were given to friends, and she was endlessly generous in her schemes for other people's houses, dresses, hats or costumes for parties. One of the last and best things she did was to paint the *trompe l'œil* images of the cook and her cat at a blind window of Biddesden House, the home of friends Bryan and Diana Guinness, to where she would ride on her pony, Belle, along the old Roman track, the Chute Causeway.

★ Michael Holroyd mentions a large writing desk, but all the photographs show a Pembroke table. Of course the desk may have been removed at Lytton's death.[67]

The Ham Spray intimates were slightly more observant about exterior details; the changing weather seemed to be a particular mark of the house's high and airy situation. They were easily cut off by snow, one heavy fall 'transforming the garden to a pantomime scene of exquisite beauty and leaving ditches and lanes brimful of drifts edged with extraordinary shapes – columns, mushrooms and pagodas'. Next morning the household put on all the clothes they could find and set out to walk to Hungerford station – 'at Inkpen the roads were full to the top with snow; the blue sky brought out curious pink lights in it and deep blue shadows; cottages were grotesquely hung with post-card icicles . . .'[70] At Hungerford the world was ordinary, bowler hats were de rigueur, and people 'gaped to see a troupe of performing Bulgarian peasants'. Carrington remained at home, bulked out in layers, trying to paint with frozen hands, but in the evening, with the fire blazing and curtains closed, the wind could howl all it willed, for she and Lytton were cosily inside, with the cats. The change from winter to spring could happen over a weekend – as James Strachey even managed to look up from his Freudian preoccupations to notice, in mid March 1925: 'Sunday morning really reminded one of life being worth living,' he wrote to his wife, Alix; 'We all sat out in the sun on the verandah in front of the house and basked without overcoats. Bees were buzzing from crocus to crocus, and the birds making a terrific din.'[71] Carrington's spring gardening was her joy, and she spent hours studying bulb catalogues, rewarded by the remembered drifts of narcissus and daffodils that surrounded Ham Spray, and her tulip garden. Once she described 'a curious world on a green stage' that she could see from her bed: 'The loves of cows, cats hunting rabbits in groves of laurels, gargantuan feasts given by black birds on the lawn, the provincial life of the rooks in Ilex tree, and last night the great brown owl padded softly through the sky past my window.'[72] During the 1926 General

Strike she felt Ham Spray distant from the world, 'marooned on a green island' – the Prince of Wales may have come home by aeroplane, the King be talking to Mr Baldwin, but there she and Lytton walked along the foot of the downs, found a wild yellow auricula, 'a cross between a cowslip and a primrose';[73] the woods were filled with bluebells, the birds in full chorus, and Lytton read Ford's *The Broken Heart*, written in 1633, in the evenings. With spring she could become very botanical – showing off to amuse Lytton's niece and her friend, Julia Strachey:

the marigolds are just coming out. I do wish you were here to see my blue irises, Musa Coccinea (scarlet banana) is a perfect sight. The Bacca Loculis have unfortunately died; the *drought* is terrible. My little Bastard Satyrium (cape orchid) is covered with blight, and my Bummonia Uncanta has the mildew . . . I do wish you were here to help . . .[74]

After the middle weekend of August 1929 Carrington reported the Ham Spray doings to Lytton, who had been socializing with Lady Horner, Katharine Asquith and Siegfried Sassoon at Mells in Somerset – the kind of society he still reserved to himself. There was an element of 'while the chief cat's away' both mice and kittens would play in the gaiety and generosity that Carrington seemed to draw unto herself: that weekend people just seemed to accumulate – the 'little' MacCarthys, Rachel and Dermot, children of Desmond and Molly, Frances Marshall, Saxon Sydney Turner, and finally (Carrington's last lover) Bernard 'Beakus' Penrose, who had brought his new film camera.[75] Suddenly they went into production, Saturday evening spent arguing and devising a playlet titled 'Dr Turner's Mental Home' (Saxon's father had actually run such a home but he didn't seem to mind being cast as villain).★

★ The film was shown at 41 Gordon Square the following Thursday.

Carrington got up at seven the next morning to find masks and props, and make the stunt-dummy cleverly substituted for Rachel when she threw herself out of an upstairs window. Rachel (stunningly photogenic, elfin-like and pretty) was the innocent victim Daisy, brought to the evil house by the dastardly Ralph Partridge looking like an undertaker and Carrington padded out as a pompous and leering matron. Discovering the victim to be incurably virtuous, Dr Turner and evil cohorts drown her – 'We didn't have lunch till 2.30,' Carrington reported, 'and the whole afternoon was given over to drowning Rachel in the bath by the greenhouse.'[76] They carried the inert Daisy and laid her in front of the big laurel hedge, sprinkling her with leaves and flowers. Ham Spray's big ginger cat, Tiberius, 'played a large part in the film with great success', Lytton was delighted to know. Tiberius was himself, Frances Marshall gambolled with riding boots on her arms as the mental home's dog.[77]

The black and white, or shades of grey, home movie both adds to the Ham Spray myth, and reveals its ordinariness: the opening scene is of the rather gaunt stucco-framed front door, the weedy gravel drive and untidy shrubs which indicate that little time or attention was given to this 'front' – where Carrington would have dreaded any provincial tidiness. The glimpse of a bedroom has a four-poster but no visible decorations; the verandah has the remains of their lunch table, a checked tablecloth hanging untidily, and an assortment of deckchairs and kitchen chairs casually pushed back. No smart garden furniture ever darkened the portals of this house! And the garden has a fellowship with all August gardens: the roses on the verandah are leggy, the planting along the foot of it – stachys, day lilies, lavender – all untidy; the big laurel hedge is shiny-leaved with health, the trees are all the heavyweights of late summer, the grass is moth-eaten and dry, the hills are hazy . . . and the last shot shows the bad doctor being chased away, down alongside the wall that accompanies the drive. Carrington herself comes to life, skittish, dancing in her white stockings, lithe in spite of her padding, pulling clown faces underneath her bell of thick golden hair.

In subsequent snatches of Beakus's film Carrington, Frances Marshall, Ralph and David Garnett are swimming in the river Kennet, and Lytton himself makes a fleeting, smiling and rather delightful appearance at a Ham Spray window – looking more wholesome and shiny-haired than one ever imagined!★

Carrington may have needed to be ceaselessly active, especially when Lytton was away, but her activities were still inspired by the innate generosity of her artistic spirit. The four Penrose brothers had been Lytton's friends since Cambridge days – Alec who farmed, Lionel the pioneer geneticist, Roland the artist and Beakus the sailor; Carrington became pregnant by Beakus (but her pregnancy too was sacrificed to the status quo at Ham Spray). For the marriage of Alec and Frances Penrose in 1930 she painted a whole fireplace of tiles, forty-one in all, a labour of loyalty and careful research; the Penrose brothers were the grandsons of Alexander, Baron Peckover of Wisbech, the Quaker banker whose illustrious and philanthropic life had ended in 1919, leaving his spinster daughters, the Hon. Alexandrina and Miss Anna Jane, in the splendid family home, Peckover House, in the centre of Wisbech.† Carrington has carefully portrayed the Penrose inheritance: delicate portraits of their houses, Peckover and Sibald's Holme overlooking the canalized Nene, flowers and birds beloved of the Misses Penrose in their lovely garden, the shell grotto at Sibald's Holme and the hermit owl, Bombie the dog and a curled-up cat,

---

★ Thanks to the persistence of Jane Hill, Carrington's biographer, these films were found, and a copy deposited with the British Film and Television Archive.
† Peckover House, Wisbech, is now owned by the National Trust.

a carriage on skis driving on the frozen fens and the full-sailed schooner in which Beakus had navigated around Cape Horn. She devised a motto, 'No Pen without a Rose', and for the pediment of the fireplace alcove 'painted mixed flowers in goblets and jugs from her own dresser and surmounted the whole with roped-up tableau curtains'.*

Carrington was an enigma, most lovingly worked out by Julia Strachey, who called her 'a modern witch' – 'a lover of marvels, a searcher for the emotionally magnificent life'. Her business, perhaps born of practice, was 'to counteract the life-frames in which she found people already mounted' – cajoling, juggling, suggesting, demonstrating, 'glowing with sympathetic magnetism and droll ideas' so that everyone felt they had met a best friend. The flamboyance of this outgoingness was the corollary to the fine distinction of her home at Ham Spray and her love for its bare and beautifully formed landscape of shifting lights and breezes. Julia seemed to understand best how Carrington 'had for long spiritually existed in the very teeth of some sort of whirlwind, too near whose path she had chanced to stray, and in whose arms, ice-pinnacled and wuthering, she had built her own nest'.[81] Was this why, as the twenties rolled to their ending, and she felt her

---

* Jane Hill's *The Art of Dora Carrington*[78] illustrates the Penrose fireplace. Noel Carrington was the only person to acknowledge his sister's work after her death: in *Design in the Home*[79] he illustrated fireplace tiles she painted for him, two morning glory plants spiralling from their pots to the sun in the central tile at the top. She was called D. C. Partridge. Boris Anrep's hermaphrodite mosaic for Lytton's bedroom fireplace at Ham Spray was also illustrated. A Ham Spray bathroom, with tiles decorated with shells, anchors, starfish and waves, by D. C. Partridge, was also included. In *Design and Decoration in the Home*[80] Noel Carrington included professionally photographed set-pieces of the dining-room and Lytton's library at Ham Spray, though neither was identified nor credited to her.

lot to be 'an eternity of dull blank skies', increasingly and ever more often she sought out the wind on the downs? She rode out on Belle – to leave Ralph and Frances to each other, to leave Lytton to the company of his last passion, for Roger Senhouse – she rode over to Biddesden to the Guinnesses, to whom riding was the most enjoyable pastime, who appreciated houses, horses and gardening rather more than those she had left behind. Riding or walking to the roof of their world became her all-purpose cure for friends, for a 'depressed' Henry Lamb, for a private chat with Dorelia John or Julia, both of whom she adored; life with Lytton increasingly centred on the doings of their beloved cats, and in the summer of 1931 she wrote a prize-winning spoof obituary of her 'venerable biographer', who 'died' in his favourite place, in his *chaise-longue* under the ilex tree on the lawn . . . she was reluctant to reveal her name, for of course they would say he wrote it for her.[82]

There was, in the end, and for all her youthful bravura at the Slade, nothing at all modern about Carrington; no speck of European modernism in art or fabric or furniture ever entered the portals of Ham Spray, apart from the *faux-moderne* of Duncan Grant, and she and Lytton lived almost entirely in the past, in their Elizabethan literature or nineteenth-century novels, where they were safest. She liked best their ordinary, domestic days; when this paradise, which she had gained, was threatened, either by other people or, at the last, by Lytton's illness in December 1931, she took to the primeval downs. They could enchant her – as once she had watched a great storm driving over from Chute Causeway in the west, lit from behind by the setting sun, until the rain came and drenched her, and there being no shelter she just sat still on Belle and watched until a rainbow fell into Combe gorge, then another echo of a rainbow 'until two great hoops stood before me barring the way'. They could comfort her –

the beechwoods drenched in gold, or 'filled with tall withered loose-strife, hung with white feathery seeds'; the ground palest green velvet with patterns made by patches of dried leaves; she was 'intoxicated with the sweet, wild beauty of the woods and valleys'.[83] Indeed, her countryside had the power to absorb her; once she had ridden all across Sheepless Hill and down her favourite Netherton valley by paths she felt were her own, to her old house at Ibthorpe. A hundred memories jostled her, the dish-like hill with juniper and hawthorn bushes that she had painted, the sunk leads of the house roof where she used to climb to watch the village on hot afternoons, the garden with the variegated hollies and the ilex, the high hedges where she had climbed to the top of the ladder, the house where she had put off her old life and taken up with the whirlwind. In the end it seemed she had only travelled those downland lanes from Hurstbourne over the ridge to Ham Spray; living in that countryside had always, she had written and said over and over again, made her very happy, and grateful.

6

Leslie Poles Hartley

The obvious connections between L. P. Hartley and my four previous subjects can be covered in one paragraph. Virginia Woolf was disdainful, merciless to the unglamorous as usual, though she respected him as a writer. Forster suffered from comparisons with Hartley, and though they often met at Garsington or in Bloomsbury drawing-rooms, Forster was wary, seeming fearful of contamination, of becoming one of Hartley's characters. Carrington, too, must have often been in the same garden or house party but she does not mention him, nor, sadly, would he have noticed her: if the faintest notion of Lytton Strachey's affection for her had reached him, he would have dismissed it as ridiculous, perhaps with a private, regretful tear on second thoughts. Brooke, whom he never met, haunted him merely because he symbolized the lost generation: Hartley wore a similar khaki, dressed with shiny leather belt and bands, and they both appeared the very image of personable Englishmen, but Hartley had a desk war and the effrontery to survive.

Hartley was more prolific than Woolf and Forster combined: he published eighteen novels and four collections of short stories, fifty stories in all.[1] But whereas Woolf and Forster delight us with their tilts and parries at the weaknesses of our species, Hartley pushes the knife deeply into humankind. Lord David Cecil thought Hartley's view 'transformed by the light of a Gothic imagination', capable of 'fanciful reverie' in a grotto-like gleam of mysterious light or in darkness, with earthly or supernatural terrors.[2] Lord David, supposed by all who knew them to be Hartley's closest friend, cannot be lightly contradicted, but Hartley never took the easy escape route into the tradition of *Vathek* and *The Castle of Otranto*; his characters are himself and his contemporaries, wrestling with 'original sin' (Cecil's term) and consequent disaster in thoroughly modern settings. The blood that flows is disturbingly red and fresh, not a watered-down and blue eighteenth-century kind.

Hartley's by-line – 'The past is a foreign country: they do things differently there' – in the context of *The Go-Between*, the story of a remembered summer of long ago, has been taken as the past of childhood. Hartley never allowed himself to stray any further. But in the context of *Spirits of Place*, there is another 'foreign country', and Hartley came from there: he is the ultimate outsider. Whereas Woolf and Forster conducted their forays from the secure emplacement of the 'intellectual aristocracy', Hartley enjoyed no such safeguards. His 'foreign country' was not only *his* past, but far out, beyond the comfortable reaches of Kensington and the Home Counties, far out in that antithesis of the mythically pretty countryside, the Fens.

Hartley was born in Whittlesey, in a room above a bank where his parents, Harry and Bessie Hartley, had their first home. Enid, the first Hartley child, had been born on Christmas Day 1892, but Leslie (or at least his anti-hero Eustace Cherrington) would have apologized profusely for missing another auspicious day, only making 30 December in 1895. He was named for Leslie Stephen – from whom the Hartleys were separated by a social and intellectual abyss – presumably because the completion of Stephen's great *Dictionary of National Biography* in that year had been celebrated

16. Henry Lamb's studio portrait of Lytton Strachey, 1914.

The ponderous woman looked through the pattern of falling words at the flowers standing cool, firm and upright in the earth, with a curious expression. She saw them as a sleeper waking from a heavy sleep sees a brass candlestick reflecting the light in an unfamiliar way, and closes his eyes and opens them, and seeing the brass candlestick again, finally starts wide awake and stares at the candlestick with all his powers. So the heavy woman came to a standstill opposite the oval shaped flower bed, and ceased even to pretend to listen to what the other woman was saying. She stood there letting the words fall over her, swaying the top part of her body slowly backwards and forwards, looking at the flowers. Then she suggested that they should find a seat and have their tea.

17. *Kew Gardens*, written by Virginia Woolf, decoration by Vanessa Bell, first published by the Hogarth Press, 1917.

. Vanessa Bell, *Summer Camp*, oils on board, 1913, captures the mood of a camp in Suffolk that summer, which included the Olivier sisters and others of the Brooke circle.

. Rupert Brooke making Helena Cornford look at the camera, Cley-next-the-Sea, August 1914. Frances Cornford on the left.

20. Asheham House Sussex, photographe in 1927 when it was the quarry manager's house: Virginia and Leonard Woolf had given up their lease 1919.

21. Vanessa Bell, *The Open Door*, oils on board, 1926, one of the many images she painted of Charleston farmhouse and its garden.

22. Vita Sackville-West in her garden at Long Barn, Sevenoaks, as she was when she met Virginia Woolf and became Orlando.

23. Knole, the Sackville family home in Kent, the Brown Gallery filled with portraits of Elizabethan notables – the historic setting for *Orlando*.

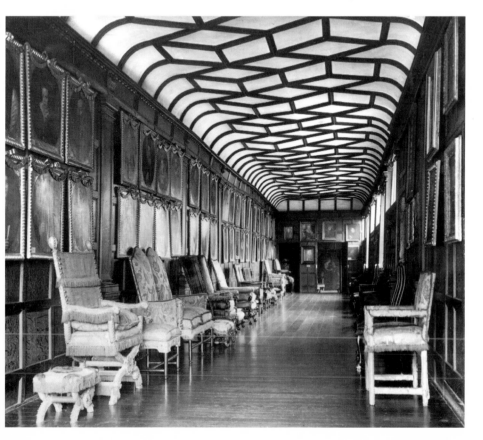

24. The Abinger Pageant, 1934, E.M. Forster and Dr Ralph Vaughan Williams – Forster said that R.V.W. looked like a wily cattle dealer getting the better of a simple rustic (himself).

25. L.P. Hartley (in the light suit) and his father at the entrance to Fletton Tower, with the directors of the Whittlesea Central Brick Company and their presentation on Harry Hartley's retirement.

26. Rex Whistler, *Conversation at the Daye House*: left to right, Edith Olivier, Lord David Cecil, Lady Ottoline Morrell and the artist; Hartley longed to be part of this world but was kept at the fringes.

27. Left to right, Carrington, Saxon Sydney Turner, Ralph Partridge, Lytton Strachey: Sunday morning at Ham Spray, 1929.

28. L.P. Hartley after receiving his CBE at Buckingham Palace, photographed by Mary Wellesley.

even in this remote corner of England. Whittlesey, to most of England, was in a foreign country, the first undeniably fenland town east of Peterborough, caught between the washes or flood channels of the partially tamed river Nene and the leams, dykes and drains of the flat black fields that chequered the country to Ramsey and the southern horizon. Whittlesey was on the edge of nowhere.

In the 1890s it was impoverished, grey and murky; a spirited and prosperous past was yielding to a dusty future as a centre of brickmaking. Whittlesey had centuries of watery prosperity based upon fishing and fowling and lucrative markets for eels, geese and heavy horses, mostly by virtue of its neighbouring and vast inland sea, or Whittlesey Mere. The Revd Charles Kingsley recalled its glories:

But grand enough it was, when backed by Caistor Hanglands and Holme Wood and the patches of the primeval forest; while dark-green alders, and pale-green reeds, stretched for miles round the broad lagoon, where the coot clanked, and the bittern boomed, and the sedge-bird, not content with its own sweet song, mocked the notes of all the birds around; while high overhead hung, motionless, hawk beyond hawk, buzzard beyond buzzard, kite beyond kite, as far as eye could see. Far off, upon the silver mere, would rise a puff of smoke from a punt, invisible from its flatness and white paint. Then down the wind came the boom of the great stanchion-gun; and after that sound, another sound, louder as it neared; a cry as of all the bells of Cambridge and all the hounds of Cottesmore; and overhead rushed and whirled the skein of terrified wildfowl, screaming, piping, clacking, croaking – filling the air with the hoarse rattle of their wings.[3]

Streets of substantial late Georgian houses testify to Whittlesey's heyday, as a 'seaside' and sailing resort, before the Mere was drained and the water gave way to the salt-laden flats where peat- and reed-cutting were the only immediate reward. The 1890s was a low point: the general agricultural depression thickened the gloom of the fen fogs, the dank airs and endemic agues – the curse of the dreaded 'miasma', the silent death rising from the stagnant waters – and forced reliance upon the white opium poppies that were grown in almost every garden. Whittlesey was a ghost of its former self, dream-walking into the next boom-time, brought about by the realization of the brickmaking properties of the lower Oxford clay, 'the clay that burns', unknowing and perhaps uncaring that the noxious dusts and relentless hammering of heavy lorries thundering through fifty years of industry would reduce the little town to a kind of ugly, living fragment of Pompeii. (A fate from which it is only now recovering.) In later life, L. P. Hartley, who so loved beauty in places and things, seemingly pushed doomed little Whittlesey out of his life, not entirely for its fenland obscurity, but more because his father had been enmeshed in its fate.

Back in the late 1890s in the rooms above the bank, the young mother Bessie Hartley, whose faith in the natural superiority of men had gushed into an obsession with her baby son, feared for his health (their daughter Enid could take her chance) from the dread 'miasma' – and the croups, asthmas and endemic malaria that were the lot of young children. Harry Hartley was a clever solicitor in his thirties, in charge of the Whittlesey branch of his principal's firm based in Cathedral Square in Peterborough: 'Could Harry not get a transfer for the sake of their son's health?' Bessie urged. Harry Hartley was in the right profession and place for a landscape of changing values – he had already become a director of the Whittlesey Central Brick Company (the foundation of the family's comfortable circumstances for the next ninety years) and in 1900 one of his clients, the Keeble family, needing to liquefy some assets, offered him their mortgage on a large house, the Victorian gothic Fletton Tower. Fletton was the southern suburb of Peterborough which would give its name to the Oxford clay brick, and from where the limitless acreages of pits, yards, kilns and chimneys would rise to feed the building booms of twentieth-century Britain.[4]

Fletton Tower belonged to an older Fletton, a rather comfortable community of tree-lined avenues and villas less than ten minutes' brisk walk from Peterborough's great Norman cathedral via the Town Bridge over the Nene and across the railway lines. This walk into town presented Edwardian Peterborough in its most pleasant light, the punts and skiffs clustering by the river bank, and the long, broad vista of Bridge Street, fringed with trees and the tradesmen's awnings, and narrowing to its closing by the cathedral's spires and the heart of everything, Cathedral Square, where the market huddled twice weekly around the Jacobean market hall. Fletton Tower represented the height of provincial achievement; it had been built in the 1840s for William Lawrence, Clerk of the Peace for the Liberty of Peterborough, and in style and crenellations it was strikingly similar to the city's gaol, later the Sessions House, in Thorpe Road, built in 1842, also 'for' Clerk Lawrence. The gaol was picturesquely designed by the Gilbertian-sounding W. J. Donthorn (*c.* 1799–1850), whose more usually credited works are Highcliffe Castle and the Leicester Column at Holkham Hall in Norfolk. History does not record that Mr Donthorn also designed Fletton Tower, a rather low-rise castle of two storeys with a three-storey central tower, sporting a billiard room and library as well as the usual count of sitting- and eating-rooms, eight large bedrooms and staff quarters, stables and outhouses all set in a large perfectly flat garden, walled in with trees and shrubs. In the sixty years of its existence Fletton Tower had been changed from an isolated grandeur to something of a cuckoo in the nest of villa-lined streets, with the Queen's Walk and the Palmerston Arms, neat respectability, clustering at its gates. The Hartleys settled in, and their third and last child, Annie Norah, was born there on 17 September 1903: Harry Hartley completed his legal acquisition of the Tower in 1908 and it was as if it had always been an ancestral home. Of course it wasn't ancestral at all, it was a well-built sham, *nouveau-riche* gothic with fake Tudor staircase of shiny wood overtopped by a panelled ceiling with imaginary armorials in the cusps. The Hartleys must have rattled around at first, but Harry Hartley soon amassed standing and substance in the Peterborough hierarchy as a solicitor and pillar of the community, and pretty little Bessie Hartley simpered and manipulated him along the road to almost half a century of married bliss.

Here Leslie Hartley grew up, in the comfortable shadow of his elder sister Enid, strong in looks and character and much braver about everything than he was, with little Norah trailing along behind. The three were marooned in a fairy-tale life; their garden was so large that they never needed to go out for a walk, and governesses and a tutor for Leslie came in. When they left home they drove down the long tree-lined drive to the Oundle Road, and the aproned little girls from the villas and their brothers with hoops and rollerskates stared in disbelief as the grand children from the Tower passed by. Leslie, who at first looked like Little Lord Fauntleroy, with ringlets and velveteen skirts, progressed into his mother's 'little man' in a sailor suit; he had a plump, pouty face and dark, self-satisfied eyes that held little humour. When their father stood his ground and was harsh, Bessie Hartley ran to her son in tears to complain and seek comfort; Leslie was highly intelligent and not a little perplexed at the mysteries of his women-ridden world. He grew up with the conviction that one day he would find friends like himself, but that they were certainly not going to be in Peterborough.

His ambivalent feelings about Fletton Tower were in contrast to his real love for the other places in his young life – his mother's family home near Crowland, in the Holland division of Lincolnshire, the farm where his father had been brought up at Alwalton, west of Peterborough, and Hunstanton, on the north Norfolk coast, where the family went for an annual seaside holiday. Hunstanton was to be immortalized as Anchorstone in the *Eustace and Hilda* trilogy. All these places he loved, but all betrayed him, or so he thought.

It was the gradual betrayal of growing up, and at Alwalton perhaps it was the worst of all. Leslie's father had been brought up by his uncle John Poles, who lived at Lynch Farm, a big sprawl of distinguished and ancient stone buildings beside the river Nene. Here was a countryside that could match any in England: the liltingly beautiful river meandered lazily through wide water-meadows, and hills rose gently on the horizon – this was most emphatically not the Fens, it was Northamptonshire, and it was (and is) deliciously lovely. Alwalton Lynch, the long river cliff that once yielded the polishable limestone known as Alwalton marble, used for church ornament, accompanied the river between Lynch Farm and the Fitzwilliams' Alwalton Hall and was the local beauty spot, the subject of a thousand picture postcards. Young and old came out from Peterborough on the train to spend Sunday afternoons at the Lynch, and it was one of the first places that the young Leslie Hartley discovered for himself; he loved watching the birds, collecting wild flowers and perhaps peeping through the willows at the lovers – observing the mysterious 'canoodling' that young Leo Colston, *The Go-Between*, did not at first understand. Leslie loved the ambience of Lynch Farm, reputedly built out of stone from the Dryden family mansion at Chesterton nearby; he loved the superiority of belonging somewhere that so many others admired as merely passers-by, and the well-run

plenteousness of the farmhouse pleased him. Most of all he loved
the smells and curiosities of the barns, carriage houses, stables and
milking parlours, where the animals and people going about their
age-old occupations appealed to his sense of history. His uncle,
John Poles, was an important man: the boy could see how orders
were obeyed, how hats were doffed and gates opened as he rode
with his uncle across the meadows to the elegant early-eighteenth-
century stone bridge at the ancient river crossing of Gunwade
Ferry, and up the drive past the sloping lawns and big trees of
Milton Park, where John Poles had immediate access to the great
Earl of Fitzwilliam in Milton Hall.★ The young Leslie weaved a
feudal fancy around Milton, his first experience of Elizabethan
battlements and the legacy of great architects striding down the
centuries, Flitcroft's Palladian south front, Talman's monumental
stables, John Carr of York's 'Adamish' libraries and Chambers's
Peterborough Dining Room with its diagonally trellised armorial
ceiling (all of which contributed in part to his fictional
Anchorstone Hall). He was overwhelmed by the Milton landau
with cockaded coachman and liveried footmen, who scattered
coins to the children who opened the Ferry Bridge gate at milady's
approach (another unbelievably feudal picture, put into *The Go-
Between*). How much of a shock therefore was it to discover his
misunderstanding, that his uncle's grand involvement in farms and
acreages, in river keeping, agricultural shows and the famous
Fitzwilliam Foxhounds, had led him into false fantasies, that his
magnificent uncle John Poles was Lord Fitzwilliam's steward, not
his friend and fellow, but his servant. The fact that the Poles and
Hartleys had formed a noble line of stewards to Fitzwilliam estates,
travelling up and down the Great North Road from Wentworth

★ William Thomas Spencer Wentworth, 6th Earl Fitzwilliam in the Irish
Creation, 4th in the English (1815–1902).

Woodhouse and their native Yorkshire, to Milton, did not count in Leslie's eyes. Alwalton and the Milton glories were scarred by servitude.

Harry Hartley could not have remotely conceived his son's snobbish disappointment over the situation at Lynch Farm, for as a young man he had plunged with alacrity into the social world of John Poles, of farming society, local cricket and Liberal politics – the society that led him to meet Leslie's mother, who was one of the six children of another stalwart farming figure, William James Thompson, of St James's Lodge near Crowland. Bessie had her own social pride: it was quite something to be one of the Miss Thompsons, buying ribbons on market day in Crowland, where everyone knew who she was, patriarch Thompson being a JP for the proud Holland division of Lincolnshire, a member of the Peterborough Board of Guardians, a good-works society, and master of several farms – a familiar figure driving his dog-cart or the smarter wagonette. Leslie enjoyed the train journey, on the Great Eastern branch line going through to Wisbech and King's Lynn (and eventually Hunstanton, once a year) – but for St James's Lodge they alighted at Eye, by the brickworks, where the wagonette met them, bowling northwards along the straight road to Crowland. Leslie rather liked the sponginess of the fenland roads, raised above fields and dykes with a precarious uncertainty: he was perfectly accurate in remembering how the straightness of the Eye to Crowland road suddenly kinks to the right, bringing the tower and squat spire of Crowland Abbey into line. Crowland fascinated the young Leslie, enough for him to make a study of it – the chequered history of the eighth-century abbey, the curious late-fourteenth-century three-arched bridge to span both rivers Welland and Nene, the companionable clustering of cottages and houses along wide streets and around greens, buildings that look innocent of much more than 200 years of habitation but harboured hearts and timbers from ancient days. St James's Lodge was out on Great Postland fen, about a mile and a half east of Crowland. Here the flat land was carved into rectangles by the dykes and ditches; one could see for miles, the land dotted with windmills but treeless, for trees were the signs of prosperous settlement, the clustering shelter belts around the old farmhouses. This was the oldest and most prosperous part of the fens, from the earliest draining of the Great North Level, and it had, even almost a century ago, a settled dignity. St James's Lodge, a big square pale brick eighteenth-century house, was typical of its kind, standing in its large garden, all protected by layers of privet, laurels, ilex and cedars, and a screen of poplars inhabited by a crowd of clamorous rooks. The rookeries, so common in the fens, were to haunt Leslie Hartley; he grew into a clever but invariably bored schoolboy, who felt himself in an alien land, rather like the Scots pine in the St James's garden, which he felt was also out of place, keeping up Scots traditions in a Sassenach land. He would wander around the garden – across the lawn not quite large enough for tennis, past the flower borders to the fruit garden where the bees hummed; with apples turning rosy faces to the July sun he felt a momentary pride, as the young man of the family, the inheritor of all this. This feeling, which came more strongly in the well-kept vegetable garden, was some compensation for the loneliness of the school holidays; the walled kitchen garden gave way to another, surrounded by a hedge, less tidy, with stalks tumbling this way and that – the apotheosis of the cabbage and its kind. So much greenery waiting to be eaten by someone, all this fetid veg-etableness – it was only a game of pretend to pass his hours, he wouldn't want a fenland cabbage patch anyway.[5]

Not wanting to be a fenland farmer for anything relieved him of all responsibility for his maternal grandparents' fate. Leslie enjoyed his farming expeditions with Grandfather Thompson –

'Besides laughing himself, he liked to make *me* laugh,' was a confession of rare pleasure. Leslie's (fictional) voice continued:

As I told you, the drains and dykes in the Fens moved in slow motion, if they moved at all . . . but there was one break in the water-torpor . . . a tributary was nearly always dammed up by a sluice, or slacker as we called it; a black wooden construction, worked by a winch, and evil-looking, like a guillotine . . . sometimes in wet weather it was raised, letting the imprisoned water gush out into the drain . . . This rare spectacle always excited me . . . my grandfather . . . would laugh uncontrollably and say, 'The mighty Niagara!'[6]

Only the comment made it so funny: perhaps patriarch Thompson was releasing the tension of the fenland farmer's reliance on 'slackers' and drains, on the legends of Morton's Leam, the Adventurers, the Bedford levels and Cornelius Vermuyden – the whole panoply of winning land from water that haunted his life. Leslie took to heart 'what the farmers were up against. *Failure*. It meant much more than the ordinary failure which each of us now dreads – not being able to fulfil ourselves, or our promise . . . It meant, besides financial ruin, a stigma . . . *suicide*, literally. They couldn't face the shame of it, for themselves or their relations.'[7] No, a fenland 'cabbage patch' was *not* for him.

For Leslie, as for Eustace Cherrington, his pinnacle was to go to a school in the south of England; for fictional Eustace it was to be Broadstairs, for Leslie it was Cliftonville, and then on to Harrow. He left behind, this increasingly snobbish schoolboy, one of the most, if not the most endearing small boys in literature, and he fixed his annual seaside holidays at Hunstanton on the map of mythology. Hunstanton, like all the best seaside places, allowed the thrill of expectation – as the train wound out from King's Lynn, through Sandringham pines and rhododendrons (it seemed the royals had brought their Surrey with them), there was that distant certainty of the blue sea. Whatever the weather inland, Hunstanton could so often be bathed in sun, under breezy blue sky. A clustered little town, with sandy beaches, it extends the treasure of being beside the sea all along the wide green lawns on top of the striped cliffs, to Old Hunstanton, with its lighthouse and paths along the dunes. This was the setting for Eustace and his elder and far more wonderful sister, Hilda; Eustace introduces himself via the smoothest inner-boy monologue in faultless prose with never a jarring adjective. 'Here was another complication . . .': Eustace's being was full of them, the momentary and critical one being that Hilda had the iron spade and he was left with the wooden one: well, that was how it was. Eustace (would it were Leslie Hartley?) – a small and rather feeble acolyte, not incapable of sparks of heroism, has his blue woollen jumper riding up in ungainly woolly folds and so a gap around his middle, baggy pants and one sock falling down; his plimsolls are wet (the worst crime). Hilda dares him to speak to the veiled and mysterious Miss Fothergill in her wheelchair, and so he is invited to Laburnum Lodge to tea and piquet. Here the real Leslie emerges, as among the pictures, ornaments and gentility he finds 'the self that he liked best'; Leslie/Eustace again relishes the idea of being an heir, for Miss Fothergill dies, leaving him an inheritance to send him to school and Oxford. Hartley needed no inheritance, but adored the idea of being special. Harry Hartley's brick investments saw to it that Leslie wanted for nothing, and had no need to work at all.

The best of Leslie Hartley is in *The Shrimp and the Anemone* – the interior monologues, the emotional journeying: a triumph of story-telling and place-making, celebrating the seaside holiday and the glories and wriggling discomforts of wet sand in everything. Miss Fothergill is a stepping-stone to the paradise on the

Hunstanton horizon, Hunstanton Old Hall, magnificently and genuinely ancient and baronial, the home of the (fictional) Staveleys, the dashing, heroic and likeable Dick, and Nancy, his cold-hearted and beautiful sister, to whom Eustace is enslaved, with whom he 'elopes' on a paper chase with the outcome of an overtaxed heart and bed for a week. He ends, where he belongs, with Hilda, marking out the beach as their entire world, promising her half his inheritance, and they gallop home, their ankles tied together three-legged, laughing and tumbling all the way.

The boy on his seaside holidays, Eustace Cherrington, rings too truly for any novelist's invention, and Hartley has presented us with the boy he believed himself to have been. After Eustace, with his wooden spade, the juggling begins, and Leslie/Eustace disappears into a gauzy tangle of fragments of people and places, where it is impossible to follow him and he justifies his own repeated protestation that his words and their characters do not reflect his real life. His books all carried that warning proviso: 'All the characters in this book are fictitious and are not intended to represent any actual persons living or dead.'* *The Shrimp and the Anemone* was dedicated to Osbert Sitwell (Hartley's friend and supporter at the time – 1944) and to 'K.A.L.', his aunt at Alwalton, Kathleen Lund. The heroine, Hilda Cherrington, has been located as a mix of Kathleen Lund and his elder sister, Enid Hartley. The real Hartley cut himself off from the continuing entanglements of Eustace, in the two following novels, simply removing himself from his family at Fletton Tower, and seeing them only on sufferance. His excuse was that he felt as if he had done something wrong in the eyes of his father, Harry Hartley. It seems rather the reverse, that Leslie himself rebuked the rather ridiculous Victorian

---

* Hartley always used this phrase in the preliminary pages to his novels, with greater emphasis than the then usual legal proviso.

gothic Fletton Tower and the brick company investments and only wanted to be the heir to something more noble and refined. His father's crime was not to be a bona fide Fitzwilliam, with an ancient pile. The question of inheritance is one of Hartley's repeated themes: he makes it quite clear that be it a picture, a vase, or a house, the source from whom the legacy comes is the most critical factor.

The war intervened for Leslie between Harrow and Oxford: he was unfit for the battlefields, but made a handsome figure, tall, dark-eyed, mustachioed, in his officer's uniform. His was a desk war – something to do with the army's postal service (which gave him a lifelong curiosity for other people's letters),★ but cast him as a spectator of the bravura and inevitable sufferings of others. (Eustace Cherrington in *The Sixth Heaven* has a desk war too: his hero, Dick Staveley from Anchorstone Hall, true to character, wins an MC, and afterwards becomes a handsome, reckless Conservative MP with tendencies to Fascism, in Oswald Mosley mode.) The misery of the war, and his own 'failure' in not becoming a hero, contributed to Leslie's increasingly rueful, sardonic view of life: there would be good reasons for supposing that his 'foreign country' of the past was now out of reach, beyond the hideous curtain of 1914–18. His immediate reaction was to hope that his delayed arrival at Oxford would mean a fresh start.

Leslie, at post-war Balliol with lots of young men of disparate ages, had the most critical meeting of his life one day in 1919 in the High Street: 'Probably we had met before, but although I did not know him, or he me, we recognized in each other what I like to think was a kindred spirit and a friendship began.'[9] His meeting

---

★ Adrian Wright in his biography[8] quotes David Horner to Christabel Aberconway on Hartley's habit of 'creeping into bedrooms and writing-rooms to read all one's letters, inspect one's clothes'.

was with Lord David Cecil, fourth child and younger son of the fourth Marquis of Salisbury of Hatfield House. Apparently Lord David 'held a torch – not for war heroes, or anti-war heroes, but for people who led quiet lives, studious and sociable, into which the idea of violence never entered'.[10] Hartley must have fulfilled this qualification: Lord David, thin, elegant, faintly dandified, ascetic, chattering in a staccato way, loving an audience (Hartley must have been that too), was . . . well, he was a Cecil, a scion of a tribe who had ruled England for aeons; did not the Cecil spires and pinnacles of Burghley House and Burghley acres shine out across the fens, were they not greater than the Fitzwilliams, were the Hatfield branch in their Tudor palace not even more aristocratic and distinguished? . . . Hartley had found his true milieu at last.

Oxford, having bestowed Lord David's friendship, with attendant visits to Cranborne and Hatfield (and Lord David photographed looking a little perplexed in the doorway of Fletton Tower), continued in her blessings. Hartley was already writing short stories and he was made co-editor of the *Oxford Outlook*, which gave him contacts with other writers – Charles Morgan, Edmund Blunden, L. A. G. Strong and St Loe Strachey, Lytton Strachey's cousin, who owned and edited the *Spectator*. A Balliol friend, Aldous Huxley, took him out to Garsington one summer afternoon in 1920 – Hartley was awestruck by Ottoline Morrell, dressed in flowered black satin over a peacock blue skirt, with white stockings and her familiar red morocco shoes, cross-gartered in the fashion. He was overwhelmed by her interest in him, her graciousness – besotted in fact – and dismissive of the 'unfortunate' Philip Morrell, convinced that Ottoline had married beneath her. He continued to pay court at Garsington, meeting E. M. Forster or Siegfried Sassoon, or almost anyone he wished: on one afternoon, with thirty-seven to tea, Virginia Woolf recorded her verdict on Hartley's friends:

Lord David is a pretty boy. Puffin Asquith an ugly one . . . Sackville West reminded me of a peevish shopgirl. They all have the same clipped quick speech and politeness, and total insignificance. Yet we asked Lord David and Puff to write for the Nation, and also a dull fat man called Hartley.[11]

Hartley left Oxford with a second class degree in modern history; he was soon reviewing for the *Spectator*, he did contribute to the *Nation*, and then went on to the *Saturday Review*, not bad progress for a young man who did not need to earn his living. He wrote home of his doings and his grand friends, but went home less and less: his younger sister Norah had come up to St Hilda's and taken her degree in English in 1925 – she made up her mind that what she wanted to do was breed dogs, which she was to do for almost seventy years!

A curiosity of Hartley's wishing to have as little as possible to do with his background led to a minor landmark in literary history. Edmund Blunden had returned to Oxford also in 1919, after a very different kind of war to Hartley's. Blunden was married, to Mary Daines, a Suffolk girl who had once served him drinks in the White Hart Hotel in Newmarket. He had never forgotten, or really left, the countryside of his childhood, the water-meadows of the Medway tributaries at Yalding in Kent, and their wild flowers, the country traditions and the village cricket, all of which contributed to his love for the rurally beautiful Mary. Their first child, a daughter named Joy, had died in the summer of 1919; Mary was pregnant again and puzzled as to why Edmund needed to chase his Oxford degree and literary fame; he knew that he needed a speedy victory. Whether he had discussed John Clare with Leslie Hartley or not, Blunden found out that there was a mass of Clare's papers in Peterborough, held by the Peterborough Natural History, Scientific and Archaeological Society (of which Harry Hartley was a leading light). So Blunden devoted three weeks of his Easter vacation to the cache – the 'kindly, rosy-faced and mildly surprised' J. W. Bodger of Peterborough Museum unlocked the cupboard and a mass of papers spilled out, the legacy of Clare's wife's family that no one had taken the slightest interest in before. Blunden spent 'three weeks of happy insanity'[12] copying out poems, his identification with Clare growing all the time. Clare's watery landscape on the edge of the fens at Helpston (those same fields that Leslie had wandered from Alwalton), a common love of the rural scene, the same mixed urges to guilt and endeavour over love of a woman named Mary – all combined into Edmund Blunden's literary coup, his first 'real discovery'.

Nothing demonstrates more clearly how Leslie Hartley abandoned his despised home countryside and all its treasures than the way Blunden stepped in: he visited the Hartleys at Fletton Tower while he was in Peterborough – which he saw as 'Bruges-like' in parts – and found Harry Hartley the most sympathetic, over the lost local hero Clare reinstated, and over their joint passion for cricket. It is Harry Hartley, clutching his trilby, who stands in the front rank of local worthies photographed on 26 May 1921, at the unveiling of a commemorative plaque on the cottage in Helpston where Clare was born, and Blunden who gave the memorial address. Blunden's publication of the Clare manuscript poems launched his own career.[13]★ Leslie Hartley always complained that he felt he had done something wrong in his father's eyes – this could have had a million sources, he did not play cricket, was not good at any game, he did not marry and take on ancestral Fletton Tower; but might there also have been a great disappointment in the old man's mind that Leslie ignored this Alwalton past, from

★ The Clare MSS at Peterborough are still being worked on, some eighty years later, for the Oxford University Press editions under the general editorship of Eric Robinson.

where Harry Hartley himself had been launched to his own successful status – at least as a big fish in the Peterborough pond? Leslie, harbouring that heartache about the servitude of his family to the Fitzwilliams, missed great treasures – not only that a world-class (for so Blunden made Clare) poet could rise wondrously from those very fields and hovels that he encountered on his drives with his uncle John Poles, but that Clare could survive even a year as a garden boy at Burghley under a brutal master of the kitchen garden, the lowest speck in the Cecils' world, to be fêted in London literary circles – of course Leslie was not interested. He also missed (as did Blunden) the excitement of Clare's archaeological friendship with Edmund Artis, the Fitzwilliams' steward – a lineal antecedent of John Poles – and Artis's excavation of the buildings of Roman Durobrivae, the Nene valley pottery town that lies beneath the Fitzwilliams' fields.[14]

The Blundens also fell on another story which might have intrigued Hartley: while they were staying at the Bull Hotel in Peterborough they chanced upon a scandal of such proportions as to shock the cathedral city out of its Trollopian ease. A great preacher, Archdeacon John Wakeford of Salisbury, was in the hotel at the same time (though why not at the Deanery? or the Bishop's Palace?), and shortly afterwards was up before a Consistory Court accused of having slept with a young lady there. The Blundens were called as witnesses for the Archdeacon's defence, for it seemed likely that a waitress had confused memories, in that Mary Blunden was not wearing her wedding ring, her finger being too thin to keep it on, and Edmund told her to keep her hand out of sight: the case turned on whether the waitress had confused Blunden and the Archdeacon. The Blundens were staunch in their support, Edmund wrote of the priest's innocence in the *Nation*, Mary set up a fund for him, but all to no avail. Archdeacon Wakeford was disgraced.

In another small and rather interior way, Blunden and Hartley were alike: they both had formed an allegiance to a river god, as Blunden freely admitted for himself, and as he noticed of Hartley. As a break from Clare's manuscripts, Blunden recalled, 'another day Leslie took us along the Nene (Clare's river) to his swimming-pool, the Forty-Foot. How icy that water was; but the novelist was in before us; comfortably, and it seemed warmly, beating along over the shoals of immemorial bream who obviously owned those deeps.'[15] Hartley would not have discussed this bond; no more would he have talked to Virginia Woolf for long enough to discover their fellowship of the seashore. For Leslie Hartley seemed to have put away his humanity with the whole background that he so disdained: he wanted nothing from the Hartleys of Fletton Tower, except his allowance. At the Tower Harry and Bessie Hartley missed him – Harry was inclined to let him go his own way, Bessie desperately wanted to be part of Leslie's life. Undoubtedly if they had lived in Gloucestershire he would have been more sociable.

Like so many of those Americans, Henry James, Edith Wharton and John Singer Sargent, who liked themselves so much more when they lived in Europe, Hartley was so completely shorn of his background that he too had to borrow another. His literary ambitions were rather Jamesian too – he needed contessas and rich widows, and so he rented himself an enviable apartment in that refuge of all dejected souls, Venice. It was excessively comfortable and looked out on to a quiet side canal: with the lease came 'a sumptuous gondola adorned with gilt and turkey carpets and a handsome gondolier'.[16] His novella *Simonetta Perkins* is a rather bitter tragedy of manners, among fading aristocrats and handsome gondoliers. Although Hartley was fast becoming unattractive himself – growing fat and balding, and paunchy for his sedentary lifestyle – his Venetian address was of appeal to a number of pleasing friends: Cynthia Asquith, Osbert and Edith Sitwell, and Lord David Cecil. Hartley had woven a fantasy around Lord David, whom he perhaps saw as an *Orlando* figure, hoping that if he wished hard enough Lord David would become a woman, and still be his close friend, perhaps even his wife? Hartley's possessiveness caused suspicion and disapproval among all their friends; it was a Lytton Strachey and Carrington variation: a provincial upstart, for all he could be both pleasant and generous, had laid hands upon their 'fairy prince' – for so Lord David, pale and interesting, dressing in romantic clothes, stuttering and dithering like an amusing and precocious child, with the head of a young god, seemed to everyone. Their friendship seemed at its closest in the early thirties, when Lord David enjoyed having a Venetian retreat, and apparently loved spending fine afternoons out on the lagoon, reading Keats aloud. Hartley's possessiveness was of deep concern to Desmond MacCarthy, who knew that his lovely daughter Rachel, the star of Ham Spray theatricals, was very much in love with Lord David. Desmond MacCarthy's chief confidante was Lady Cynthia Asquith, also a 'friend' of Hartley's – 'a great comfort to me when I worried about her possible– probable disappointment . . . and it would have been through you that I would have tried to disentangle her – at the cost of I'm afraid deep pain.'[17] Never has poor Leslie seemed more of an outsider: he wrote only once of the complete mutual trust and happiness of love – 'Together-ness – how well the Latins under-stand it' – in Italy, in *Poor Clare*.[18] While Lord David lingered in Venice, Rachel plied him with letters on the charms of England; Leslie was in his seventh heaven; Desmond MacCarthy to Lady Cynthia again: 'On the whole I thought it likely that she would have to go without David,' he wrote. Then, on a hot Tuesday evening in the summer of 1932, MacCarthy walked home to Wellington Square to find Lord David there: 'I am surprised to see you. I thought you were in Italy,' said MacCarthy. 'Yes I was,' replied Lord David, 'and I've another surprise for you. I'm going to marry Rachel.'[19] This is all the evidence that remains to explain that Hartley suffered a shattering blow, a betrayal of some kind, at this time, and the pain remained with him for the rest of his life. Perhaps it was the blow that sent him scurrying down the lanes of memory, to that foreign country of the past, where he found his other, fictional self, Eustace Cherrington.

He gave up his Venice palazzo apartment and settled back in England in advance of the war. In memory of Alwalton and the sleepy meanders of the Nene, his priority was a house by a river, and the river was of most importance. He rented Court House at Lower Woodford, in that exquisite stretch of the Avon valley just north of Salisbury. Here he was tactically placed, between David and Rachel Cecil settled at Rockbourne, and their circle, which included Cecil Beaton at Ashcombe, Edith Olivier at Wilton (a cousin slightly removed of the Oliviers at Limpsfield), and her young protégés, Laurence and Rex Whistler, all passing to visit Stephen Tennant at Wilsford, just north of Lower Woodford. Rex Whistler painted a conversation piece of himself, Lady Ottoline Morrell – in a picture hat with tulle drapes – Lord David and Edith Olivier in her elegant sitting-room at the Daye House in Wilton's park: somehow Leslie Hartley would not have fitted in.★ Indeed, it is hard to imagine how his rather doleful and unkempt presence – Leslie never seemed to deviate from a crumpled suit and shirtsleeves, with or without a woollen pullover – fitted in with any of these vivacious and exotic young people. Yet again he was an outsider, a voyeur at their games.

In the summer of 1941, he moved to the Cecils' West Hayes at

★ This conversation piece later appeared as the frontispiece in Edith Olivier, *Without Knowing Mr Walkley* (1937).

Rockbourne, which he rented for the remainder of the war. (The Cecils were in London or Oxford, escaping to Ham Spray for long weekends, where Ralph Partridge, now married to Frances Marshall, kept open house.) Leslie was very happy at Rockbourne, both in Lord David's house and in the village community, where he felt he made many friends – who regarded him, warmly, as Lord David's friend. He saw *The Shrimp and the Anemone* into print there (1944) and wrote *The Sixth Heaven*: Eustace has grown into an undergraduate at Oxford. There he meets his boyhood hero again, Dick Staveley MC, MP, by now, and he and Hilda are invited to Anchorstone Hall as bona fide guests – in fact Dick and Hilda's escapade in his aeroplane to Holland seems the seal of acceptance. Anchorstone Hall shifts from the Fitzwilliams' Milton to look very like the Cecils' Hatfield House. In the third volume, *Eustace and Hilda* (1947), Eustace, now a literary fellow, discovers Italy: Hartley includes a rather wonderful figure, Lady Nelly, a hybrid of Ottoline and perhaps Lady Ida Sitwell, as coal mines in Derbyshire are mentioned. These three works, a trilogy, are Eustace Cherrington's biography. Having completed that one life, Leslie Hartley began a series of others: in his own he bought an eighteenth-century house, Avondale, in Bathford, near Bath. The Avon flowed through his garden, and it was almost as far from Fletton Tower as it was possible to be in England.

Hartley and Morgan Forster were wary of each other; Hartley recalled that once they were at the same Garsington party and he skulked in the bushes, fearful of finding himself in Forster's next novel. It was an empty fear. With *A Passage to India*, which was published in the summer of 1924, Forster's spate of novel-writing came to an end. With a geographical neatness, life on the astral plain of Weybridge ended too, with the death of his aunt Laura Forster, who left Morgan her house, the house that his father,

Eddie Forster, had built, West Hackhurst at Abinger Hammer. His mother did not want to leave suburbia, but was eventually persuaded – and, as history repeating itself, mother and son once more packed their belongings, including the mahogany 'knick-knack' fire surround from Rooksnest, and took themselves to the country. Well, not entirely. Morgan, aged forty-five, made a bid for some freedom by taking himself a flat at 27 Brunswick Square in Bloomsbury, in the house belonging to Frances Marshall's mother, so that he could have some social life of his own.

The association with Abinger was to attach itself to Morgan Forster, with *Abinger Harvest*, a collection of essays published in 1936, and the Abinger edition of his works. West Hackhurst, which somehow melds itself into the vision of Howards End, was much prettier than Rooksnest: deep-roofed, tall-chimneyed, tile-hung, with a tiled rooflet over the big sitting-room bay window and garden door, and a herringbone brickwork terrace for sitting in the sun and enjoying the view. The view, southward over the village of Abinger Hammer, over the roofs of the roadside cottages, across the immortal A25, the Dorking to Guildford road, to the Tillingbourne and the cricket green at the corner of the lane to Felday, the old name for Holmbury St Mary. Abinger Hammer, named for the hammer ponds of its iron-working past, was one of three Abingers, in the elongated parish that stretched from the scarp of the North Downs, behind West Hackhurst, and southwards through the valley fields and woodlands to the sandstone hills of Pitch, Holmbury and Leith on the Sussex rim. This – despite the newcomer Lord Farrer at Abinger Hall (where Lily Forster had once been companion to Ida Farrer), next door to West Hackhurst – was Evelyn country. The family of the diarist John Evelyn (merely a younger son) had ruled their farms, woods and gunpowder mills along the Tillingbourne, from Wotton House, since the days of Elizabeth I (and still do). Felday Lane wound through the heart of Evelyn territory, to Sutton Abinger, Abinger Common and Holmbury St Mary – the latter already purloined by Forster as the home of the Honeychurches in *A Room with a View*. Forster had explained how Lucy Honeychurch's father, 'a prosperous local solicitor', had been one of the firstcomers; another was the painter Richard Redgrave, from the house opposite the Stephens in Hyde Park Gate, who had first come to Abinger Common in the 1850s and was to think no other place so restful or so paint-worthy. Indeed, it was lovely, perhaps from centuries of the tree-conscious Evelyns managing their beechwoods, coppices of oak, sweet chestnut and hazel, quarrying their own sandstone for the cottages and houses and honouring the grazing rights on the turf- and flower-covered hills. In the 1870s the architect of the Law Courts in the Strand, George Edmund Street, had built a house for himself, Holmdale, on Holmbury Hill (next to Windy Corner), and paid for the building of Mr Beebe's church, St Mary's on the triangular Felday green: the rectory was beside the green with a few cottages, including the new slate-roofed 'Albert' and 'Cissie' villas, one of which Forster imagined for George Emerson and his father:

It was a Saturday afternoon, gay and brilliant after abundant rains, and the spirit of youth dwelt in it . . . All that was gracious triumphed. As the motor cars passed through Summer Street they raised only a little dust, and their stench was soon dispersed by the wind and replaced by the scent of the wet birches or of the pines. Mr Beebe, at leisure for life's amenities, leant over his rectory-gate

with Lucy's brother, Freddy . . . 'Suppose we go and hinder those new people opposite for a little.' And so they turf out George and, swinging up the lane, find the pond 'set in its little alp of green', with masses of rose-bay willowherb in seed, and aromatic balsam

– here they were tempted to take a dip and were cavorting, naked, when Mrs Honeychurch, Lucy and her prim fiancé, Cecil Vyse, having come round the hill to call on old Mrs Butterworth, found them, prompting one of the most amusing Forsterian scenes.[20]

A Room with a View, written with the insight of the Bob Trevelyans who occupied the Honeychurch house in real life, perfectly captures the rare atmosphere; it had a great deal to do with the heavy influx of prosperous, do-gooding and social people who chose to live at Holmbury and Abinger, the breadwinners commuting to Gomshall or Dorking stations. By the time Forster settled at Abinger Hammer in the mid-twenties, almost every Arts and Crafts architect – the successors of Street and Eddie Forster's master Sir Arthur Blomfield – had built in the area. The very coincidence of people who were willing to pay for Richard Norman Shaw, Voysey, Alfred Powell, Baillie-Scott and Edwin Lutyens to build in the golden sandstone and English oak, with Dorking bricks and Ockley tiles, was a blessing on the countryside: with no planning authorities to persuade them, they had built superbly in context – which is why 'Albert' and 'Cissie' villas of harsh bricks and slated roofs were so despised.[21] The Arts and Crafts philosophy was quickly absorbed into the persons of wives and daughters, or spinsters of independent means who lived here, who were interested in nature, music and education and inserted an inspirational layer in between the patriarchal Evelyns and their cottagers. In many an instance they were Forsterian heroines come alive. Such energies filled the villagers' years with activities, sporting clubs, societies, flower shows and improving entertainments of every kind, of which the high point was the annual Abinger pageant or medieval fair. The year 1934 was an especially good one, with the pageant performed in July, in the natural amphitheatre of the Old Rectory garden, where there was a tulip tree reputedly planted by John 'Sylva' Evelyn: the 1934 pageant was written by Forster, who modestly gives most of the credit to the producer, Tom Harrison, with music by Ralph Vaughan Williams, and the part of the narrator, the Woodman, spoken by Wilfrid Grantham.[22]★

The prologue – after shooing away the sheep from the stage – introduces a 'history of a village lost in the woods' . . . do not expect great histories here . . . 'Lords and ladies, warriors and priests will pass, but this is not their home, they will pass like the leaves in autumn but the trees remain.' The first episode evokes the clashes between Ancient Britons (the neolithic camp on Holmbury Hill), the Romans (a villa site near Abinger Hall), and Saxons (who won a battle over the Danes at Ockley), all smoothed into peaceableness by the Normans (who built St James's church and a motte and bailey at Abinger Manor†). Episode two features King John, who gets a bad press in the Abinger area for raping and pillaging at Paddington manor house (now farm) and who is followed by the local boy who becomes Cardinal-Archbishop Stephen Langton, remembered at Friday Street for saving a lovely young girl from drowning in the big hammer pond. The central episodes – with Vaughan Williams's hymns fading and songs of Merrie England taking their place – celebrated the iron industry, smithing and charcoal-burning, how the trees contributed to the defeat of the Armada and the clashes of the Civil War, all brought to peace once again with the Restoration and the age of John Evelyn. 'Haste to the Wedding', 'Seventeen Come Sunday' and the Surrey folk song 'The Sweet Nightingale' accompany the

★ The producer of the pageant was Tom Harrison or Harrisson, but I have been unable to establish if this was a member of the Harrison family in Abinger Common or Tom Harrisson, soon to be the founder of Mass Observation, who was a friend of the Trevelyans at Holmbury.

† Dr Louis Leakey had not, in 1934, excavated the mesolithic pit dwelling at Abinger Manor, the oldest 'house' in England, which he did in the 1960s.

news that the first larch tree in England was planted at Parkhurst, where another 'queer fish', Jean-Jacques Rousseau, in exile, was also taking refuge. Smugglers and exotic characters from Bulwer-Lytton novels, small boys in the village stocks (carefully preserved with a roof over them outside the church), bring Victorian England into the frame, with some verses from Psalm 84 and 'O God Our Help in Ages Past' sung by the whole company.

Forster's epilogue, spoken by the Woodman, follows in full:

THE EPILOGUE

Houses, houses, houses! You came from them and you must go back to them. Houses and bungalows, hotels, restaurants and flats, arterial roads, by-passes, petrol pumps and pylons – are these going to be England? Are these man's final triumph? Or is there another England, green and eternal, which will outlast them? I cannot tell you, I am only the Woodman, but this land is yours, and you can make it what you will. If you want to ruin our Surrey fields and woodlands it is easy to do, very easy, and if you want to save them they can be saved. Look into your hearts and look into the past, and remember that all this beauty is a gift which you can never replace, which no money can buy, which no cleverness can refashion. You can make a town, you can make a desert, you can even make a garden; but you can never, never make the country, because it was made by Time.

Centuries of life amongst obscure trees and unnoticed fields! That is all our Pageant has tried to show you, and it will end as it began among country sights and sounds. Farewell! and take back its lesson with you to your houses, for it has a lesson. Our village and our woods bid you farewell.

Forster's sentiments had never changed, not since he had said goodbye to Howards End: this, his last cry for England, was targeted carefully. The Abinger audience were villagers whose names had existed in the local records since records began; there were townees who came by charabanc to take lunch and tea at the Abinger Hatch hostelry, and there were the newcomers, the merchant-banking Gibbs from Goddards on the green, the City accountant Waterhouse at Feldermore, the Brookes from Leylands (the Brooke Bond tea family, whose son Justin was close friends with Rupert (no relation) Brooke), the colonial administrators, the pottery Wedgwoods, the Misses Vaughan Williams, Judge Christmas Humphries and countless others of influence. Forster knew that there were plenty of Henry Willcoxes here – who would justify their fortune-making on behalf of wife and children, nice house and looking after their patch of rural peace, defending it from all-comers, or later-comers: equally he knew that though he might wish the feudal system could have lasted for ever, 'social relationships based upon the ownership or occupation of land are at an end'. He debated this subject with Hilton Young, Lord Kennet, in letters in the opening months of the war: 'I love my books as dearly as you can love yours,' protested Morgan, 'but it is typical of us that whereas you should stick in armorial bookplates, I should only write in mine "E.M. Forster, at West Hackhurst." I don't feel *of* any where. I wish I did. It is not that I am déraciné. It is that the soil is being washed away.'[23]

He was 'at West Hackhurst' until the end of the war: Lily Forster died on 11 March 1945, and by the autumn he had cleared out the house and was preparing to leave for Cambridge. He was both surprised and pleased that the village gave him a 'wonderful' farewell party with dancing and games and a commemorative book filled with over 100 names. King's College found an honorary fellowship for him, and rooms to go with it, a sunny sitting-room with big gothic windows in Bodley's Building. His books, his piano and the Rooksnest fire surround and all its ornaments took to the road for the last time. Forster loved being at King's – it must have been the forerunner of one of those mansions with apartments where the elderly can take all their best belongings, be waited upon, and be quiet or sociable as the mood inspires. Once again Cambridge had taken him, soothed and warmed him (though perhaps he was too distinguished to be laughed at now), as she had done to the young 'Rickie', fifty years before.

Leslie Hartley had no such homecoming: settled on the opposite side of England from his native fens, he remained at Bathford, writing and reading, at his happiest in his garden and messing about in a boat on the Avon. Avondale was a tall stone house, comfortable and unpretentious, with the distinction of having once belonged to Dr Oliver, of Bath Oliver biscuit fame. It was (and is) rather too close to the road, but securely walled: Avondale's garden and its stretch of river were to be the solace of the twenty-six years remaining to Hartley's life – they were productive years and the garden and the river were his frequent themes:

Mid-August was a dull time in my garden – the drought had seen to that . . . the Japanese anemones looked like shillings, not half-crowns. Because the garden lay beside the river, and sometimes, in wet seasons, under it, people thought that the subsoil must be moist, but it was not; the rain ran off the steep slope without sinking in, the river drained the ground without irrigating it.

But the river-banks had just been in full glory, two interminable winding borders on which grew willow-weed and loosestrife, the lilac clusters of hemp agrimony, deep yellow ragwort, lemon-yellow chick-weed, the peeling purple of the woody nightshade, the orange drops of the ranunculus, the youthful, tender teazle-cones of palest pink contrasting with their hard, brown, dried-up predecessors of the year before – and, a new comer . . . the tall white balsam.[24]

The balsam, threatening to dominate all the others, is a sinister literary device – as Hartley is not writing a nature study, he leaves it as a threat . . . but continues his river-garden picture. On the river's grey-green surface 'floated the earliest victims of the year's decline, yellow willow leaves tip-tilted like gondolas, that twirled and sported in the breeze'.[25] The garden was long and narrow for its length. From an outward-curving terrace in front of the house he could watch the water – 'a mirror broken here and there by tree-trunks, and darkened by the reflections of the trees on the farther bank; or maybe by the image of a cow, suspended in mid-water upside-down, the shadowy feet seeming almost to touch the real feet'.[26]

It may have been simply the half-century, or perhaps some notion of nostalgia in the preparations for the 1951 Festival of Britain, that made him decide to exploit his treasured memories of his 'enchanted' summer of 1900 for *The Go-Between*:

I wanted to evoke the feeling of that summer, the long stretch of fine weather, and also the confidence in life, the belief that all's well in the world, which everyone enjoyed or seemed to enjoy before the First World War.[27]

Hartley was five years old in 1900; there was a tremendous heatwave, and the talk at Fletton Tower, and even removed to breezy Hunstanton, was of the newspaper headlines: High Court judges were bareheaded – 'it was too hot for wigs' – the troops at Aldershot and the Peterborough omnibus horses were supplied with sunhats, damsons hung so heavily the branches broke on the trees. On 25 July it was 93° Fahrenheit in the shade, and a great thunderstorm broke the weather.[28] Hartley 'never forgot that summer' and its promise – to a five-year-old – of a Golden Age: 'almost literally, for I think of it as being the colour of gold. I didn't want to go back to it, but I wanted it to come back to me, and I still do,' he wrote. So he used the golden wheatfields and sun-browned grasses of the river meadows for the Norfolk setting for Leo Colston, the boy who carries messages between the daughter of the grand house where he is staying, and her farmer-lover. That Leslie Hartley has once again portrayed himself in a setting – an eighteenth-century Palladian mansion this time, and among people who reflected the self he liked best, takes second place to the euphoria of 1900, the new century, a fresh start, and how it all crumbled away. The prefix of the years may change: human nature remains the same.

Hartley's first collection of short stories, *The Travelling Grave*, had appeared in 1951, *The Go-Between* in 1953, and a second collection, *The White Wand*, followed in 1954. From the fifties to the sixties the novels and stories poured as a prolific stream: his reputation was secure, but his relations with his publisher had been stormy: *The Go-Between* was his first book for Hamish Hamilton, who was to remain with him to the end of his life. A rare photograph, taken at his Avondale breakfast table in the 1960s, complete with raffia mats and honeypots, shows a dyspeptic, chinless, portly but pensive elderly man[29] – an image which brings to life another of Hartley's *alter egos*, the distinguished and elderly novelist Richard Mardick, the subject of a supposedly autobio-graphical novel, *The Brickfield*, published in 1964. In this con-fessional novel he paints a barren and unloving picture of Mardick's fenland origins, juggling names unconvincingly (and unnecessarily) – painting a landscape devoid of love, or charm, and reeking of bitterness. Much of *The Brickfield* tells of the young 'Mardick's' love for a neighbour (he uses the neighbouring farm to St James's Lodge on Postland Fen as her home) named Lucy Soames, who is drowned in a flooded brickpit – a loss which has marked his life. (Tragic drownings were all too common in the pits and drains, and the boy Leslie Hartley must have heard these things discussed; whether Lucy Soames had any real-life parallel I do not know.) Mardick dwells at great lengths on the miseries and misunderstandings of his (fictional) life, but rather less for the benefit of the reader than to forward the intense relationship with his amanuensis, Denys, to whom he is dictating the story: Denys is twenty-eight,★ with a conscious elegance, long legs, a long oval face with slightly upturned nose, a delicate complexion and blue eyes. Mardick is clearly entranced, revelling in tangential discussions of emotions, indulging in Denys's mannerisms, his deft juggling of gold cigarette case and lighter, Mardick's gifts, with palpable frissons of pleasure. Progress with the story is understandably slow, so Hartley allowed himself a sequel, *The Betrayal* (1966), in which the languorously aristocratic Denys manoeuvres Mardick's death.

Perhaps it was unsurprising, therefore, that Lord David Cecil, in his introduction to *The Collected Short Stories* (1968), should dwell on Hartley's 'Gothic imagination'. Lord David concludes on the one story 'that ends well', 'The Price of the Absolute', in which Timothy Carswell recklessly purchases a Celadon vase and feels himself the possessor of 'Absolute beauty incarnate. Can this mean, we wonder, that Hartley thinks that art is to be trusted even if life is not?' This seems, Lord David says, implicit in the tone of his description:

Who can describe perfection? I shall not attempt to, nor even indicate the colour; for, like a pearl, the vase had its own colour, which floated on its surface more lightly than morning mist hangs on a river . . .

★ In the opening of *The Brickfield*, the description of Denys has many parallels with Lady Mary Clive's memoir of David Cecil[30] when he too was twenty-eight.

illuminated, the vase shone as if brightness had been poured over it. It might have been floating in its own essence, so insubstantial did it look. Through layer on layer of soft transparency you seemed to see right into the heart of the vase.[31]

Lord David suggests that this is Hartley's art 'at its beautiful best' as well as a 'memorable' illumination of his beliefs. It seems appropriate that such a watery image of beauty, whether from the dreaming Nene, a Venetian lagoon or the grey-green mirror of the Avon, should be his end, as it was his beginning. L. P. Hartley died in London in December 1972, and with the inevitable sophistry of death all his worldly goods were returned to Fletton Tower.

7

Spirits of Place

My five subjects all trod lightly on this earth, and none of them wished to weight it with heavy memorials. Virginia Woolf's ashes were set beneath an elm tree in Monk's House garden at Rodmell, and were joined there by Leonard's in 1969. Morgan Forster left King's College to die in the home of his beloved Bob and May Buckingham, his 'family' for nearly forty years, in Coventry. His ashes were scattered on their rose bed. Carrington's have merged with the downland soil at Ham Spray.★ Leslie Hartley too was cremated, and has no known memorial. Rupert Brooke's friends buried him beneath a cairn of stones and a wooden cross in an olive grove on Skyros, and most of his friends still in England thought that best: but who could gainsay poor Mrs Brooke for wanting marble, bereft of all of her three sons when Alfred was killed in France in the summer of 1915, let alone Winston Churchill's eulogizing of Rupert as one of

★ Michael Holroyd says that Carrington left a letter for Ralph Partridge asking that her ashes should be put beneath the laurel hedge with Lytton's nearby under the ilex, in his favourite sitting place. She left £100 for Stephen Tomlin to design a stone, which Ralph Partridge vetoed; Gretchen Gerzina says that no one remembered what happened to her body or anything else; Jane Hill says that James Strachey took Lytton's ashes, and that Carrington was cremated but no one remembers what became of her ashes.[1]

'England's noblest sons' in the cause of war propaganda? Frances Cornford came to think that his Skyros memorial had the unfortunate look 'of an advertisement for Elliman's embrocation',[2] and Morgan Forster fell out with International PEN because they gave publicity to a commercial cruise to see it, which he felt 'aggravated by every circumstance of bad taste'.[3] Rupert had often joked himself that the space on the wall of Rugby School chapel next to Lewis Carroll was for him, and it was duly filled.

But of course ashes and stones were not their endings.

Leslie Hartley's would make one of his own stories: he left no will and everything was returned to his surviving sister, Norah, at Fletton Tower (with the exception of his manuscripts, which ended up in the John Rylands Library at the University of Manchester).[4]* Norah Hartley, by then a famed breeder of rangy grey champion deerhounds, appears in her photographs as a sweet-looking if grizzled old lady – much adored, at least according to her obsequies, for her olde-worlde kindnesses. But was there something ruthless in the twinkle in her dark eyes, something about the stretched skin of her forehead that hinted at the spideress? – for she saw off a pretender, a Mrs Dreda-Owen, complete with Hartley's 'daughter', who claimed his wealth,[5] and dealt with his 'expectant circle' of friends and still amassed some 3 million pounds into her web (or so the local papers said). Norah Hartley lived on into her sprightly nineties, until 27 September 1994. Two years before her death she allowed Adrian Wright, for whom Hartley had been a childhood hero, to use some of the papers for a biography, *Foreign Country*, which was published in 1996. There was a condition, that all the papers would be subsequently

---

* Hartley appointed Walter Allen as his literary executor and though he changed his choice to Francis King it was not valid. Walter Allen sold the manuscripts to the John Rylands Library.

destroyed; Wright's closing words are that Norah left her affairs in perfect order, all the deerhounds were to be cared for, and 'According to her instructions, the family papers, including the great archive of Leslie Poles Hartley's life, were burned.'[6]

It was said that nothing had changed for decades at Fletton Tower except the extra digits added to the phone number, and the names of the deerhounds. The rather dull rooms, with their old-fashioned arrangements of mediocre antiques and repro-ductions, worn rugs, Chinese porcelain and uninteresting paint-ings, were on view on Saturday, 18 February 1995, and were photographed for Peterborough Museum before everything was packed off for Sotheby's auction at Summers Place, Billingshurst, in Sussex later that year. I looked in vain for the Girtin cityscape of Paris with the luminescent Seine, for the Vuillard of a peasant woman and her daughter, the Munnings girl on a horse and the Rembrandt etching *Death of a Virgin*, all so lovingly and essentially part of Hartley's novel *Poor Clare*: perhaps they were plums for legatees or an international sale? Perhaps they were only in Hartley's imagination – or seen at Cranborne or Milton or Hatfield after all? Peterborough Museum, as guardians of the world from which Hartley sprang, made a modest request for a memento – perhaps his silver cup won for long-jumping at Harrow in 1911, his school boater, hymn-book or an inscribed volume from his childhood? Any of these might have sparked the imagination of a future novelist, but the request was not granted. Forty lots of Hartley's books were auctioned by John Bellman at Wisborough Green – in far-off, salubrious Sussex once again – on 24 May 1995. They were not particularly revealing, inscribed volumes from writers and poets who had passed through his life – Evelyn Waugh, Dorothy Wellesley, Edmund Blunden, Stephen Tennant, Robert Frost, Virginia Woolf, D. H. Lawrence, Anthony Powell, Arthur Waley, and more substantial evidences of his admiration for Henry James, Dickens, Dr Johnson and Conrad. Tiny insights were a first edition of 1902 of Kenneth Grahame's *Dream Days* (a Eustace Cherrington kind of book) and volumes of Lewis Carroll, Edward Lear and Max Beerbohm. Otherwise it was just encyclopedias and a writer's quick reference on castles, armour, orchids, butterflies, grasses, the English or Italian lakes – blind and silent books.★

Hartley went to such great lengths to obscure his tracks through this world: what was his terrible secret? Norah Hartley dreaded him being called a Fenland writer, much preferring him to be known as a Venetian writer! I wonder if she had ever read any of her brother's books at all, for neither pigeonhole could possibly contain him.

In *The Brickfield* (1964), supposedly semi-autobiographical, Hartley/Richard Mardick, the author dictating his story, talks of some dark secret of which he would like only the shadow to fall across his life-story. Adrian Wright's real-life biography, *Foreign Country*, acknowledged what he thought this to be and hoped he had honoured Hartley's wishes.[7] Those who were interested assumed that the secret was Hartley's homosexuality, though it is puzzling how this could be so terrible to a Bloomsbury familiar. In provincial strait-laced Peterborough perhaps it was different, perhaps he felt his sisters should be protected; and yet included in the Fletton Tower paintings, given house room by Norah Hartley for over twenty years, was a Glyn Philpot portrait of a handsomely moustachioed gondolier, Pietro Busetti, commissioned by Hartley as a Venetian memento. Hartley's mother and his elder sister, Enid (who had predeceased him, dying in 1968), did visit Venice, but the more worldly Norah could not be persuaded: it was after all difficult to leave the deerhounds. Hartley's mildly homosexual

---

★ These sale catalogues, etc. are in the Hartley file in Peterborough Museum.

novel *The Harness Room* appeared in 1971, the same year (and perhaps intentionally) as Forster's posthumously published *Maurice*, and the year before Hartley's own death. *The Harness Room* is a hackneyed tale, rather on the level of a late Friday night comedy spot on television, and difficult to take seriously (but for its bitter Hartley ending). With Hartley, as with so many others, sexuality has been over-played to the point of missing the more likely betrayal, in Hartley's case a betrayal of class and place. The traumatic moment in his young life (which he never did adapt to fiction) was that adolescent discovery at Alwalton, when for all his mother's spoiling, for all the grandeur of Fletton Tower, his specialness, his 'difference' from other children, this pompous, sensitive, inordinately proud boy realized that he had no atavistic past, no grand relations, and as he looked down on the boys who opened the Milton Park gates, so the lordly Fitzwilliams looked down on him. For all his fantasies, he had only the drab monotony of the fens and dingy solicitors' offices and Methodist meeting-houses as his heritage; though his father's money might send him to Harrow and Oxford, his case was only exacerbated, for the things he wanted could not be bought. In retrospect all Hartley's dreams and desires were balked by his shame, and his life was permanently darkened by this shadow. He lived out his life in exile, all the more pathetically because much of it was in a world of social renegades, where the ruthless chose themselves new roots and social identities at will.

All the more sadly because his countryside needed Hartley: this countryside where I am sitting now, in the ancient Soke of Peterborough, between the stone belt quarries of majestic names, Ketton, Colley Weston and Barnack, and the flat, black fenland fields. The countryside of Ermine Street and Boudicca, of the Water Newton hoard and Saxon saint-princesses, of broken-hearted queens (Catherine of Aragon and Mary, Queen of Scots) and Cromwellian feuds, this countryside of John Dryden and John Clare, of fabulous skies and the meandering, temperamental river Nene – it is a countryside of unwritten stories, with a kind of cultural hole in its heart. While Eustace Cherrington, the dishevelled boy with the wooden spade and his socks falling down, keeps the treasured memories of seaside holidays, and Leo Colston, breathless and with pounding heart, dashes through the golden Norfolk meadows with all the fervency of questing sexuality, it is Leslie Hartley who fails his homeland. Peterborough and the fens are left with the determinedly miserable, dyspeptic Richard Mardick, disillusioned novelist, who never wished to come home.

Unsurprisingly, Peterborough has carried on without him: a small town, subjected to centuries of buffeting by larger forces, marauding Danes, squabbling Saxons and rich and despotic abbots of a Benedictine monastery that was as magnificent as any in Europe.[8] These were followed by the railway kings, bartering with the spiritual and temporal landlords for the rights of way and marshalling yards at the crucial meeting-point of the main line to Edinburgh and the corn, stock and brickfields immediately to the east and west. Unlike Rupert Brooke's Rugby, Peterborough had no great school to uphold its cultural, historic heart, and at the critical moments the lords and canons of the Church of England retired into a Trollopian seclusion in the cathedral precincts: behind the walls all the sleepiness of Barchester lived on, well after the nineteenth century had passed away. Then it was the planners; like the market town of Andover in Hampshire, which had once so enchanted Mark Gertler, Peterborough was deemed so devoid of any charms that it could be demolished and rebuilt differently, with vast square blocks of shops and offices, thousands of acres of new housing estates, all hung together in the heyday of the motor car by swirling parkways and numberless, identical traffic roundabouts. Local opinions are still totally divided as to whether the new town revamping of Peterborough was a good or bad thing; undoubtedly much was lost in the particularly philistine invasion of the nineteen-sixties to the eighties: the 'cathedral' of this age is the glitzy, warm and colourful Queensgate shopping centre, with integral multi-storey car parks. The names of these are significant, introducing local heroes into everyday lives: Clare, Cavell (Edith Cavell was brought up in Peterborough, and she 'has' a hospital too), Royce (Henry Royce earned his living selling newspapers in the streets here until he met Charles Rolls) and Perkins (the inventor of the diesel engine, still one of the city's major companies).

Leslie Hartley does not have a car park, nor any other remembrance that I can find; only the historian Mary Liquorice's booklet, *The Hartleys of Fletton Tower*, published by Cambridgeshire Libraries, alerts anyone – as it did me – to him. Would he have been so horrified at the thought of a car park named for him? I persist in thinking not, for the only begetter of Eustace Cherrington cannot have been entirely an alienated snob. If Hartley had given Peterborough cause to remember him, there is much he would now be proud of, for it is a city arising from the almost vanished dust of the brickworks and asserting itself once more: the children of the sixties and seventies have matured to a vibrant enthusiasm for the wonderful landscape, the now emparked valley of the Nene, and there are far too many interest groups, clubs and societies of a cultural or active kind for any single lifetime. The very traditions and customs of the fens are unearthed and polished off, as fascinating as any other histories, reborn into present entertainments. Travellers who have only passed by, speeding up the A1 or glimpsing the spires and pinnacles of the cathedral only from the train, who now stop awhile, discover convenient modern pleasures, shopping and eating, but also unsung and almost secret places of the past. The Hartleys' Fletton Tower, now an (unfortunately) listed elephantine presence, its decaying grandeur ever more alien – and therefore vulnerable – in a workaday suburb, has a problematic future, as the costs of its maintenance will always exceed any income. Even if it acquired a Hartley blue plaque, no one would ever see it behind trees, shrubs and locked gates; a future as a literary shrine seems remote; what would Hartley have thought of that? – I feel he would rather it was demolished.

Among his books was an architecture of Northamptonshire – of course, Peterborough was in Northamptonshire in his day, but I feel he really kept it for Alwalton, as the place by the river that he would have most liked to call home. He would recognize the village today, carefully conserved – but not overtly so – between the massive palaces of Pearl Assurance and the A1. Hartley's parents, Harry Bark Hartley (1860–1954) and Mary Elizabeth, his wife (1863–1943), were joined in the cemetery opposite St Andrew's church by Norah in 1994, but there is no mention of Leslie. Other Hartleys are there too, with the proud Poles connection with Wentworth Woodhouse in Yorkshire remembered: Leslie never apparently had any interest in 'ancestral' Wentworth at all. But Alwalton would please him, even now, well enough, with its quiet cottages and pretty gardens, discreetly tree-shaded vicarage, and the almost secret pathways down to Alwalton lock and the Nene, and the water-meadows that both John Clare and the young Leslie loved. Perhaps he would even enjoy the cemetery too, a pleasant spot where the ghost of Leo Colston can still peek at illicit-looking lovers who park their cars next door for a lunch-hour tryst by the river.

It was a coincidental irony that the year of Leslie Hartley's death, 1972, saw the apotheosis of John Clare, the local hero he had spurned. What Edmund Blunden had begun in 1920, in unearthing unpublished poems and songs from Peterborough's dusty archive, was confirmed by John Barrell in his scholarly landmark *The Idea of Landscape and the Sense of Place 1730–1840*.⁹ Barrell approached Clare through the accepted cultural idea of the eighteenth-century 'landskip', of paintings, aristocratic parks and Augustan poetry – greensward, groves and Gainsborough ladies: he then proceeded through the parallel but earthier business of agricultural improvements, stockbreeding and enclosures, all chronicled by farming commentators Arthur Young and William Marshall. He examined Clare's technique and imagination in the real context of the poor country boy in the farming fens, who had little use for the word 'Picturesque' and could only apologize for the lack of any sublime rockiness in his home landscape:

> Swamps of wild rush-beds, and sloughs' squashy traces,
>   Grounds of rough fallows with thistle and weed.
> Flats and low valleys of kingcups and daisies,
>   Sweetest of subjects are ye for my reed.¹⁰

Barrell gave academic credence to Clare as a poet of importance, despite his love for a culturally unusual – to say the least – countryside. Clare's fragile genius has continued to sparkle over Helpston and Northborough and his other places, even over Northampton, where he was incarcerated in the asylum.* He has remained a poet of relevance and controversy: even to meet his naïve and open gaze from a holographed image on a concrete wall

---

* Recent work has been done on the records of Northampton Asylum, where Clare was a patient: after Blunden's publications of Clare's work, editing was taken over by J. W. and Anne Tibble and Geoffrey Grigson, until re-editing began all over again under Eric Robinson, who is general editor of the current Oxford University Press editions. There are several biographies, the most popular by Edward Storey (1982). The John Clare Society issues an annual journal and a quarterly newsletter.

in weekly visits to Peterborough's Clare car park keeps his memory alive.

Thirty years ago John Barrell concluded that Clare was too deeply identified with his 'doughy sloughs' and squashy fens to appeal to mainstream tastes – 'we are all tourists now,' he wrote, and preferred eighteenth-century poets such as Thomson and Cowper and sometimes Wordsworth, who 'compared to Clare, moved as tourists through the places they wrote about'.[11] Thomas Hardy, Barrell purported, was determined 'that his own place in the landscape is that of guide, and ours that of tourists'.[12] After Barrell a flow of books and exhibitions illustrated the favoured places, as seen through the eyes of culturally approved people – Constable, the Pre-Raphaelites, Wordsworth, William Kent, the Revd Gilpin, poets, painters, landscapists, the viewers were almost always the same.[13]

One of the contentions of this book is that other viewers are important makers of myths and memories in places, even though they are not the usual paid-up members of the travellers' or countryside guilds. Virginia Woolf's sense of identity with her places has been emphasized in Chapter 1, with an intended emphasis on her love of London and St Ives: but, in the ever more crowded twentieth century, jostling for visual images, as a writer of St Ives she has been rather crowded out by a vigorous group of modern artists.

The story resumes, as it so often does, at the death of Rupert Brooke. Katharine Cox, to whom Rupert had written one of his last letters as 'the best I can do in the way of a widow',[14] married the marine painter Will Arnold-Forster in 1918; they had a son, Mark, and lived in Cornwall, between St Ives and Zennor, at Eagle's Nest, perched on its pinnacle of rocks overlooking the fields of Tregerthen and the sea. Virginia had been tempted to rent one of the Tregerthen cottages – next door to where D. H.

Lawrence wrote much of *Women in Love* – when she knew that she had to give up Asheham, but she found Monk's House instead. In 1921 she and Leonard visited the Arnold-Forsters: 'Ka and Will are the great people of the neighbourhood,' she reported to Vanessa, 'in a large solid house, views from every window, water closets, bathrooms, studios, divine gardens, all scattered with Logan rocks' – that is, the rocks that are balanced so delicately that they move when touched.[15] Eagle's Nest commanded a landscape of gorse hills and scattered farmsteads, all safely built in sheltered hollows; it was most definitely a stoically artistic house, and the Woolfs, visiting again in 1926, found it bitterly cold – Cornish cold being of a more intense variety than their own Sussex chill at Monk's House. Katharine Arnold-Forster lived out her life there, a public-spirited life in which she became a JP and a member of the county education committee; when she died, in 1938, she was only fifty-two.

Eagle's Nest has a companion on its eyrie, the older and more roughly-built Zennor Poor House, for another 'class' of Victorian outcasts. In 1875 the Penzance Union Guardians had sold their bleak house to Barbara Leigh Smith Bodichon, the artist, feminist pioneer and co-founder of Girton College, Cambridge – and it was her beloved painting retreat, shared with many friends, including Gertrude Jekyll, for the rest of her life.[16] Barbara Bodichon too had been scarred by a tumultuous love affair, with John Chapman, a Byronic literary man,[17] some fifty years before Katharine's involvement with Rupert: both – across the years – had settled for this wild seascape, and the achievements of a useful life, and they make a companionable pair of ghosts.

Eagle's Nest is tied tightly into the fate of Virginia's St Ives: in 1927 the Arnold-Forsters let it to a friend, a Fabian and Yorkshire industrialist, Tom Heron, and his family. Heron became a partner with the textile-designer Alex Walker in his silk-printing works,

Cryséde, which was first at Newlyn but expanded into new premises in former fishermen's lofts on the Island in St Ives: the silk printing, allied to Bernard Leach and Shoji Hamada's pottery, was part of an economic upturn, an Arts and Crafts revival in the 1920s, which gave work to the artists and local people, and consolidated the artistic future of the little town.[18] The Victorian Royal Academicians with painting retreats and gentlemanly ideas had given way to a brisker desire to succeed that was the mood of the twenties: a newcomer, of course, a marine painter and naval commander who had won a DSO in the war, George Bradshaw, led the way to the formation of the St Ives Society of Artists, to support a permanent gallery in a building overlooking Porthmeor beach – for selling to the increasing numbers of visitors, but also forging a wider creative community. In March 1929 the Society had over 100 members, and opened forty-one studios on show days: the *St Ives Times* was pleased to announce:

There is nothing eccentric about the art of the St Ives colony. Cubism and such schools have not found their way down here yet. The art of St Ives is eminently sane and handsome . . .

The artists were still taking the same traditional views of the beauty spots and sea coast, in the light of dusk and mornings, on boats and harbour scenes, which were the order of the days.[19]

It is a quirk of St Ives's history that perhaps would not have appealed to Virginia that the real source of its twentieth-century fame was an inarticulate and wizened little dwarf of a failed fisherman, whom she just may have noticed calling for 'old iron' in the streets of her childhood. Or perhaps seen his rag-and-bone cart outside his store in Quay Street, with its crudely painted board: 'A. Wallis Dealer in Marine Stores'. Alfred Wallis, a widower in his late sixties, had retired to a little terraced house in Back Row

West, in the early twenties, and painted 'for company'. He was a figure of fun to local boys, ignored by the artists, 'a solitary friendless man' who put his paintings out for sale: he painted on anything he could find, on china and old furniture, on flotsam wood and cardboard given to him by the grocer, which he would cut into shapes to fit his designs. (His paintings had an obscure fellowship with Vanessa Bell's at Charleston, at the same time, but far away in miles and class.) He painted the harbour and Godrevy lighthouse, 'placing the flattened shapes of houses and boats as in an ancient map or a child's drawing', using old tins of boat paint of deep greens, blues and blacks donated by the fishermen, always with a disarming simplicity, sometimes with a transforming clarity, as *The Fishing Fleet* in full sail, black boats and black sails against the rising blush of a dawn sky (and on cardboard), with 'always the whitened transparency of the sea moving and tossing in his visionary world'.[20] In August 1928 two young painters, Ben Nicholson and Christopher Wood, were having an interesting day exploring St Ives when they came upon Wallis's open doorway and his paintings. Nicholson, determined to escape from the stylish sophistication and fame of his inheritance, especially of his painter father William Nicholson, was struck by Wallis's 'direct creative energy' and simple clarity. In painting so naïvely the only world he knew, Wallis had captured the spirit of the St Ives seascape; Ben Nicholson found the colours – a lively dark brown, shiny black, fierce grey, strange whites and a 'pungent Cornish green' – derived as they were from the old boat paints, especially intriguing. The very moulded, plastic – tactile – quality of Wallis's pieces of wood and card inspired him, merging with influences from Miró, Braque and Picasso. Captivated by the intense possibilities of the spirit of this place, he immersed himself in it – Ben Nicholson in fact repeated the process that Virginia Stephen had experienced and projected into her writing, only he pursued a visual expression. The complexity of Nicholson's love affair with St Ives is explored by Christopher Neve, who finds him the most brilliant *evocateur* of the spirit of his place:

. . . gradually the world beyond the studio found its way into the work as surely as the tide comes in. Nicholson began scraping and scouring the surfaces of his forms, rubbing colour on to them with rags or brushing them with successive layers of thin pigment and then scouring and scratching it away again with razor blades to uncover the ground beneath, as though the erosion of rock by weather was something he could experience himself. . . Sometimes the coloured areas were regular geometric shapes . . . At others the line twitched because he had been out on the cliffs, drawing, at Pendeen and Lelant, where the engine-houses with their chimneys make their forlorn, abandoned geometry against the sea, or above the patterned farmland spread among its battered nervous system of walls around Trendrine. He looked for the taut lines of telegraph wires, the verticals of poles and chimneys and church-towers which accorded with his precise geometry; but on bicycle rides to Carbis Bay and Zennor, and on walks up Trencrom Hill, he was lassooed by a much less ruly line, in the curve of the road, the swell of the hills, the crescents of harbours and hulls, a line of which the loose end would snake in the wind if he let it.

Neve continues on Nicholson's colours 'that seemed to have been made from the landscape, in the same way that it is possible to boil up lichen to dye wool. Red-brown sails, mauve foxgloves, sage and seaweed, sand, pebble, rust, rock, the finger-nail pink of shells, the absolute blue of sky' – colours not merely used to describe forms but 'become them'.[21]

In *Painting the Warmth of the Sun*,[22] Tom Cross chronicles St Ives from 1939, when Ben Nicholson and Barbara Hepworth settled there (Nicholson leaving for a studio overlooking Lake Maggiore in 1958), until 1975, the year Hepworth, Bryan Wynter and Roger Hilton all died. They, with Peter Lanyon and Patrick Heron (who had bought Eagle's Nest from Mark Arnold-Forster in 1955, and whose daughters now own it and the Poor House), made the fishing village into an art mecca. The pity of it is that there is all too little recognition of Virginia Woolf's prose in St Ives's great status: her walks (and Ben Nicholson's) out over the gorse-lined paths to Treveal and Trendrine are secure, with much of the coastline in the ownership of the National Trust; her beloved Talland House is spruced and neat (too neat for her), catering for holiday pilgrims, although much of the many-layered garden has become a car park. I don't imagine that Nicholson ever read *To the Lighthouse*, or anything of Virginia's prose, but the failure to connect, to see that he was merely achieving in painted expressions the same spirit of St Ives that she had captured in words, seems all our losses. Justice would be served by images of the town and great gobbets of her words splashed across the walls of Tate St Ives.

The influence of St Ives returned to Cambridge via a young art historian named Jim Ede, an assistant at the Tate Gallery in London in the 1920s, where he first met Ben Nicholson and his first wife, Winifred Dacre. 'Oddly enough,' wrote Ede in 1970, 'I turned out to be one of Ben Nicholson's very few admirers at that time,' and any paintings that he failed to sell, or tired of, came Jim Ede's way. He found the freshness of modernism enchanting, especially Winifred's belief in the fusion of art and living that they had experienced in Paris:

We lived in white houses with new large windows, we ate simple foods – the fruits of the earth. We wore sandals and ran barefoot along the boulevards. We talked in the cafés of the new vision, the new scale of music, the new architecture – unnecessary things were to be done away with and all was to be functional. How young we were![23]

Jim Ede and his wife Helen came home to Cambridge in the 1950s with a collection of paintings from Alfred Wallis, dozens of Ben Nicholsons, and more of their St Ives successors, pottery by Lucie Rie and Katherine Pleydell-Bouverie (one of Leach's first pupils), sculptures, some antique and modern furniture, old china, toy-like treasures, pebbles, rocks and plants, which they wanted 'in a modest way' to conspire into a living place – an experience for young and older, of 'a continuing way of life from these last fifty years'. This translated into the conversion of four slum dwellings at Kettle's Yard in Cambridge, at the corner of Castle and Northampton streets, north of Magdalene Bridge. Jim Ede spent the remainder of his life as 'curator' of his own home collection, which has passed to the University of Cambridge and is carefully and lovingly maintained as he intended, still playing its educational role, both in the university and the wider world.[24] His exquisite house demonstrates the impact of the modern movement on English traditions; it is, as he said, the reflection of a particular kind of mind through the first fifty years of the twentieth century. It is one of the places in Cambridge, where – lounging in the Windsor rocker, sunk deeply into the white armchair – one may be certain of finding the ghost of Rupert Brooke.

It was Mrs Brooke who saved the Old Vicarage at Grantchester, buying it for £1,250 in 1916 and making it over to Rupert's friend Dudley Ward, with the legal provision that the house and garden 'should be kept in their now existing state without any alterations or additions as a memorial to her said Son'.[25] Dudley and Anne-marie Ward, and their son Peter, were to keep Mrs Brooke's charge for over sixty years: for a while, and in the best Widnall tradition, Peter Ward used the gothic ruin as a workshop for making musical boxes and mechanical singing birds. Next door, the Orchard Tea Gardens were launched on 'a long and golden era' from the 1920s, the goal of the 'Grantchester Grind', the river walk

from the shaven lawns of the Backs to the billowing grasses of the
river meadows, and the scenes of generations of May Ball break-
fasts. They still punt and row as Rupert did, shooting Silver Street
Bridge★ into the unruly pool where Cam and Granta meet, the
Granta stream spilling out of King's Mill (still loading Beale's corn
barges in his day). In his day, too, George Darwin and his American
wife Maud du Puy were living in the old granges along the
Newnham bank (now Darwin College): nasturtiums hung over
the garden wall, planted by their daughter Margaret (who married
Geoffrey Keynes), and all the young then bathed in the deep pool
at the end of Little Island, which was itself a wild garden mixture
of peonies, lilacs and cherry blossoms. After Little Island the river
momentarily passes the garden of the Hermitage, built by Swann
Hurrell, one-time monarch of this watery empire and of a great
deal of Cambridge city life – in Rupert's day it was the home of
the Widow Cobb, to be serenaded with . . . all together . . .

> On the road to Mandal . . . a . . . ay,
> Where the flying fishes play . . . a . . . ay . . .

for she lived on the royalties of Cobb's settings of Kipling's *Barrack
Room Ballads*. Past the Darwins' green painted footbridges, beyond
Big Island to Lammas Land, freed from grazing cattle on Mondays
and Tuesdays so that the university washing could flutter in the
river breeze, until the Darwins bargained it for an archery ground.
Beyond the washing the Granta brewery, and clear of close buildings the Cam ran wide to join the Granta at Coe Fen – the public
bathing places where the boys ran pink and naked, and, *quelle*

★ The Silver Street bridge in Brooke's day was iron (1841), replacing the
wooden bridges kept by a hermit: the iron bridge has now been replaced by
Lutyens's 1932 design, erected in 1958–9.

horreur for dons and Darwins, a ladies' bathing place too. After that the rower settles into the meandering way to Grantchester, not much more than a land mile or so, and mooring and the stroll across the meadow path to the Orchard, with green deckchairs still set amid the leaning apple trees, as though the twentieth century had hardly been at all.

In the late eighties the Orchard had been threatened with a housing estate – 'exposed to the cold reality' of the unceasing Cambridge property boom – but after a considerable outcry and a great deal of rallying round in Grantchester, it was saved, restored and reopened. With only a lightweight wooden pavilion added to save staff and patrons from the weather, it offers a wholly romantic and insubstantial view of life's pleasures: it has an air of unbelievable innocence (and awfully good soups and cakes – the essence of its charm). Since launching day, 24 August 1999, the Orchard has been home to the Rupert Brooke Society, who keep a small museum, equally appropriately housed in a lightweight wooden 'summerhouse'.★

Significantly, Brooke's 'fantastic ruralism' has continued as a thread of Cambridge life which can be traced back to his friends and time. When his friend Gwen Raverat wrote her famous *Period Piece* (1952), her memoir of her Cambridge childhood, she ended with a picnic that she and her cousin Frances had arranged for their Darwin parents, aunts and uncles, who were rowed to a meadow beside Grantchester Mill. The elders, muffled and furred, convinced they were catching their deaths from cold, contended with nettles, cowpats and ants in sheer misery, enduring tepid sweet tea from flannel-clad bottles: Gwen Raverat drew them, huddled in a row beside the fence – except for her father, George

---

★ The Rupert Brooke Society, 45–47 Mill Way, Grantchester, Cambridge CB3 9ND, tel. 01223 845788; email: rbs@callan.co.uk.

Darwin, who had set off to walk home in disgust – with a backdrop of the elms and willows that sheltered Byron's Pool. The picnic was in June 1909 – Rupert, Gwen and Frances were about to cross the generational void and banish huddled miseries in the open air. Even the 'elders' met today at the Orchard are likely to be wearing sandals, and enjoying crusty brown bread in the chill June air. A plundering of 'The Great Lover' (1914) – a poem Laurence Olivier performed once and never forgot – confirms Brooke's 'loves' for white china ringed with blue, crusty bread, flowers, cool sheets, rough blankets, grainy wood and woodsmoke, old clothes and hair that shines and voices that sing and laugh, which conjure a familiar twentieth-century style.

The Cornfords, Francis and Frances, at Conduit Head on the Madingley Road, reared their children playing barefoot in the garden, with insistence upon fresh air and healthy food: they named one son Rupert John, but dropped the Rupert as too romantic (though the brilliant, passionate, poetic John Cornford became a romantic hero, killed in the Spanish Civil War). Frances, who suffered from Darwin depressions, 'was tangled in Brooke's legacy for many years', consoling his lovers and acting as inter-mediary between Mrs Brooke and the makers of the Brooke legend – 'For Frances he was not a legend, but a deeply mourned friend.'[26]

All Brooke's loves had to find the rest of their lives: of Katharine Cox we know. The actress Cathleen Nesbitt, whose fragile beauty belied her courage, continued to play starring roles on the London stage, and eventually in Hollywood. She lived to be ninety-four.[27] Phyllis Gardner had worked in Admiralty intelligence after his death, but she seemed never to recover, taking to wood-engraving and breeding Irish wolfhounds – she died in 1939 from breast cancer, aged forty-eight.[28]

Those modern women the Oliviers bravely pursued their

courses. The musical Daphne married Cecil Harwood and founded the first Rudolf Steiner school in England; Bryn the beautiful, married first to Hugh Popham (their daughter Anne married Vanessa's son, Quentin Bell), and then to Raymond Sherrard, worked hard at farming. Noel, who feared that she would never marry for love after Rupert's death, qualified as a doctor in 1917 and married for love a Welsh colleague, Arthur Richards, with whom she had a son and four daughters. Noel became a busy and successful physician, MRCP in 1922 and a consultant at Westminster Children's Hospital. She gave up work to care for her husband, who died in 1962, and she outlived him by seven years. Margery, the eldest and cleverest, paid an all-too-common price, being confined in a mental hospital from 1922 – she was there for over fifty years, outliving all her sisters.[29]

At Limpsfield Chart life at The Cearne continued its fruitful course; on a warm May afternoon in 1926, Edward Garnett, a 'puffy asthmatical glinting bear', walked yet another nervous young writer from Oxted station across Limpsfield Common to The Chart. This was Herbert Ernest Bates, twenty-one, fluttering out from a puritanical Midlands country upbringing on the strengths of his first novel, *The Two Sisters*: H. E. Bates long remembered how they emerged from the pinewoods, fringed with bluebells, rose campion and bright spring ferns, into the little orchard at The Cearne, where he saw Constance (whom he'd feared would be a she-bear), a small white-haired woman with 'a sort of intense and homely frailty' that reminded him of his grandmother; how the garden was ablaze with scarlet poppies, blue aquilegias, pinks, violas, lupins, and how he and Constance immediately slipped into 'horticultural fandangles' and flower talk, she revelling in – at last – a successor to D. H. Lawrence as an author with a real love of flowers. Bates became a regular at The Cearne; he 'got into the way of helping . . . picking raspberries, weeding, cutting grass, sowing and collecting seeds, fetching leaf mould from the woods behind the house'. Within a few years he came to Kent, buying an old granary, and like a songthrush let out of a cage 'he planned lawns, rock gardens, flower beds, pergolas and potato patches, reviewed prodigious quantities of books, wrote stories and planned novels'. The blossoming and ripening of life in a country hybridized from his native Northamptonshire and Kent brought H. E. Bates enduring success and celluloid fame with *The Darling Buds of May* (1958) and other novels.[30]

David Garnett, escaping from the Charleston ménage, had married Frances Marshall's sister Rachel, 'Ray', in 1921, and written his first novel, *Lady into Fox* (1922), which had been inspired on a visit to The Cearne and on a walk back into his memories of watching fox cubs at play. The novel's success enabled the young Garnetts to house-hunt, and the first copy of *Country Life* that they bought advertised an 'interesting' house – which sent them scurrying to St Ives in Huntingdonshire in their two-seater Morris to view Hilton Hall. They were (as Virginia had been) 'a good deal charmed' by St Ives, enchanted by Hilton – a rambling village around a big green, tree-fringed (the legend, which one would like to be true, has the trees disposed by 'Capability' Brown, lord of the manor of Fenstanton next door), and a turf maze, cut rashly (it might be supposed) to mark the Restoration of 1660 in this Parliamentary countryside. The Garnetts tried to be wise, but lost their hearts to the old brick Hall, part colour-washed in ochre yellow and reddish ochre, with Jacobean stair, old garden, pigeon-cote, stables and orchard of old apples and pears.[31] They took possession in October 1924, at the same time that Lytton and Carrington and Ralph Partridge moved into Ham Spray, and Hilton Hall became a less-known but equally frequented Bloomsbury house. David Garnett, full of a country-man's curiosity, dug himself into local life, willing to wade in the breast-high grasses on the green and the equally mysterious village lore: the Garnetts were 'surprised' that the boys came to the door singing on wintry Plough Monday, that St Valentine's day brought the girls 'Good morrow to you Valentine, Shake your locks as I shake mine,' followed by Mayday garlands of cowslips from which dangled a small doll, symbol of fertility, and the song 'We've brought the summer home today'. David Garnett found this 'deep harmony existing between the labouring people and the life they led, a hard one, but full of nature which brought poetry into their lives'.[32] His fourth novel, *Go She Must!* (1927), is lovingly evocative of this eccentric life: the story of Anne Dunnock, the rector's daughter, imprisoned by the beauty of the countryside and her longed-for escape to Paris, which is art, music, life, cafés, parties, everything that Hilton is not. Paris is also a maelstrom of jealousies, between men and men and men and women, and it is when Anne has come through, with an unexpected husband, that they return to the fen edge village and 'happiness ever after'. David Garnett is telling his own story in a mirrored version; his upbringing by Constance at Limpsfield had given him a deep and practical sympathy with the immutable traditions, where a whole community of disparate ages was tied together through long, long lives, so that the ensuing loves and jealousies were twisted and ingrained – more curious than the city-bred passions of youth on the fling. Garnett caught, in 1927, the dilemma of the countryside – the Hardyesque dramas of Linton Fair, the pleasant, dullard young farmer whose horizon spread no farther than his fields, whom his heroine was expected to marry, and the consequent urge of the young to taste the wider world. This urge was no different in 1927 than it had been for the wandering tribes of Iceni or medieval pilgrims, it just demanded less determination, as it was facilitated by car and motor bus.

The Garnetts settled in at Hilton Hall (David's son, Richard

Garnett, is there still) – typifying a new breed of sympathetic intellectual, with an income from working at home, involved with the community, not isolated from it. Surprisingly, it was much the same at Ham Spray, where Lytton Strachey would wander into Ham village and sip beer in the sunshine, always good for a donation towards the boy scouts' outing or policemen's ball; at Rodmell the Woolfs too were absorbed, eccentrics in a world of rural eccentrics – the villagers passing to their allotments could see Virginia at work in her writing-room, nor did they disturb her. At Abinger Hammer, Lily Forster and 'Mr Morgan' were part of the village by the very act of going to the post-box or Morgan's walking to Gomshall station. These people, odd by everyday standards, possessed a curiosity which took their rural retreats on their own terms: this included – as David Garnett put to practical use in his novels – a healthy respect for the old beliefs. In June 1927 the Garnetts, Woolfs, Carrington and Vita and Harold Nicolson made the expedition to Giggleswick in Yorkshire, which was the best place to see the total eclipse of the sun. David Garnett was not the only one to be deeply disturbed by the experience: as the light grew dim they gazed, using pieces of exposed film, at the arc of the moon biting into the flaming rim. By unearthly light that set the lambs bleating, he saw the corona, 'the writhing nobs of scarlet' that were 'obscene' and horrible: the larks were silent, the cold was polar, the crowd were hushed and huddled – and then the first slant of warm, familiar, sunlight broke out and everybody began to cheer and chatter with excitement.[33] Stonehenge, Avebury and other standing stones drew them too: at Stonehenge, sitting on the altar stone eating an apple – as Morgan Forster and Virginia had done, separately – was seen as far from sacrilege, and most likely 'the other thing', something approaching a communion. Unfortunately establishment suspicions had already been aroused, and dodging the duty policeman, as Virginia had noted in 1906, was part of the excitement. That Stonehenge has become, like a prized toy taken away, a talisman for twentieth-century battles in the green and pleasant land is due to that lone policeman, undoubtedly put there by a good Christian Chief Constable, town bred and in terror of the First Commandment.

The fate of Stonehenge was compromised almost throughout the century by the need for the use of Salisbury Plain as a military training ground: and, so much more, was Rupert Brooke's Lulworth Cove, where he danced and salved his soul, and where literary reading parties took their walks to Mupe and Worbarrow Bay. His last weeks in England, through the winter of 1914–15, were spent at Blandford Camp with the Hood Battalion, imprisoned in 'miasmic' huts and gruelling routines, back in his all too familiar guise of being far removed from – out of reach of – real life. Only once, briefly, he seemed even to realize he was in Dorset, telling Violet Asquith of his only 'solace' in a local guidebook, disjointedly, cherry-picking in a guidebook way: 'The Tower that had Two on it is not far away. And at Tarrant Crawford a Queen is buried. And Badbury Rings – which we attack weekly – is the scene of one of Arthur's greatest victories.'[34] Even while Brooke and his battalion slaved over field warfare, the first newly invented tanks were *en route* to Dorset, installed at Bovington in 1916 and confirmed as the Royal Tanks Corps and part of the British Army in 1923. Like unbroken colts or wild elephants, these secret weapons were led to exercise on a territory viewed from Whitehall as tactically suitable and as a lightly populated stretch of the Dorset coast, with coves that could be fired across and projecting rocks for target practice. If only Rupert had still been dining in Downing Street; for the first outcry arose from an error in announcing the boundary of the ranges on the *west* side, instead of the *east* side of Lulworth Cove. East was bad enough, imprisoning the fossil forest below Bindon Hill, the Mupe ledges

and the cove Arish Mell, all along the sweeping cliffs to Worbarrow and Brandy Bays, and inland engulfing the village of Tyneham, and Hardy's Creech and Holme heaths. The *Daily Mail*
called it, in outrage, that 'most exquisitely beautiful stretch of the
Wessex coast'.[35] There was an irony that Rupert's 'The Soldier'
had been used to win the war, but no one cared to look into his
earlier poems to win the peace of Lulworth: his lilting burial of
'Day That I Have Loved':

> I bear you, a light burden, to the shrouded sands,
> Where lies your waiting boat, by wreaths of the sea's making
> Mist-garlanded, with all grey weeds of the water crowned.[36]

Or, datelined Lulworth, 8 July 1907, 'Pine-trees and the Sky':

> Then from the sad west turning wearily,
> I saw the pines against the white north sky,
> Very beautiful, and still, and bending over
> Their sharp black heads against a quiet sky.
> And there was peace in them; and I
> Was happy, and forgot to play the lover,
> And laughed, and did no longer wish to die;
> Being glad of you, O pine-trees and the sky![37]

His place at Westminster dinner tables had been taken by
another hero, who turned up at Bovington as a lowly member of
the Royal Tank Corps, in 1923, Private T. E. Shaw, the *alter ego*
of Lawrence of Arabia. Lawrence liked his rural retreat at Clouds
Hill Cottage, at the edge of Moreton woods, just north of the
camp, not because it was part of a beloved landscape but for its
anonymity and hidden qualities. Many travellers in thrall to the
desert quite understandably find England prissy and restrictive:

Lawrence neither knew Dorset nor saw the need to defend it in high places — his very attitude to the land was of suppressed violence and modern recklessness — 'When my mood gets too hot and I find myself wandering beyond control I pull out my motor-bike and hurl it at top-speed through these unfit roads for hour after hour.'[38] When he was feeling sociable he attracted quite a literary salon around the ageing Hardy at Max Gate, on the edge of Dorchester, where he too hid behind a high wall and screen of Austrian pines; Forster, the Woolfs, Edmund Blunden, Siegfried Sassoon, Robert Graves and Lawrence, a regular and beloved of the Hardy's fox-terrier, Wessex, all sipped tea in the Brookeless world and thought not of saving Lulworth. When Hardy died in 1928 his native Dorset suddenly realized the great man's legacy — his first novel, *Desperate Remedies*, and *Far from the Madding Crowd* were dusted off for their mentions of Lulworth Cove, and literature rather ineffectually entered what had become the most bizarre contest in English landscape history. Bemused fishermen and shepherds, the Welds of Lulworth Castle, the Committee for the Preservation of Rural Dorset, retired majors and helpless local authorities, the villagers of Tyneham, the literati — Theodore Powys, Valentine Ackland and Sylvia Townsend Warner (supported by David Garnett) at East Chaldon, Gerald and Gamel Brenan, returned from Spain, the idealistic rural revivalists of Rolf Gardiner's Springhead community, the journalist H. J. Massingham and novelist A. E. W. Mason — all and many more were to be involved in the raids and skirmishes that constituted the long battle for the Lulworth ranges, the fantastic story told by Patrick Wright in *The Village That Died for England*.[39] Twentieth-century direct action was invented in the Lulworth campaign; hearts and friendships were broken, blood was spilled, lives were lost, and room upon room was filled with dusty files. Similar battles have been fought over Dartmoor and other Defence lands — they are the most inane and debilitating of struggles, by a people who love their country against their country's forces of defence.

Winston Churchill came to south Dorset, grim-faced, in May of 1935, to Lawrence's funeral in Moreton church; another eulogy – 'one of the greatest beings of our time' – on another hero, in the cause of another war effort.[40] Seven years later, in the dark days of 1942, he returned to watch 'his' Churchill tanks being put through their paces. Churchill had no love for Dorset (after all, he had his own private paradise with a view, tucked into the tree-girt hills of Sydney Olivier's 'holy land' west of Limpsfield Chart, at Chartwell). The Lulworth ranges were, incontrovertibly, in the national interest, and with the Second World War the Ministry of Defence consolidated their territory, with the promise to the villagers of Tyneham that one day they would be able to return. (To this day they have not, and the range areas are marked with thick warning lines on the Ordnance Survey maps.[41]) Nor, back in the 1930s, was everyone happy with Lawrence's arrival in Moreton cemetery, his grave attracting a trail of tourists from the first: the press whipped up sinister rumours, that his crash on his Brough Superior motorcycle was no accident, that he was not dead at all, but spirited away to be Churchill's spymaster. Some of Lawrence's friends, including Morgan Forster, thought Moreton, in the valley of the Frome, an 'alien meadow' for him to lie in anyway, and that 'the place he will never cease to haunt' was Clouds Hill, on the Dorset heath, which had an empathy with the sands of Arabia.[42]

The voices that call over the downs and valleys of south Dorset today are persistently those of Thomas Hardy, Lawrence, and more faintly, Rupert Brooke. A momentary experience can set them whispering along with the 'old sad kings', of Maiden Castle, or Chalbury, whom Rupert chaffed could be heard if you put your ear to the grass on Lulworth downs. To find Hardy's gaunt brick house, Max Gate, open to visitors, as I did one warm May day at the start of work on this book, offers the passport: the house is now tucked away from the roar of bypass traffic in a cul-de-sac. Visitors are invited to open the front door and walk in: it is an awakening experience, putting a hand on Hardy's front door-handle, something a visiting stranger would never have done, except to retrieve something forgotten from the car, or by being leader returning from an inspection of the garden. The door-knob turns back time: the house is not as the Hardys left it, but evocative enough when one is standing on the same spot of entry as Yeats, the Woolfs, Morgan Forster . . . of Carrington I'm not sure, but Lytton Strachey came, and surely – though not recorded – Brooke, who requested Hardy's poems to be sent to him half-way across the world in 1913. Max Gate and its garden, with Wessex the terrier and his canine fellows buried in the shrubbery, leads to Hardy's birthplace at Higher Bockhampton, to Stinsford church, where his heart is buried, and into the well-documented Hardy countryside,[43] and on to Clouds Hill and Moreton cemetery and Lulworth Cove heritage centre: West Lulworth's narrow hilly street of stone houses is still much as Rupert would remember it, but the Cove itself betrays his memory. This place of natural beauties has been distorted into 'heritage' at its worst portrayal – bulky brick buildings of the supermarket school of architecture, with shopping-mall 'landscaping', disgrace the relict of a little harbour strewn with rusty oil-cans and bramble-encrusted boat-trailers. The mix of squalor and commercialization presented to the Cove's visitors suggests that neither the local authority nor the Weld Estate are fit to look after Lulworth Cove. And yet, on balmy afternoons of the thick sea mist which obscures so much of twenty-first century pilgrimage comes the rumble of the guns, much as Virginia heard them on the Sussex downs almost a century ago.

Virginia's downs – those mountainous green seas that flank the flat valley of the Sussex Ouse – have been protected mainly by their barren steepness and inaccessibility, and the desire to rush past to the seaside. It is still possible to walk the heights of Itford or Highdole hills, and feel and see the things she felt and saw, on the green ground of a blue world, between sky and sea – even if the opportunity should be taken on quiet days in spring or autumn. The Ouse, which she knew instinctively at her ending would return her to the embrace of her beloved sea, has protected her villages and their views, with its marshy flats. Only Asheham House has gone, and it seems that its fate was sealed before Virginia and Leonard found it – and it was only available to them because of a long-term interest in the chalk-quarrying. The illustration of Asheham [20] shows it in the 1920s (the Woolfs had left in 1919) as the quarry manager's house: chalk-quarrying was at a peak then, feeding a building boom and largely unrestricted by any planning legislation or protection of the downland landscape, which did not come into force until well after the 1947 Town and Country Planning Act.* Quarrying was scaled down, and Asheham House was let to a series of tenants until the mid-seventies.[44] When quarrying ceased, the landfillers moved in and the house – which had not escaped the hawk-eyed researchers of Ian Nairn and Nikolaus Pevsner's *Sussex* volume of *The Buildings of England* (1965) – had become listed as of architectural and historic interest, even though it was progressively more derelict. By 1994 it was in such a bad condition that it was allowed to be demolished, though by then the Virginia Woolf connection had given teeth to the conservation argument, and a large sum of compensation was subscribed to uphold the Bloomsbury connections in the area. The money went towards the upkeep of Monk's House, which after Leonard Woolf's death had slipped quietly into the

---

* Asheham quarry was playing a vital role, pioneering new kiln-firing techniques for the industry.

ownership of the National Trust, and of Charleston Farmhouse. Monk's House, as a small house, down a quiet narrow village street (Virginia ended her life as she began it, in a cul-de-sac), is a tenanted property of the National Trust, open at certain times★ but clearly fragile and sensitive to too much visiting. Though it was acquired in the days when a brisk attitude to efficient maintenance rather overruled sensibilities to atmosphere in the Trust's management – and Monk's House is consequently rather too spruce (though more sound than probably Virginia ever knew it) – this quiet protection suits it well. The pilgrims find an oak footgate leading to a white door in the white clapboarded front: they find sombre, green-shaded rooms, mementoes, treasures, some painted furniture and china, and a peaceable, quiet house. A big glass verandah along the back (partly added by Leonard after Virginia's death) leads to the garden, on which they both worked, but he most of all. Like many shrines, so much depends upon what the pilgrim hopes to find, but many do find a benign presence – perhaps the ghost of Virginia – in this quiet place.

Charleston Farmhouse, the painted house, on the other hand, was the subject of a courageous and flamboyant campaign which revolutionized the techniques of restoration of houses and gardens during the last quarter of the twentieth century. Vanessa Bell, matriarch of a large and complex family, had died at Charleston on 7 April 1961, and was buried in Firle churchyard. Duncan Grant lived on in an ever-decreasing space and, at the last, Quentin Bell recalled, 'almost entirely in his studio; the walls were damp, the roof leaked, but it was habitable and, thanks to a large stove, it was one of the few rooms in the house which was not very cold'. Beyond the studio the water poured in all over the place,

★ Only two afternoons a week: consult current listing or tel. 01892 890651 (NT Regional Office).

'the decorated wall surfaces mouldered, the painted woodwork began to serve a vast population of pests, the pictures decayed and, where they were painted on three-ply, became alive with woodworm, fabrics crumbled'.[45] In the garden the plaster figures melted in the rain or were broken by frosts, and in summer covered by encroaching weeds. In 1978 Duncan died and joined Vanessa in Firle churchyard. At that time the 'Bloomsberries' were deeply out of fashion, but Quentin Bell quite rightly believed that it is not our duty to judge, but it is our duty to leave the option open to posterity. The National Trust recognized Charleston's value, but declined to take part without a very large endowment.

Quentin Bell felt everyone was waiting for a miracle, or expected one of him, and then the miracle came – 'burst through our front door' – in the person of Deborah Gage:[46] the Gage family at Firle Park were – and had always been – the owners of the farmhouse, which was ever only sub-let to Vanessa and Duncan. Deborah Gage was determined that it should be saved, and she gathered and formed the Charleston Trust, registered as a charity for the saving of the farmhouse in April 1980. For the next six years, through tremendously hard work and many heartbreaks – the wiseacres saying that it could not be done – the Charleston campaign became a passionate and inclusive operation. From the outset, via leaflets, broadcasts, and advertisements and a modest typed newsletter, the plan was to appeal to as many people as possible, the Bloomsbury constituency all over the world – giving supporters a voice through the Friends of Charleston, courting everyone from the most modest local volunteer to the presidents of philanthropic American corporations, and saying thank you, again and again, all the time. The rejuvenation of the crumbling house and the painstaking, surgical processes of samplings, analysis, liftings, peelings, stabilizing, remounting, repairing, restoring, endless time-consuming tinkerings with painted surfaces – not merely paintings, but painted walls, doors, floors, beds, cupboards, tables – painting almost anything, was the old joke, 'that did not move' – was eventually completed and the house was ready for opening to the public at the beginning of June 1986.

The garden restoration was equally inspirational: with its own funding from Lila Acheson Wallace, the American owner of *Readers' Digest*, and with committed volunteers under the direction of the architect and landscape architect Sir Peter Shepheard (who has had a long teaching connection with the University of Pennsylvania), the garden processes were equally surgical, of fingertip delicacy. Having examined Vanessa's paintings and the innumerable family snapshots taken in the garden – looking behind the shoulders and beneath the elbows to see what was going on behind the sitters – the picture of Vanessa's garden was reconstructed. After that it was a gentle hand-clearance of the weeds, and a scrabbling in the beds and paths to find surviving roots, which often appeared of their own accord once given light and air – a forensic rebirth of her favourite flowers. The intention was, Peter Shepheard remarked, to recall the garden in such a familiar way 'that the ghosts might wish to return'.★

Charleston triumphant – and it has been an undoubted triumph – has gone from strength to strength: books, exhibitions, revived fabrics and ceramics, embroidery kits, the now elegant *Charleston Magazine* edited by Frances Spalding, the Charleston Festival and the Bloomsbury Trail. This includes the little medieval church at Berwick, at the foot of the downs just east of Charleston, where Vanessa Bell, her son, Quentin, and Duncan Grant painted murals, at the request of Bishop Bell of Chichester, in 1942 and 1943. Vanessa's Annunciation and Nativity, Quentin's altar decorations

---

★ The Charleston Trust, Charleston, near Firle, Lewes, East Sussex BN8 6LL, tel. 01323 811626. Visitor information 01323 811628.

and the Sacraments, and Duncan's Crucifixion and Christ in Glory, all unmistakably Bloomsbury in style, have a simplicity that accords with this ancient building: they seem a painted echo of Virginia's 'genesis of myth' of 1916,[47] an offering by sophisticated people to age-old protectors from the depths of war.

The saving of Charleston created its own world, which dazzled and enchanted all who touched it for well over a decade: it has been a uniquely vivacious enterprise for the sober circles of the conservation movement, and it was hardly surprising that even Charleston's most distinguished and staunchest supporters might sometimes wonder what they'd done. Noel Annan, the late Lord Annan, Leslie Stephen's biographer, sometime Provost of King's College, Cambridge, recalled his Bloomsbury connections in an early Charleston newsletter, beginning when he was eleven with an accidental reading of Lytton Strachey's *Queen Victoria* and the feeling that 'I had been let into a secret.' He dances through decades of friendships and fashions, to Edward Albee's play *Who's Afraid of Virginia Woolf?* of 1962 – shortly afterwards 'Marc drew a cartoon of one of his N.W.1 characters saying to another "Afraid of, no. Marginally bored with, yes."' Lord Annan concluded:

But for thousands . . . it is as if a new country has been discovered. As I watch the throng who tour through Virginia Woolf county alone, I stand amazed. I am a bit critical of some of the tourists and the litter they leave behind them; but on the whole delighted at the pleasure that the opening up of this territory has given. Until, of course, I recollect that I too have been a tourist for 50 years.[48]

For Carrington's more northerly downland and her more discreetly painted house, Ham Spray, there was to be (thankfully) no such transfiguration. Ham Spray was willed to Ralph Partridge by Lytton, and he loved the place and wanted to live there after

Carrington's death. Ralph married Frances Marshall and they stayed there happily until his death in 1960, after which Frances sold it.

With Carrington, as with all people who really love a country-side and cross and re-cross it by their own pathways as she did, her momentum carried on. She was far from forgotten at Biddesden House, about a nine-mile drive and a rather shorter ride south by Tidcombe and Chute, where she had recognized in Bryan Guinness someone who loved his house as much as she loved Ham Spray: the Guinnesses had coveted the house for years but only won it in 1931 so they were last friends, and Carrington's *trompe l'œil* of the wistful maid at the window with the canary-fixated cat (for which her own beloved Tiberius was the model), painted in the cold and the wet, became a Biddesden conversation piece, along with General John Richmond Webb's bell, looted from Lille in 1708, in its crenellated tower and the carved stone trophies adorning the house front.[49] Trophies, bell, Tiberius and the maid, and the Guinness family are all still there. (General Webb built Biddesden *c.*1711 with the spoils of war; his quarrel with Marl-borough over the credit for the victory at Wynendaele is in Thackeray's *Henry Esmond*, and so the reel winds back to Leslie Stephen's life and the beginning of this book.)

Carrington, like the Woolfs and Leslie Hartley, had become accustomed to her car by the mid-twenties (troublesome though it may have been), which extended her range, and brought her into a fellowship with us. Her car conveyed picnics into Savernake Forest, sped them the few miles into Marlborough for the markets and fairs, and to buy buns at Polly's Tea Rooms. Out of sheer curiosity, she may well have driven south from Newbury to Burghclere, to watch her old Slade colleague Cookham Spencer working on his murals for the Sandham Memorial Chapel,★ where

★ Bookings and inquiries to The Custodian, Sandham Memorial Chapel, Burgh-clere, Newbury RG 20 9 JT, tel./fax 01635 278394. Restricted opening hours.

he was for nearly four years. How comparable were their talents? How different had been their lives? Spencer's Burghclere Chapel, covered with the images of war, the prosaic, often comical route-marching, bivouac, kit inspection, inevitably moving into the turmoil of battle, the tumbling white crosses, and the convoy of the wounded arriving at the Beaufort hospital gates – with rhododendrons in flower occupying half the canvas and salving the scene – is a *tour de force* generally accorded as his greatest achievement. Spencer was elected to the Royal Academy on the strength of it and fêted as 'the native returned in triumph' at Cookham in the spring, as Carrington died.[50] Burghclere is perhaps the natural eastern boundary of her world: the chapel is such a momentous and horrific offering simply because it is in this mute, unchanging countryside . . . indeed, Spencer had to balance the more traumatic images of his murals by painting the outside world, the rhododendrons and *Cottages at Burghclere*, with their russet roofs and lopsided gates, and great mounds of topiaried yews. Westward the drifting downs, beyond Highclere, to Walbury Fort where she walked so often and which she thought so fine, along the Inkpen ridge to Ham itself; westward still, down the tangle of re-entrant combes, truly the country of old sad kings, barrows and mounds by the score, a forgotten Roman road, and the tiny church of Tidcombe below its down, another favourite place. All survive much as Carrington knew them, though all survive despite – or because of – what is on the Burghclere Chapel walls, which let in a gentrification of the working villages she loved.

So many questions abound. Carrington's passion for motor-cycles and cars might insist that she would have taken to flying, all the rage: it was the threatening gloom of Lytton's illness that made her regret giving too little time to the young Garrow Tomlin, who was killed practising spins.[51] Her most frequent journeys were along the by-roads to Collingbourne, then down the A338 to Salisbury, stopping off with Henry and Pansy Lamb at Brookside beside the Ebble in Coombe Bissett, and ending with Augustus and her dearest Dorelia John at Fryern near Fordingbridge. Bryan Guinness had called the Lambs' half-way house 'between the sophistication of Ham Spray and the wildness of the Visigoths'[52] at Fryern. It was the Visigoth Johns who imported modern architecture, bringing Ben Nicholson's brother Kit to design the sleek white studio-cum-library for Fryern. Kit Nicholson was crazy about gliding, never stopped talking about it – and somehow the air seems the natural element for Carrington too?

It is infuriating when worlds just fail to collide, but worse if we don't recognize when they do: we cannot tell if Rupert Brooke could have changed the Lulworth story, and perhaps too many expectations rise from his legendary shade? Should Morgan Forster's moral tales have reached beyond the literary, into a landscape that was not merely parcelled out as good or bad, to be saved or squandered as politicians and planners deemed, but regenerated more sensitively, according to its needs? One thing is certain, and I trust evident by now, that Rupert and Virginia, Morgan and Carrington (and Leslie Hartley if he were a little more trusting of our opinion of him), loved their particular places, the wild seashore, the downs, Cornwall, Sussex, ancient Wiltshire and Berkshire, the soft water-meadows of the Cam, Ouse and Nene, with a supreme objectivity of a passion without possessiveness, for places they could never own. Here is the crux of my search for these spirits of place: instead of recognizing Brooke's odes, Virginia's evocations, Forster's warnings and Carrington's salvation as messages of relevance, posterity has confined them to academic ghettos, to whole university courses devoted to Virginia's *bête noire*, literary geography. Passions for places are easily confused with human loves and hatreds: the chaos of Rupert Brooke's love life had much to do with his efforts to unite both a person and place in the scale of his emotions; Virginia's marriage to Leonard Woolf was founded on his love for *her* in the settings that *she* loved; Morgan Forster sacrificed all his beloved places for love, which was the key to his detachment; Carrington substituted the one for the others. And yet, though these are evident enough in their words and actions, posterity has thought their places only relevant in retrospect, in terms of the inspiration of their arts, rather than the voices from their hearts.

Their passions were all in place by the time Morgan Forster gave his warning in the Woodman's epilogue to the Abinger Pageant in 1934; and yet his warnings went unheeded. No little irony that the same Hilton Young, who stuck armorial bookplates in his books, whose comfortable cottage The Lacket at Lockeridge had been visited by the majority of people in this book as the stepping-stone to their walkings on the downs, and visits to the talismanic Stonehenge, should, as Lord Kennet, be a pioneer of the conservation of the countryside in the mid-twentieth century.* The idea that places should be respected for themselves and their associations was so quickly distorted by a division of the spoils between the Henry Willcoxes and Harcourt Worters, the new men in the countryside who wanted to push the housing and arterial roads away from their weekend gardens, and the witterings of landed aristocrats, who feared losing their bastions of privilege and intended much the same. With the ingrained obeisance of the flock, these natural leaders of men and women were elevated into the presidencies of conservation societies and causes for the good of their names. The overwhelming ethos of a century-long conservation movement in Britain has thus been based upon maintaining

---

* Lord Kennet (1879–1960) married Kathleen Scott in 1922, becoming stepfather to Peter Scott, the naturalist; also their son, Wayland Young, maintained the family interest in conservation.

property values. The bitter debates, the battle for the Lulworth ranges multiplied over and over again, have wasted so much energy, based as they were on a false pretence, which itself fanned the flames of 'right to roam' opposition. We have undervalued Hartley's, Woolf's and Forster's novels, Brooke's poetry and Carrington's distillation of her love of a landscape into a pattern for living; we have in many senses betrayed them.

For what is a land but for living in, rather than seeking impossibly to set in aspic or shift pawns as on a chessboard? And what are the purposes of poets and artists but to seek out the spirits of a place, hone and polish legends and stories, and heal violence and defilement so that we seekers who follow after have something to find? As I was leaving T. E. Lawrence's gaunt tomb in Moreton cemetery I met a party of people who had come on purpose to see the church: inside, with them and all of us in wordless wonder, I found why. St Nicholas at Moreton is an ancient church, badly damaged by a stray bomb in 1940. After much debate it was decided to spend some of the war damage compensation fund to commission the glass-engraver Laurence Whistler (whose artist brother Rex had been killed in the war) for new windows to replace the conventional stained glass.[53] From five new windows in 1955, the idea progressed through individual donations to the completion of all fourteen windows in 1984, with an additional memorial pane by Simon Whistler in 1996. Inside the building the light is the first surprise, and light was the chosen theme for all the windows – candlelight, sunlight, jewel-light, starlight and lightning are all included, with the characteristic Whistlerian love for exquisitely detailed portraits of birds, animals, flowers and buildings. The experience inside St Nicholas's church is rare, a fragile, sparkling enchantment, as if one were living inside a crystal bowl. Laurence Whistler has used his revival of an ancient craft to celebrate the features of a landscape with which we are familiar, because it is of our own time.

As I set out along the valley of the Frome, glimpsing square, grey Moreton House, which has its portrait miniature in the Findlay family's Seasons window, the metaphor of the windows lingered: the most poignant is perhaps that of the Trinity Chapel, a memorial to an unnamed airman killed in 1940 in the Battle of France. Elements of the air fill most of the panels, the haloed sun, clouds, vapour trails and soaring eagles, but below, far below, is the pilot's eye view of southern England – the Channel coast, Salisbury Cathedral teetering in a grove of trees, his cottage home, the home of one year of marriage, in its Surrey garden. Hares play on the downs, oblivious of the broken wing and shattered propeller, the blade bearing the initials 'RG'.

The unknown 'RG' clearly loved a landscape of places he could not possibly own, and died for them. He could represent well the hundreds of thousands who followed down the twentieth century in the wake of Rupert Brooke, Virginia Woolf, Morgan Forster and Carrington, for it is not the prerogative of poets and artists alone to create a palimpsest of myths and memories that binds the living to the dead, the present to the past.

At the beginning of this book I set out to find the memories of Virginia Woolf, Morgan Forster, Rupert Brooke and Carrington in the places they loved, but suspected that I might find something more. Surely they have proved to be leaders of modern cultural and social history, piping us into an imagery of the world as they saw it? Woolf, Forster and Brooke were so intrinsically a part of the 'intellectual' aristocracy, and Carrington adopted their mores in her loyalty to Lytton, that they were able to break the bonds of the traditional point of view, which was entirely based upon landowning and inheritance. When they set out across the face of England it was not to inspect agricultural improvements, admire Palladian houses and well-manicured parks, or even to drool over the delicious wildness of the Lake District or the Welsh mountains.

The complete 'heritage' of old and outdated tastes was set aside by them: they opted for socially modest settings, and many of the places they most loved – west Cornwall, the sands of Dorset and the New Forest, the Surrey hills, the watery meadows of the fen edges, the Berkshire downs – were immured and almost lost in years of agricultural stagnation. The 'lostness' had immense appeal but perhaps the consequences of being found were more beneficial in the general scheme of things. The Fabian tinge to their youthful tastes was no stronger than the generally democratic drift of twentieth-century beliefs, and had nothing to do with nationalism or politics. When E. M. Forster refuted the armorial bookplates, saying that he never felt 'of' anywhere, but simply 'at' somewhere, it was no less a belonging: but it was the antidote to the curse of half a century of environmental civil war – the dreaded 'nimbyism', the 'not in my back yard' syndrome that landowners taught to garden owners, and even those with only window-boxes. (Leslie Poles Hartley emerges as the 'control' in my experiment, his life shadowed by his unhappy enslavement to a dream of a noble name and pile.)

Many of the poets, novelists and artists of every kind of the last 100 years are expert voices and we should heed them, more so than politicians, planners and lobbyists wearing green wellington boots. They cannot do a worse job. I am finishing this book to the strains of Peter Maxwell Davies's piano interlude, *Farewell to Stromness*: it is a 'protest' work, the composer's reaction to the controversy over siting a uranium smelter in that remote seascape. I have never seen Stromness, but can perfectly well allow that the outrage was in the concatenation of perceived evil and innocent natural beauty, much as has been fought over in other places, including Lulworth Cove. When all is said and done, those piano notes will linger, long after the passion and folly have passed away.

Notes

Introduction

1. Edith Cobb, *The Ecology of Imagination in Childhood*, New York, 1977, p. 18.
2. ibid., p. 23.
3. William M. Curtin (ed.), *The World and the Parish: Willa Cather's articles and reviews, 1893–1902*, 2 vols., Lincoln, Nebraska, 1970, vol. 2, p. 728. Quoted by Hermione Lee in her introduction to *Short Stories of Willa Cather*, London, 1989.
4. Rupert Brooke, 'The Chilterns', in *The Complete Poems*, London, 1932, pp. 109–10.
5. Richard Garnett, *Constance Garnett, A Heroic Life*, London, 1991, p. 30.
6. Michael Holroyd, *Lytton Strachey: A Biography*, London, 1967, latest edition 1994.
7. L. P. Hartley, *The Go-Between*, London, 1953.
8. William Camden, *Britain, a Chorographical description of the most flourishing Kingdoms of England, Scotland and Ireland*, London, 1610.

Chapter 1: Virginia Stephen

1. Noel Annan, *Leslie Stephen, The Godless Victorian*, London, 1984, p. 15.
2. Bridget Cherry and Nikolaus Pevsner, *The Buildings of England, London 3: North West*, London, 1991, p. 450.
3. F. H. W. Sheppard (general editor), *The Survey of London, The Museums Area of South Kensington and Westminster*, London, 1975, p. 32.
4. Cherry and Pevsner, *London 3*, p. 509.
5. ibid., pp. 535–7.
6. Guy Williams, *The Royal Parks of London*, Chicago, 1985, p. 116.
7. Caroline Dakers, *The Holland Park Circle, Artists and Victorian Society*, London, 1999, pp. 102–3.
8. Both Vanessa and Virginia wrote their memories of 22 Hyde Park Gate, and these are from Vanessa Bell, 'Notes on Bloomsbury' (1951), in S. P. Rosenbaum (ed.), *The Bloomsbury Group, A Collection of Memoirs and Commentary*, Toronto and London, 1995, pp. 102–5, and from Lia Giachero (ed.), *Sketches in Pen and Ink*, London, 1997, p. 81.
9. Bell, 'Notes on Bloomsbury', in Rosenbaum, *The Bloomsbury Group*, p. 104.
10. See note 1 above.
11. Annan, *Leslie Stephen*, p. 2.
12. ibid., p. 98.
13. Virginia Woolf, 'Old Bloomsbury' (*c.* 1922), in Rosenbaum, *The Bloomsbury Group*, pp. 41–4.
14. Rudyard Kipling, 'The English Flag', 1891.
15. Nigel Nicolson and Joanne Trautmann (eds.), *The Flight of the Mind*, vol. 1 of *The Letters of Virginia Woolf*, 6 vols., London, 1975–80, p. 12.

16. Quentin Bell, *Virginia Woolf, A Biography*, 2 vols., London, 1972, vol. 1, p. 32.

17. Tom Cross, *Painting the Warmth of the Sun, St Ives Artists, 1939–1975*, Tiverton, 1995, p. 14.

18. Tom Cross, *The Shining Sands, Artists in Newlyn and St Ives, 1880–1930*, Tiverton, 1994, p. 12.

19. Cross, *Painting the Warmth of the Sun*, p. 17.

20. Hermione Lee, *Virginia Woolf*, London, 1996.

21. Cross, *The Shining Sands*, p. 105.

22. Annan, *Leslie Stephen*, p. 116.

23. Anne Olivier Bell and Andrew McNeillie (eds.), *The Diary of Virginia Woolf*, 5 vols., London, 1977–84, vol. 1, 11 January 1897.

24. ibid., 25 January 1897.

25. ibid., 29 January 1897.

26. Virginia Woolf, *Between the Acts*, London, 1941, p. 56.

27. Andrew Birkin, *J. M. Barrie and the Lost Boys*, London, 1979.

28. Bell and McNeillie (eds.), *Diary*, vol. 1, 23 October 1918.

29. These parallel lives are all portrayed in Edward Shils and Carmen Blacker (eds.), *Cambridge Women, Twelve Portraits*, Cambridge, 1996; Hugh Lloyd-Jones, 'Jane Ellen Harrison, 1850–1928', pp. 29–72. There is also a new biography by Mary Beard, *The Invention of Jane Harrison*, Cambridge, Mass., 2000.

30. Maxine Berg, 'Eileen Power, 1889–1940', in Shils and Blacker (eds.), *Cambridge Women*, pp. 159–82.

31. Mitchell A. Leaska (ed.), *A Passionate Apprentice, the Early Journals of Virginia Woolf*, London, 1990, p. 136, 4 August 1899.

32. ibid.

33. ibid.

34. ibid., p. 137.

35. ibid., pp. 150–52, revised and published in the *Charleston Magazine*, Spring 1990.
36. Nicolson and Trautmann (eds.), *The Flight of the Mind*, p. 27, 12 August 1899.
37. ibid.
38. Leaska (ed.), *A Passionate Apprentice*, p. 187, and Margaret Newbolt, *The Later Life and Letters of Sir Henry Newbolt*, London, 1942, p. 88, for the story of Harriet Grove.
39. Leaska (ed.), *A Passionate Apprentice*, p. 188.
40. 'Romsey Abbey', in ibid., pp. 202–3.
41. 'Stonehenge Again', in ibid., pp. 203–5.
42. 'Life in the Fields', in ibid., p. 203. The complete Netherhampton pieces are: 'Netherhampton House'; 'Wilton – From Outside the Walls'; 'The Water Meadows'; 'The Downs'; 'Salisbury Cathedral'; 'Evening Service (missed)'; 'Wilton from Inside (open day)'; 'The Talk of Sheep'; 'Stonehenge'; 'The Wilton Carpet Factory'; 'Romsey Abbey', 'Life in the Fields'; 'Stonehenge Again'; 'Country Reading'; 'The Storm'; and 'Wilton Fair'.
43. Margaret Newbolt, *The Later Life and Letters of Sir Henry Newbolt*, p. 80.
44. Nicolson and Trautmann (eds.), *The Flight of the Mind*, p. 43, 8 August 1901.
45. ibid., p. 73, April 1903, to Violet Dickinson.
46. Leaska (ed.), *A Passionate Apprentice*, p. 35, 13 February 1897.
47. 'The Downs', in ibid., p. 192.
48. 'A Priory Church', in Andrew McNeillie (ed.), *The Essays of Virginia Woolf, vol. 1, 1904–12*, London, 1987, p. 53, first published in the *Guardian*, 26 July 1905.
49. Nicolson and Trautmann (eds.), *The Flight of the Mind*, pp. 137–8, 4 April 1904, to Violet Dickinson.
50. ibid., p. 138, 25 April 1904, to Emma Vaughan.

51. Leaska (ed.), *A Passionate Apprentice*, p. 215, Christmas 1904.
52. Virginia Woolf, 'Old Bloomsbury', in Rosenbaum (ed.), *The Bloomsbury Group*, p. 44, and Vanessa Bell, 'Notes on Bloomsbury', in ibid., pp. 102–5.
53. Nicolson and Trautmann (eds.), *The Flight of the Mind*, p. 326, letter 407 to Clive Bell, 20 April 1908.
54. 'A Walk by Night', in Andrew McNeillie (ed.), *The Essays of Virginia Woolf*, vol. *1, 1904–12*, pp. 80–82, first published in the *Guardian*, 28 December 1905.
55. Leaska (ed.), *A Passionate Apprentice*, p. 282, 11 August 1905.
56. ibid.
57. A review published in *The Times Literary Supplement*, 10 March 1905, of *The Thackeray Country* by Lewis Melville and *The Dickens Country* by F. G. Kitton, in McNeillie (ed.), *Essays*, vol. *1*, p. 35.

Chapter 2: Edward Morgan Forster

1. E. M. Forster, *Marianne Thornton, 1797–1887, A Domestic Biography*, London, 1956.
2. Margaret Richardson, *Architects of the Arts and Crafts Movement*, London, 1983, p. 94.
3. Forster's 'Rooksnest Memoir' (1894) is reprinted in the 1989 Penguin edition of *Howards End*, ed. Oliver Stallybrass, pp. 333–43.
4. Forster's plan of Rooksnest was also published in Francis King, *E. M. Forster and His World*, London, 1978.
5. E. M. Forster, *Where Angels Fear to Tread*, Abinger edition, London, 1975, pp. 26–7.
6. 'Rooksnest Memoir'.
7. 'Rooksnest Memoir' and *Howards End*, as quoted in Nicola

Beauman, *Morgan, A Biography of E. M. Forster*, London, 1993, p. 42.

8. Walt Whitman, 'There was a child went forth', from *Leaves of Grass and Selected Prose*, ed. Ellman Crasnow, 1993, and also in Cobb, *The Ecology of Imagination in Childhood*, p. 31.

9. Beauman, *Morgan*, p. 185.

10. ibid., pp. 118–19.

11. ibid., p. 118.

12. ibid., pp. 55–6.

13. ibid., p. 76.

14. Richard Keynes, 'The Darwins in Cambridge', in Richard Mason (ed.), *Cambridge Minds*, Cambridge, 1994, pp. 110–25.

15. Gillian Sutherland, 'Emily Davies, the Sidgwicks and the Education of Women in Cambridge', in Mason (ed.), *Cambridge Minds*, pp. 34–47.

16. Jane Brown, *A Garden of Our Own, A History of Girton College Garden*, Girton College Friends of the Garden, Cambridge, 1999.

17. Virginia Woolf, *Roger Fry, A Biography*, London, 1940, p. 50.

18. E. M. Forster, *The Longest Journey*, Edinburgh and London, 1907, p. 5.

19. ibid., p. 74.

20. ibid., pp. 2–3.

21. ibid., pp. 4–5. The authenticity of Forster's fictional view is fully confirmed in Paul Levy, *G. E. Moore and the Cambridge Apostles*, London, 1979.

22. Mary Lago and P. N. Furbank (eds.), *Selected Letters of E. M. Forster, vol. 1, 1879–1920*, London, 1983, p. 48, letter 38, 30 October 1901.

23. ibid., p. 51, letter 39 to G. L. Dickinson, 15 December 1901.

24. ibid., p. 53, note to letter to Dickinson.

25. ibid., p. 52, letter 40 to G. L. Dickinson.

26. ibid., p. 53, to G. L. Dickinson from Rome, February/March 1902.

27. ibid., p. 59, letter 44, to E. J. Dent.

28. E. M. Forster, *The New Collected Short Stories*, intro. by P. N. Furbank, London, 1985, p. 14.

29. ibid.

30. Lago and Furbank (eds.), *Selected Letters of E. M. Forster, vol. 1*, p. 61, letter 46, 14 November 1904.

31. E. M. Forster, *The Celestial Omnibus and Other Stories*, London, 1911, p. 56.

32. Lago and Furbank (eds.), *Selected Letters of E. M. Forster, vol. 1*, p. 61, letter 46.

33. Barbara Jones, *Follies and Grottoes*, London, 1974 edn., p. 159.

34. Lago and Furbank (eds.), *Selected Letters of E. M. Forster, vol. 1*, p. 78, letter 57 to Arthur Cole, 7 July 1905.

35. Forster, 'The Story of a Panic', in *The Celestial Omnibus*, 1911, pp. 1–42.

36. Forster, 'The Celestial Omnibus', in ibid., pp. 54–83.

37. Forster, 'Other Kingdom', in ibid., pp. 84–128.

38. Forster, *A Room with a View*, Penguin edn., 1955, p. 65.

39. Lago and Furbank (eds.), *Selected Letters of E. M. Forster, vol. 1*, p. 97, letter 74 to Malcolm Darling, 14 October 1909.

40. Leslie de Charms, *Elizabeth of the German Garden*, London, 1958, p. 104.

41. Lago and Furbank (eds.), *Selected Letters of E. M. Forster, vol. 1*, p. 72, letter 53.

42. ibid., p. 78, letter 57, 5 July 1905, to Arthur Cole.

43. Forster, *Howards End*, Penguin edn., 1989, p. 329.

44. Margaret Olivier (ed.), *Sydney Olivier: Letters and Selected Writings*, London, 1948.

45. Francis Lee, *Fabianism and Colonialism: The Life and Political Thought of Lord Sydney Olivier*, London, 1988, pp. 31–3.

46. ibid., p. 219.
47. Richard Garnett, *Constance Garnett: A Heroic Life*, London, 1991, p. 51 for her love of Sussex countryside.
48. David Garnett, *The Golden Echo*, London, 1953, pp. 16–18; Richard Garnett, *Constance Garnett*, pp. 154–5.
49. David Garnett, *The Golden Echo*, p. 21.
50. Peter Gray (ed.), *Limpsfield Ancient and Modern*, 1997.
51. Pippa Harris (ed.), *Song of Love, The Letters of Rupert Brooke and Noel Olivier, 1909–1915*, London, 1991, p. xxiii.
52. David Garnett, *The Golden Echo*, pp. 30–31.
53. W. M. Whiteman, *The Edward Thomas Country*, Southampton, 1988 edn., p. 23, and also unpublished notes on Bedales and its buildings by David Ottewill, 1980, Richard Holder for the Victorian Society, 1990, and Alistair Langlands.
54. Marjory Allen, Lady Allen of Hurtwood, *Memoirs of an Uneducated Lady*, London, 1975.
55. C. C. Cotterill, *Human Justice for those at the Bottom. An Appeal to Those at the Top*, London, 1907.
56. Harris (ed.), *Song of Love*, letter 28 May 1909.

Chapter 3: Rupert Chawner Brooke

1. The photos of the clock are in E. W. Timmins, *Rugby, A Pictorial History*, Chichester, 1990. The description of Rupert Brooke's death aboard the *Duguay-Trouin* is in Geoffrey Keynes, *The Letters of Rupert Brooke*, London, 1968, pp. 684–5, W. Denis Browne to Edward Marsh.
2. Christopher Hassall, *Rupert Brooke: A Biography*, London (1964), 1984 edn., p. 35.
3. ibid., p. 81.

4. H. C. Bradby, BA, *Rugby (Handbooks to the Great Public Schools)*, 1900, p. 28.

5. ibid., pp. 188–9.

6. ibid.

7. J. B. Hope Simpson, *Rugby since Arnold: a History of Rugby School from 1842*, London and New York, 1967, p. 11.

8. ibid., p. 42.

9. ibid., p. 46.

10. Roger Dixon and Stefan Muthesius, *Victorian Architecture*, London, 1978, p. 206.

11. Simpson, *Rugby since Arnold*, p. 107.

12. ibid., p. 116.

13. Hassall, *Rupert Brooke*, pp. 28–9.

14. ibid., p. 55.

15. Bradby, *Rugby*, p. 142.

16. ibid., p. 54.

17. Ian Hamilton, *A Gift Imprisoned: The Poetic Life of Matthew Arnold*, London, 1998, pp. 22–3.

18. ibid., p. 32.

19. Matthew Arnold, 'Thyrsis' (A Monody to commemorate the author's friend, Arthur Hugh Clough, who died at Florence, 1861), in *The New Oxford Book of English Verse*, chosen and edited by Helen Gardner, 1972, pp. 696–702.

20. Hamilton, *A Gift Imprisoned*, p. 69.

21. ibid.

22. Hassall, *Rupert Brooke*, p. 87.

23. ibid., p. 65.

24. Keynes (ed.), *The Letters of Rupert Brooke*, p. 79, Good Friday 1907, to St John Lucas.

25. Hilaire Belloc, 'Sonnets of the Twelve Months', in *Sonnets and Verses* (1896), from Hilaire Belloc, *Complete Verse*, intro. by A. N. Wilson, London, 1991, p. 4.

26. Keynes (ed.), *The Letters of Rupert Brooke*, pp. 84–5, May 1907, to Francis McCunn.

27. ibid., p. 89, Sunday (July 1907), to Andrew Gow.

28. E. Townshend (ed.), *F. H. Keeling, Letters and Recollections*, London, 1918, p. 22.

29. ibid.

30. Hugh Dalton, *Call Back Yesterday, Memoirs 1887–1931*, London, 1953.

31. Ben Pimlott, *Hugh Dalton*, London, 1985.

32. ibid., p. 57.

33. Geoffrey Keynes (ed.), *The Letters of Rupert Brooke*, London, 1968; Christopher Hassall, *Rupert Brooke: A Biography*, London, 1964.

34. Alison Waley, *A Half of Two Lives: A Personal Memoir*, London, 1982.

35. Keynes (ed.), *The Letters of Rupert Brooke*, p. 127, 11 May 1908, to Mrs Brooke.

36. Norman and Jeanne Mackenzie, *The Life of H. G. Wells: The Time Traveller*, London, 1987, p. 234.

37. Keynes (ed.), *The Letters of Rupert Brooke*, pp. 128–9, 25 May 1908, to Mrs Brooke.

38. See Helen Fowler, 'Frances Cornford 1886–1960', in Shils and Blacker (eds.), *Cambridge Women*, 1996, pp. 137–58.

39. Hassall, *Rupert Brooke*, pp. 163–5.

40. John Milton, *Comus*, lines 123–4, 143–5.

41. A long letter, entirely in this vein: Keynes (ed.), *The Letters of Rupert Brooke*, pp. 163–5, April 1909, to Jacques Raverat.

42. ibid.

43. ibid., pp. 159–60, 25 March 1909, to Erica Cotterill.

44. Hassall, *Rupert Brooke*, p. 238.

45. Keynes (ed.), *The Letters of Rupert Brooke*, pp. 172–3, Sunday (July 1909), to Erica Cotterill from The Orchard, Grantchester.

46. ibid., p. 230, 27 March 1910, to Dudley Ward from 24 Bilton Road.

47. ibid., p. 229, 23 March 1910, to Hugh Dalton from School Field, Rugby.

48. ibid., p. 233, 12 April 1910, to Edward Marsh from Cove Cottage, Lulworth.

49. Hassall, *Rupert Brooke*, p. 107.

50. Keynes (ed.), *The Letters of Rupert Brooke*, p. 236, 9 May 1910, to Edward Marsh from The Orchard, Grantchester.

51. Hassall, *Rupert Brooke*, p. 277, quoting Frances Cornford's opinion.

52. ibid.

53. Hilaire Belloc, *Milton*, London, 1935.

54. Hassall, *Rupert Brooke*, p. 277, quoting Frances Cornford's opinion.

55. Keynes (ed.), *The Letters of Rupert Brooke*, p. 314, 18 September 1911, to Erica Cotterill from the Old Vicarage, Grantchester.

56. Margaret Keynes, *A House by the River: Newnham Grange to Darwin College*, privately printed, Cambridge, 1976, pp. 5–6.

57. Mary Archer, notes on The Old Vicarage, April 1999, and *Rupert Brooke and The Old Vicarage, Grantchester*, Cambridge, 1989.

58. F. A. Reeve, *Cambridge from the River*, Cambridge, 1977, p. 28.

59. Archer, notes on The Old Vicarage.

60. Rupert Brooke, 'The Old Vicarage, Grantchester', in *The Complete Poems*, pp. 93–7.

61. ibid.

62. Archer, notes on The Old Vicarage.

63. David Garnett, *The Golden Echo*, pp. 175–6.

64. Hassall, *Rupert Brooke*, pp. 230–31.

65. Brooke, 'The Old Vicarage, Grantchester', in *The Complete Poems*, pp. 93–7.

66. See Martin Green, *New York 1913, The Armory Show and the Paterson Strike Pageant*, New York, 1988.

67. Keynes (ed.), *The Letters of Rupert Brooke*, p. 482, 9 July 1913, to Edward Marsh from Ottawa.

68. ibid., pp. 513–14, 1 October 1913, to Edward Marsh from San Francisco.

69. Hassall, *Rupert Brooke*, p. 414.

70. Brooke, *The Complete Poems*, p. 121.

71. Keynes (ed.), *The Letters of Rupert Brooke*, p. 553, 17 December 1913, to Cathleen Nesbitt from Grand Hotel, Auckland.

72. Brooke, 'Tiare Tahiti', in *The Complete Poems*, p. 137, and 'The Great Lover', in ibid., pp. 132–4, dated Mataia, 1914.

73. Keynes (ed.), *The Letters of Rupert Brooke*, p. 591, 9 June 1914, to Jacques Raverat from Bilton Road, Rugby.

74. ibid., p. 599, July 1914, to Lady Eileen Wellesley from Rugby.

75. Paul Freyberg, *Bernard Freyberg V.C., Soldier of Two Nations*, London, 1991.

Chapter 4: Virginia Woolf and Orlando

1. Nicolson and Trautmann (eds.), *The Flight of the Mind*, pp. 448–9, 1 January 1911.

2. Michael Holroyd, *Lytton Strachey, A Biography*, London, 1980 edn., p. 465.

3. Hermione Lee, *Virginia Woolf*, London, 1996, p. 316.

4. ibid., p. 317.

5. ibid.

6. Frederic Spotts (ed.), *The Letters of Leonard Woolf*, London, 1989, p. 67, to Lytton Strachey, 16 December 1904.

7. Lee, *Virginia Woolf*, p. 317.

8. [Virginia Woolf] 'Heard on the Downs, the genesis of myth',

anonymous contribution to *The Times*, 15 August 1916, reprinted in McNeillie (ed.), *The Essays of Virginia Woolf, vol. 2, 1912–18*, 1987.

9. From Charlotte Brontë, *Jane Eyre*, Ch. 12, quoted by Virginia Woolf in *The Times Literary Supplement*, 13 April 1916, reprinted in McNeillie (ed.), *The Essays of Virginia Woolf, vol. 2*.

10. David Garnett, *The Golden Echo*, pp. 210–11.

11. David Garnett, *Flowers of the Forest*, London, 1955, p. 112.

12. ibid., p. 115.

13. ibid., p. 114.

14. ibid.

15. Angelica Garnett, 'Charleston Remembered', in *Antique Collector*, May 1986, pp. 67–71.

16. Richard Garnett, *Constance Garnett*, p. 296.

17. Jane Dunn, *A Very Close Conspiracy, Vanessa Bell and Virginia Woolf*, London, 1990; the chapter 'Sons and Lovers' reveals Vanessa's feelings about the triangular relationship.

18. Angelica Garnett, 'Charleston Remembered'.

19. Leonard Woolf, 'The Beginnings of the Hogarth Press', in Rosenbaum (ed.), *The Bloomsbury Group*, p. 149.

20. Judy Moore, *The Bloomsbury Trail in Sussex*, 1995, SB Publications, 19 Grove Road, Seaford, East Sussex BN25 1TP.

21. ibid.

22. Lee, *Virginia Woolf*, p. 422.

23. ibid., p. 424.

24. ibid., p. 422.

25. ibid.

26. 'Blo' Norton 1906', in Leaska (ed.), *A Passionate Apprentice*, p. 311.

27. ibid., p. 310.

28. ibid.

29. McNeillie (ed.), *Essays of Virginia Woolf, vol. 2*, pp. 30–31, *The Times Literary Supplement*, 13 April 1916.

30. Virginia Woolf, 'Old Bloomsbury', in Rosenbaum (ed.), *The Bloomsbury Group*, p. 58.

31. Miranda Seymour, *Ottoline Morrell: Life on the Grand Scale*, London, 1992, p. 236.

32. ibid., p. 230.

33. ibid., pp. 230–31.

34. ibid., p. 232, quoting Ottoline Morrell.

35. Jane Brown, *Eminent Gardeners*, London, 1990.

36. Seymour, *Ottoline Morrell*, p. 232.

37. Victoria Glendinning, *Vita*, London, 1983, and Jane Brown, *Vita's Other World*, London, 1985.

38. Louise de Salvo and Mitchell A. Leaska (eds.), *The Letters of Vita Sackville-West to Virginia Woolf*, New York, 1985, p. 23, quoting Virginia's diary.

39. ibid., p. 24, also quoting Virginia's diary.

40. ibid., p. 26.

41. Vita Sackville-West's two Persian books, *Passenger to Teheran* (1926) and *Twelve Days* (1928), were published by the Hogarth Press.

42. De Salvo and Leaska (eds.), *Letters of Vita Sackville-West to Virginia Woolf*, p. 139, 15 September 1926, Virginia to Vita from Monk's House, Rodmell.

43. Jane Brown, *Vita's Other World* (see note 37 above).

44. De Salvo and Leaska (eds.), *Letters of Vita Sackville-West to Virginia Woolf*, p. 237, 9 October 1927, Virginia to Vita from 52 Tavistock Square, London WC1.

45. ibid.

46. ibid., p. 25.

47. Brown, *Vita's Other World*, p. 99.

48. De Salvo and Leaska (eds.), *Letters of Vita Sackville-West to*

Virginia Woolf, pp. 288–9, Vita to Virginia from Long Barn, Weald, Sevenoaks, 11 October 1928.

Chapter 5: Carrington

1. A. W. Coysh, *The Hamlet of Ibthorpe, its history, buildings and people*, privately printed, 1988, typed MS in Local Studies Collection, Hampshire County Library at Andover.
2. A. B. Connor, *Highways and Byways in Hampshire*, London, 1908, quoted in Coysh, *The Hamlet of Ibthorpe*.
3. Gretchen Gerzina, *Carrington: A Life of Dora Carrington, 1893–1932*, London, 1989, p. 201.
4. Holroyd, *Lytton Strachey*, 1980 edn., p. 292.
5. ibid., p. 43.
6. ibid., p. 51. Michael Holroyd goes into the endless ramifications of the intellectual aristocracy, but see also Noel Annan, *Leslie Stephen, The Godless Victorian*, London, 1984, and *The Dons*, London, 1999, which contains his essay 'The Intellectual Aristocracy' as an Annexe.
7. Holroyd, *Lytton Strachey*, p. 45.
8. Noel Carrington, 'Carrington's Early Life', in David Garnett (ed.), *Carrington, Letters and Extracts from her Diaries*, London, 1970, p. 504.
9. Nikolaus Pevsner, *The Buildings of England, Bedfordshire, the County of Huntingdon and Peterborough*, London, 1968, p. 51.
10. Gerzina, *A Life of Dora Carrington*, p. 23.
11. Illustrated in Noel Carrington, *Carrington, Paintings, Drawings and Decorations*, Oxford, 1978, and also in Jane Hill, *The Art of Dora Carrington*, London, 1994.
12. Holroyd, *Lytton Strachey*, p. 481.
13. ibid.

14. Gerzina, *A Life of Dora Carrington*, pp. 23–4.
15. Noel Carrington (ed.), *Mark Gertler, Selected Letters*, London, 1965, letter to Carrington, 24 September 1912.
16. Mark Gertler to William Rothenstein, undated 1909, postmark Andover, in ibid.
17. Christopher Neve, *Unquiet Landscape: Places and Ideas in 20th Century English Painting*, London, 1990, essay on Stanley Spencer.
18. Mark Gertler to Carrington, quoted in Ronald Blythe, *First Friends*, London, 1999.
19. Hill, *The Art of Dora Carrington*, p. 23.
20. Blythe, *First Friends*, and also Sir John Rothenstein, *John Nash*, London, 1983.
21. Carrington (ed.), *Mark Gertler, Selected Letters*, p. 33.
22. Mark Gertler to William Rothenstein, in ibid.
23. Mark Gertler to Carrington, letter July 1914 from the Old Coastguard Cottage, Pett Level, near Hastings, in Carrington (ed.), *Mark Gertler, Selected Letters*, pp. 70–71.
24. Hill, *The Art of Dora Carrington*, pp. 25–6.
25. ibid., p. 25.
26. ibid., p. 26.
27. David Garnett (ed.), *Carrington, Letters*, pp. 18–19, May 1915, to Mark Gertler from Ibthorpe House.
28. Hill, *The Art of Dora Carrington*, p. 27.
29. Coysh, *The Hamlet of Ibthorpe*, has the Jane Austen connection; also various references in David Cecil, *A Portrait of Jane Austen*, London, 1980 edn.
30. Diana Farr, *Gilbert Cannan, A Georgian Prodigy*, London, 1978.
31. Birkin, *J. M. Barrie and the Lost Boys*.
32. Mary Ansell, *The Happy Garden* and *Happy Houses*, both London, 1912.
33. Farr, *Gilbert Cannan*.

34. ibid., p. 98.

35. Ansell, *The Happy Garden*, introduction.

36. Farr, *Gilbert Cannan*, p. 95, quoting Ottoline Morrell's *Early Memoirs*.

37. ibid., p. 65.

38. ibid., p. 109.

39. David Garnett (ed.), *Carrington, Letters*, p. 21, to Mark Gertler, December 1915, from 87 Carlisle Road, Hove, Sussex.

40. ibid., p. 62, on a note from Lytton Strachey, 23 March 1917.

41. ibid., p. 30, Carrington to Lytton Strachey, 19 June 1916.

42. ibid.

43. ibid., p. 42, 16 September 1916.

44. ibid., p. 83, 20 October 1917.

45. ibid., pp. 90–91, 18 November 1917.

46. Gerzina, *A Life of Dora Carrington*, p. 122.

47. David Garnett (ed.), *Carrington, Letters*, p. 87, 9 November 1917.

48. ibid., p. 129, diary entry, 14 February 1919.

49. ibid.

50. ibid., p. 137, diary entry, Sunday in May, 1919.

51. ibid.

52. ibid., pp. 182–4, Lytton Strachey to Carrington, from Villa I Tatti, Settignano (Berensen's), Friday night, 20 May 1921.

53. Hill, *The Art of Dora Carrington*, especially Chapter 5, 'The English Tradition of Popular Art', pp. 65–72.

54. ibid., p. 66.

55. John Fothergill, *My Three Inns*, London, 1949, pp. 19–21.

56. Gerald Brenan, *A Life of One's Own: Childhood and Youth*, London, 1962, p. 242.

57. David Garnett (ed.), *Carrington, Letters*, pp. 194–5, Tuesday 14 September 1921, to Gerald Brenan from the Mill House, Tidmarsh.

58. ibid.

59. ibid., p. 237, 20 December 1922, to Gerald Brenan.

60. ibid., p. 247, 28 May 1923, to Gerald Brenan.

61. Gerzina, *A Life of Dora Carrington*, p. 201.

62. David Garnett (ed.), *Carrington, Letters*, pp. 264–5, 19 November 1923, to Lytton Strachey from the Mill House, Tidmarsh.

63. ibid., p. 287, 2 April 1924, to Gerald Brenan.

64. Richard Shone, *The Art of Bloomsbury*, London, Tate Gallery, 1999, p. 200, cat. no. 119, *Juggler and Tightrope Walker*, bought by Lytton Strachey in 1920. Also cat. no. 118, *Venus and Adonis*, pp. 196–8, in Lytton Strachey's possession by February 1929.

65. David Garnett (ed.), *Carrington, Letters*, p. 328, 26 September 1925, to Lytton Strachey.

66. Holroyd, *Lytton Strachey*, pp. 868–9.

67. ibid., p. 868.

68. Frances Partridge, *Memories*, London, 1981, pp. 123–4.

69. Holroyd, *Lytton Strachey*, p. 868.

70. Partridge, *Memories*, p. 140.

71. Perry Meisel and Walter Kendrick (eds.), *The Letters of James and Alix Strachey, 1924–1925*, London, 1986, p. 235, 16 March 1925.

72. David Garnett (ed.), *Carrington, Letters*, p. 335, May 1926, to Gerald Brenan from Ham Spray House.

73. ibid., pp. 336–7, Thursday 6 May 1926, to Gerald Brenan from Ham Spray House.

74. ibid., p. 337, Thursday in 1926, to Julia Strachey from Ham Spray House.

75. ibid., pp. 413–14, Saturday and Monday, 17 and 19 August 1929, Carrington to Lytton Strachey from Ham Spray House.

76. ibid., p. 414.

77. ibid.

78. Hill, *The Art of Dora Carrington*, p. 72.
79. Noel Carrington, *Design in the Home*, London, 1933.
80. Noel Carrington, *Design and Decoration in the Home*, London, 1952.
81. Julia Strachey, *Julia, A Portrait by Herself and Frances Partridge*, London, 1983, pp. 118–19. Julia's posthumous memoir of Carrington was written in 1932.
82. The 'First Prize' biography is printed in David Garnett (ed.), *Carrington, Letters*, p. 467.
83. David Garnett (ed.), *Carrington, Letters*, pp. 344–5, Monday evening 11 o'clock, 23 November 1926, to Gerald Brenan.

Chapter 6: Leslie Poles Hartley

1. Besides his novels and short stories Hartley wrote *The Novelist's Responsibility; Lectures and Essays*, London, 1967.
2. Lord David Cecil, introduction (first published 1968) to *The Complete Short Stories of L. P. Hartley*, London, 1973, p. vii.
3. Charles Kingsley, *Prose Idylls*, London, 1874.
4. Mary Liquorice, *The Hartleys of Fletton Tower*, Cambridgeshire Libraries, 1996.
5. L. P. Hartley, *The Harness Room*, London, 1971, pp. 6–7.
6. L. P. Hartley, *The Brickfield. A novel*, London, (1964), 1968 edn., p. 23.
7. ibid., p. 22.
8. Adrian Wright, *Foreign Country, The Life of L. P. Hartley*, London, 1996, pp. 165–6.
9. ibid., p. 60.
10. *David Cecil, A Portrait by His Friends*, collected and introduced by Hannah Cranborne, Wimborne, 1990; Lady Mary Clive on her first impression, when Cecil was twenty-eight.

11. Wright, *Foreign Country*, p. 75.

12. Barry Webb, *Edmund Blunden, A Biography*, New Haven and London, 1990, pp. 116–17.

13. Edmund Blunden, *John Clare: Poems, chiefly from manuscript*, London, 1920, and *John Clare: Madrigals and Chronicles*, London, 1924.

14. Steven Tomlinson, 'The Antiquary and the Poet, Edmund Artis and John Clare', in *Durobrivae*, a review of Nene Valley archaeology, no. 6, 1978, and subsequent papers etc. in Peterborough Museum.

15. Webb, *Edmund Blunden*, p. 118.

16. Wright, *Foreign Country*, pp. 91–4, on Venice, and Elizabeth Longford's memoir in *David Cecil, A Portrait by His Friends*.

17. The letter to Cynthia Asquith from Desmond MacCarthy, 20 August 1932, is printed in *David Cecil, A Portrait by His Friends*, p. 49.

18. L. P. Hartley, *Poor Clare*, London, 1968, p. 124.

19. Desmond MacCarthy to Cynthia Asquith, as above, note 17.

20. E. M. Forster, *A Room with a View*, London, 1947 edn., Ch. 12, pp. 152–63.

21. See Terence O'Kelly, *The Villages of Abinger Common and Wotton in Surrey*, Horsham, 1988; Jane Brown, *Lutyens and the Edwardians, An English Architect and his Clients*, London, 1996.

22. E. M. Forster, 'The Abinger Pageant', in *Abinger Harvest*, London, 1936.

23. Mary Lago and P. N. Furbank, *The Letters of E. M. Forster*, *vol. 2, 1921–70*, London, 1985, 17 November 1939 and 15 February 1940, to Hilton Young.

24. L. P. Hartley, 'Two for the River', in *The Complete Short Stories of L. P. Hartley*, p. 463.

25. ibid., p. 464.

26. ibid.
27. Wright, *Foreign Country*, pp. 7–8.
28. ibid.
29. Photograph by Janet Stone for the cover of *Poor Clare*, 1968.
30. *David Cecil, A Portrait by His Friends*, 1990.
31. David Cecil, introduction to *The Complete Short Stories of L. P. Hartley*, pp. ix and x.

Chapter 7: Spirits of Place

1. Holroyd, *Lytton Strachey*, p. 1078; Gerzina, *A Life of Dora Carrington*, p. xxiv; Hill, *The Art of Dora Carrington*, pp. 132–3.
2. Fowler, 'Frances Cornford 1886–1960', in Shils and Blacker (eds.), *Cambridge Women*, p. 143.
3. Lago and Furbank (eds.), *Selected Letters of E. M. Forster, vol. 2*, pp. 100–101, Letters 280 and 281, to Herman Ould.
4. Wright, *Foreign Country*, p. 269.
5. ibid., p. 270.
6. ibid., p. 274.
7. Wright, *Foreign Country*, p. 4.
8. Donald Mackreth, *Peterborough History and Guide*, Stroud, 1994.
9. John Barrell, *The Idea of Landscape and the Sense of Place, 1730–1840: an Approach to the Poetry of John Clare*, London, 1972.
10. ibid., p. 148, quoting John Clare, 'Song', in *The Poems of John Clare*, 2 vols., ed. J. W. Tibble, 1935, vol. 1, p. 253.
11. Barrell, *The Idea of Landscape*, p. 188.
12. ibid., p. 187.
13. For instance: Leslie Parris, *Landscape in Britain, c.1750–1850*, London, 1973; Ian Jeffrey, *The British Landscape 1920–1950*, London, 1984; Raymond Williams, *The Country and the City*,

London, 1985; Jay Appleton, *The Experience of Landscape*, London, 1975; Stuart Wrede and W. Howard Adams (eds.), *Denatured Visions, Landscape and Culture in the Twentieth Century*, New York, 1991. A refreshing change of view is provided by Christiana Payne, *Toil and Plenty, Images of the Agricultural Landscape in England 1780–1890*, New Haven and London, 1993.

14. Keynes (ed.), *The Letters of Rupert Brooke*, p. 669, 10 March 1915 from SS *Grantully Castle*.

15. Martin Gayford, 'Still Winding and Wonderful: Zennor's Literary and Artistic Connections', *Charleston Magazine*, Spring/Summer 1999, pp. 5–14.

16. Pam Hirsch, *Barbara Leigh Smith Bodichon, 1827–1891, Feminist, Artist and Rebel*, London, 1998, p. 284.

17. ibid., pp. 105 ff., on John 'Byron' Chapman, the *Westminster Review* and Barbara.

18. Cross, *The Shining Sands*, pp. 206–7.

19. ibid., p. 209.

20. ibid., p. 213.

21. Neve, *Unquiet Landscape*, pp. 134–5.

22. Cross, *Painting the Warmth of the Sun*.

23. ibid., p. 25.

24. Jim Ede, introduction to *Kettle's Yard, an Illustrated Guide*, 1982 edn.

25. Archer, notes on The Old Vicarage.

26. Fowler, 'Frances Cornford', in Shils and Blacker (eds.), *Cambridge Women*, p. 143.

27. Cathleen Nesbitt, *A Little Love and Good Company*, London, 1974.

28. Andrew Wilson, 'Rupert Brooke's hidden love', *Daily Telegraph*, 11 March 2000.

29. Harris, *Song of Love, The Letters of Rupert Brooke and Noel Olivier*.

30. H(erbert) E(rnest) Bates (1905–74), *Edward Garnett*, London, 1950, pp. 28–30.

31. Richard Garnett (ed.), *Sylvia & David, The Townsend Warner/ Garnett Letters*, London, 1994, pp. 7–8, September 1924.

32. David Garnett, *Go She Must!*, London, 1927, p. 39.

33. David Garnett, *Flowers of the Forest*, pp. 42–5.

34. Keynes (ed.), *Letters of Rupert Brooke*, pp. 658–9, Rupert Brooke to Violet Asquith from Hood Battalion, 2nd Naval Brigade, Blandford, Dorset, 25 January 1915.

35. Rodney Legg, *Lulworth Encyclopaedia*, Wincanton, 1998, p. 58.

36. Rupert Brooke, 'Day That I Have Loved', in *The Complete Poems*, pp. 7–8.

37. Rupert Brooke, 'Pine-trees and the Sky: Evening', in ibid., p. 12.

38. Rodney Legg, *Lawrence in Dorset*, Wincanton, 1997, p. 43.

39. Wright, *The Village That Died for England*, London, 1995.

40. Legg, *Lawrence in Dorset*, p. 115.

41. Wright, *The Village That Died for England*, early chapters, and OS Outdoor Leisure 15, Purbeck & South Dorset, where the range areas are marked in thick purple.

42. Legg, *Lawrence in Dorset*, p. 132, quoting E. M. Forster.

43. F. P. Pitfield, *Hardy's Wessex Locations*, Wincanton, 1992.

44. Moore, *The Bloomsbury Trail in Sussex*.

45. Quentin Bell, foreword, 'Charleston Preserved', in Quentin Bell et al., *Charleston Past and Present*, London, 1987.

46. ibid., p. 10.

47. See Chapter 4, note 8.

48. Noel Annan, 'Some Thoughts on Bloomsbury', Charleston Newsletter no. 14, March 1986, pp. 7–11.

49. Bryan Guinness, *Potpourri from the Thirties*, Burford, 1982.

50. Duncan Robinson, *Stanley Spencer*, Oxford, 1990, p. 55.

51. David Garnett (ed.), *Carrington, Letters*, p. 478, notes the death

of Stephen Tomlin's brother Garrow Tomlin; letter to Rosa-
mund Lehmann, November 1931, from Ham Spray House.

52. Guinness, *Potpourri from the Thirties*, p. 62.

53. *St Nicholas, Moreton, The Engraved Glass Windows*, booklet in
the church, printed at the Friary Press, Dorchester, with plates
from *Scenes and Signs on Glass*, 1985, being the fifth book on
Laurence Whistler's work published by the Cupid Press of
Woodbridge, Suffolk.

Bibliography

Selected sources, in addition to the works noted in the introduction:

Annan, Noel, *Leslie Stephen, The Godless Victorian*, London, 1984.

Archer, Mary, *Rupert Brooke and The Old Vicarage, Grantchester*, Cambridge, 1989.

Beauman, Nicola, *Morgan, A Biography of E. M. Forster*, London, 1993.

Bell, Anne Olivier, and McNeillie, Andrew (eds.), *The Diary of Virginia Woolf*, 5 vols., London, 1977–84.

Bell, Quentin, *Virginia Woolf, A Biography*, 2 vols., London, 1972.

Blythe, Ronald, *First Friends, Paul and Bunty, John and Christine – and Carrington*, London, 1999.

Carrington, Noel (ed.), *Mark Gertler, Selected Letters*, London, 1965.

De Salvo, Louise, and Leaska, Mitchell A., *The Letters of Vita Sackville West to Virginia Woolf*, New York, 1985.

Farr, Diana, *Gilbert Cannan, A Georgian Prodigy*, London, 1978.

Forster, E. M., *Marianne Thornton 1797–1887, A Domestic Biography*, London, 1956.

Garnett, David, *Flowers of the Forest*, London, 1955.

Garnett, David, *The Golden Echo*, London, 1953.

Garnett, David (ed.), *Carrington, Letters and Extracts from Her Diaries*, London, 1970.

Garnett, Richard, *Constance Garnett, A Heroic Life*, London, 1991.

Gerzina, Gretchen, *A Life of Dora Carrington 1893–1932*, London, 1989.

Harris, Pippa, *Song of Love, the Letters of Rupert Brooke and Noel Olivier 1909–15*, London, 1991.

Hassall, Christopher, *Rupert Brooke, A Biography*, London, 1964.

Hill, Jane, *The Art of Dora Carrington*, London, 1994.

Holroyd, Michael, *Lytton Strachey*, London, 1967 (latest edition 1994).

Keynes, Geoffrey (ed.), *The Letters of Rupert Brooke*, London, 1968.

Lago, Mary, and Furbank, P. N. (eds.), *Selected Letters of E. M. Forster*, 2 vols., London, vol. 1 (*1879–1920*), 1983 and vol. 2 (*1921–70*), 1985.

Leaska, Mitchell A. (ed.), *A Passionate Apprentice, the Early Journals of Virginia Woolf*, London, 1990.

Lee, Hermione, *Virginia Woolf*, London, 1996.

McNeillie, Andrew (ed.), *The Essays of Virginia Woolf, Vol. 1, 1904–12*, London, 1986, *Vol. 2, 1912–18*, London, 1987.

Nicolson, Nigel and Trautmann, Joanne (eds.), *The Letters of Virginia Woolf*, 6 vols., London, 1975–80.

Rosenbaum, S. P. (ed.), *The Bloomsbury Group, a Collection of Memoirs and Commentary*, Toronto and London, 1995.

Seymour, Miranda, *Ottoline Morrell, Life on the Grand Scale*, London, 1992.

Wright, Adrian, *Foreign Country, The Life of L. P. Hartley*, London, 1996.

Index

Index

Whichelo; mother of Edward
Morgan Forster), 45–6, 49, 51,
52, 57, 61, 223, 228, 259
Foster, Birket, 62
Fothergill, John, 182–3
Fox How, 91
Franklin family, 48–9
Frederika of Prussia, Duchess of
York, 61–2
Freyberg, Bernard, 120
Friends of Charleston, 267
Fripp, Alfred, 108n.
Fritham House, 31
Frome, valley of the, 263, 275
Frost, Robert, 116, 239
Froxfield, 78
Fry, Roger, 54, 70, 166
Fryern, 272
Furse, Charles, 27, 28–9
Furse, Henry, 27, 29
Furse, Katharine, 29

Gage, Deborah, 267
Galsworthy, John, 74, 117
Gardiner, Rolf, 262
Gardner, Phyllis, 113 and n., 255
Garnett, Constance (née Black), xvi,
71–2, 73, 74–5, 128, 130, 132,
133, 134, 256, 258
Garnett, David 'Bunny', xv, xvi, 72,
73–4, 75, 98n., 108, 111,
127–30, 132–3, 187, 195,
257–9, 262
Garnett, Edward, 72, 73, 74, 256
Garnett, Rachel (née Marshall) *see*
Marshall, Rachel

Garnett, Dr Richard (grandfather of
David Garnett), 72
Garnett, Richard (son of David
Garnett), 258–9
Garsington Manor, 143–4, 145–7,
169, 170, 173, 175, 176, 201,
215, 222
Gauntlett family, 27
George II, King, 5
George III, King, 34
George, IV, King, 5
George V, King, 81, 98
George, Henry, 69
Georgian Poetry, xvi, 106, 115
Germany, 65–7, 128
Gertler, Golda, 164
Gertler, Louis, 164
Gertler, Mark, 144, 145, 163–4,
165–6, 168–9, 170, 171, 173,
177, 180, 242
Gerzina, Gretchen, 237n.
Gibbs, James, xvi, xvii
Gibbs family, xv, 228
Gibraltar, 158
Giggleswick, 259
Gill, Eric, 77
Gill, Marjory, 77
Gilpin, Revd, 246
Gimson, Ernest, 76, 183
Girtin, Thomas, 239
Girton College, Cambridge, 22–3,
53, 86, 247
Glasgow Boys, 17
Gloucester Road, 3
Gnoll, the, 97
Godalming, 77